Ma

lonely planet
phrasebooks
and
Anthony Garnaut

Mandarin phrasebook
5th edition – September 2004

Published by
Lonely Planet Publications Pty Ltd ABN 36 005 607 983
90 Maribyrnong St, Footscray, Victoria 3011, Australia

Lonely Planet Offices
Australia Locked Bag 1, Footscray, Victoria 3011
USA 150 Linden St, Oakland CA 94607
UK 72-82 Rosebery Ave, London, EC1R 4RW

Cover illustration
Pouring the dragon's brew by Daniel New

ISBN 1 74059 179 8

text © Lonely Planet Publications Pty Ltd 2004
cover illustration © Lonely Planet Publications Pty Ltd 2004

10 9 8 7 6 5 4

Printed through Colorcraft Ltd, Hong Kong
Printed in China

acknowledgments

Lonely Planet Language Products and editor Francesca Coles would like to thank the following for producing this phrasebook:

The scholarly Anthony Garnaut for providing the translations, transliterations and cultural and linguistic expertise for this book. Anthony studied physics at Beijing University, sought his fortune in Hong Kong then returned to campus life and is currently doing his PhD in Asian Studies at the Australian National University. The editor would like to thank him for being a pleasure to work with.

Karin Vidstrup Monk as commissioning editor then publishing manager and managing editor for her contribution to the project on a celestial scale.

Karina Coates as commissioning editor for following the fortunes of this book in myriad ways.

Project managers Fabrice Rocher and Glenn van-der-Knijff for taming the wild dragon and ensuring that the constellation of talents coalesced to produce this book on time.

Fellow editors Piers Kelly, Annelies Mertens and Quentin Frayne for companionship and sage advice on the editorial journey. A special thanks to Piers for his earnest proofing.

Layout designer John Shippick for applying his feng shui to the layout task. Layout manager Adriana Mammarella and acting manager Kate McDonald for layout checks and assistance.

The inscrutable Yukiyoshi Kamimura for series design. Proxy series designer Brendan Dempsey for balancing the Yin and the Yang in Yuki's absence. Daniel New for the cover design and for harmonious inside illustrations. Maria Vallianos and Patrick Marris for additional inside illustrations.

Thanks also to Elizabeth Chong for providing additional material for the culinary reader, Wayne Murphy, Mark Germanchis and Ben Handicott for production support, Nick Stebbing for macro magic and LP's print production department for getting the book to the printer.

make the most of this phrasebook ...

Anyone can speak another language! It's all about confidence. Don't worry if you can't remember your school language lessons or if you've never learnt a language before. Even if you learn the very basics (on the inside covers of this book), your travel experience will be the better for it. You have nothing to lose and everything to gain when the locals hear you making an effort.

finding things in this book

For easy navigation, this book is in sections. The Tools chapters are the ones you'll thumb through time and again. The Practical section covers basic travel situations like catching transport and finding a bed. The Social section gives you conversational phrases, pick-up lines, the ability to express opinions – so you can get to know people. Food has a section all of its own: gourmets and vegetarians are covered and local dishes feature. Safe Travel equips you with health and police phrases, just in case. Remember the colours of each section and you'll find everything easily; or use the comprehensive Index. Otherwise, check the two-way traveller's Dictionary for the word you need.

being understood

Throughout this book you'll see coloured phrases on the right-hand side of each page. They're phonetic guides to help you pronounce the language. You don't even need to look at the language itself, but you'll get used to the way we've represented particular sounds. The pronunciation chapter in Tools will explain more, but you can feel confident that if you read the coloured phrase slowly, you'll be understood.

communication tips

Body language, ways of doing things, sense of humour – all have a role to play in every culture. 'Local talk' boxes show you common ways of saying things, or everyday language to drop into conversation. 'Listen for ...' boxes supply the phrases you may hear. They start with the phonetic guide (because you'll hear it before you know what's being said) and then lead in to the language and the English translation.

CONTENTS

5

social 107

CONTENTS

mandarin

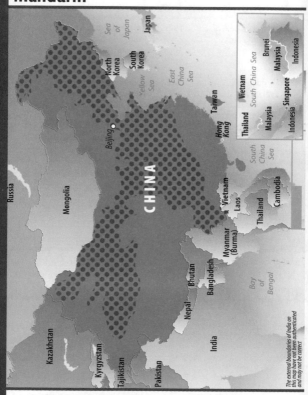

The external boundaries of India on
this map have not been authenticated
and may not be correct

- •ᵃ first language
- widely understood
- official language

For more details see the **introduction**.

It may surprise you to learn that Mandarin is not really the name of a language. The term Mandarin actually refers to one of the seven Chinese dialect groups – Mandarin being the largest of those groups. What most English speakers refer to when they use the term 'Mandarin' is more accurately described as modern standard Chinese or *Putonghua* – to give it its Chinese name. So, although this phrasebook has 'Mandarin' emblazoned on its cover, the language contained in it is best described as Modern Standard Chinese.

What exactly is Modern Standard Chinese-cum-Mandarin and why is it the most useful form of Chinese for the traveller? Modern Standard Chinese is based on the Beijing dialect of Mandarin. Its grammar, vocabulary and pronunciation reflect the norms of the capital. It's the main language used in official contexts, in the media and in education. Just about everyone in China therefore has exposure to the standard language and can read, speak and understand it.

Its Chinese name is *Putonghua* which means 'the common dialect' and it's been a powerful force for linguistic and political unity in a country with countless dialects, many of them mutually unintelligible.

at a glance ...

language name:
Mandarin Chinese

name in language:
Putonghua (China),
Gouyu (Taiwan) & *Huayu*
(Singapore)

language family:
Sino-Tibetan family

approximate number of speakers: 800 million plus

close relatives:
other dialects of Chinese including Hakka, Gan, Yue, Min, Xiang & Wu

donations to English:
tea, chopsticks, Japan, ketchup, kowtow, kung fu, wushu, tai chi & silk

introduction

Wherever you go in China you should be understood using the *Putonghua* given in this phrasebook. As all Chinese dialects share a common written language the Chinese script in this phrasebook can be read by all literate Chinese people too.

Aside from its use in mainland China, modern standard Chinese has official status in Taiwan (where it's called *Gouyu*) and Singapore (where it's called *Hanyu*). In addition, hundreds of thousands of people in migrant communities around the world speak Mandarin in one form or another. The total number of speakers worldwide is in excess of 800 million, making Mandarin the most widely spoken 'language' in the world.

There can be no doubt about the practical advantages of taking this Mandarin phrasebook on a trip to China with you. It contains all the useful words and phrases to help make your trip as hassle free as possible. Another compelling reason to bring it with you are the social words and phrases which will open up a world of possiblities for social interaction and cultural exchange with the locals.

By taking the time to acquaint yourself with China's national language you'll also be accessing a vital part of a rich and ancient culture and a dynamic modern society. Add to this the aesthetic appeal of its writing system and the logical simplicity of its grammar and you'll be richly rewarded for your efforts.

TOOLS > pronunciation

发音

For speakers of English, the sounds of Mandarin are quite easy to produce. There are relatively few of them and many of them have equivalents in English. One aspect of the language that may prove a little challenging is the use of tones. In Mandarin you can change the meaning of a word by altering the pitch level (tone) at which it is spoken. (See **tones** on page 14 for an explanation of how this works).

vowel sounds

元音

Mandarin vowel sounds are straightforward and you'll notice that there's quite a lot of overlap with English vowel sounds. Note that a changes to u before n and ng as these 'n' sounds influence the vowel. A similar thing happens with ee which changes to i before n and ng.

symbol	english equivalent	mandarin example
a (un, ung)	father (lun, sung)	la (lùn, lǔng)
ee (in, ing)	peel (pin, ping)	pèe (pǐn, pīng)
er	her	ger
ew	similar to new pronounced with rounded lips	yèw
ir	girl but with an 'r' sound	zir
or	more	bor
oo	tool	shoo
u	cut	fǔng

pronunciation

vowel/consonant combinations

双元音

Mandarin has quite a few vowel and consonant combinations (sounds where the sounds y and w and vowels meld together) and diphthongs (composite vowels). Again you'll notice that quite a few of these have counterparts in English.

symbol	english equivalent	mandarin example
ai	**ai**sle	kai
air	l**air**	lyair
ao	M**ao**	tao
ay	p**ay**	pay
o	l**ow**	shŏ
ya	**ya**rd	syà
yen	**yen**	syen
wen	**wen**t	ywěn

Note that vowels and consonants can be used in a variety of combinations not represented here. We've given you all the sounds you need to pronounce Mandarin but for a fuller treatment of sound combinations see the Pinyin chart under **romanisation & the Pinyin system** on page 16.

consonant sounds

Mandarin consonants should be quite easy for you to get your tongue around as they'll all be familiar from English.

symbol	english equivalent	mandarin example
b	**b**it	**b**ùng
ch	**ch**in	**ch**ir
d	**d**og	**d**ò
f	**f**un	**f**êrng
g	**g**o	**g**ûn
h	**h**ot	**h**ǎi
j	**j**ump	**j**ōong
k	**k**id	**k**ěr
l	**l**ip	**l**ín
m	**m**ap	**m**ín
n	**n**o	**n**érng
ng	si**ng**	mú**ng**
p	**p**ig	**p**áy
r	**r**un	**r**ìi
s	**s**ip	**s**ěe
sh	**sh**op	**sh**ǎo
t	**t**op	**t**óo
ts	ca**ts**	**ts**èr
w	**w**in	**w**ùng
y	**y**ou	**y**ó
z	la**ds**	**z**ir

tones

音调

Many words in Mandarin have the same basic pronunciation. The thing that distinguishes these 'homophones' is their tonal quality – the raising and lowering of pitch on certain syllables. Mandarin is commonly described as having four tones, but it's more accurate to think of it as having five tones, including the neutral tone. Tones are indicated in our pronunciation guides by the use of diacritics (symbols) over the vowels as shown here.

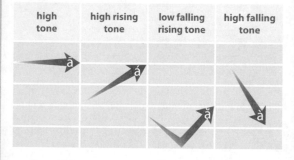

high tone	high rising tone	low falling rising tone	high falling tone
ā	á		
			à
		ǎ	

The table below shows how one 'word' ma can have five different meanings distinguished by tone.

tone	example	meaning
high	mā	mother
high rising	má	hemp
low falling-rising	mǎ	horse
high-falling	mà	scold
neutral	ma	question marker

TOOLS

Tones in Mandarin allow for some amusing tonally based tongue twisters such as the following based on the example words above:

Mother rides a horse. The horse is slow. Mother scolds the horse.

妈妈骑马，马慢，
妈妈骂马。

mā·mā chée mǎ, mǎ mùn,
mā·mā mà mǎ

(lit: mother ride horse, horse slow, mother scold horse)

Bear in mind that tones are not absolute in pitch but are relative to your natural vocal range. So don't feel inhibited – just experiment with the contours of your natural voice. English speakers do this anyway to a small extent. When you pronounce 'What?' you're getting close to a Mandarin high rising tone and when you say 'Damn!' you're approximating a high-falling tone.

There's no need to feel daunted by this 'foreign' system. There's nothing obscure or mysterious about tones – over half of the world's languages use them. You might have mixed success in getting your meaning across to start with, but remember that patient repetition is all it takes to learn. Even if your tones are slightly off, the meaning you wish to convey will often be clear from the context.

A Chinese listener might find it easier to understand you if you ignore tones altogether than if you come out with upside-down tones, so you could give this strategy a go. Failing that, you can always point to the word or phrase you're aiming for in this phrasebook.

romanisation & the Pinyin system

汉语拼音

In 1958 the Chinese officially adopted a system known as Pinyin which is a way of writing Chinese using the Roman alphabet. Pinyin played an important role in overcoming obstacles to communication and development by providing access to a common language in a vast country with countless dialects.

correspondence between Pinyin and the Lonely Planet system			
vowels & vowel combinations		consonants	
pinyin symbol	our symbol	pinyin symbol	our symbol
a (an, ang)	a (un ung)	b	b
ai	ai	c	ts
ao	ao	ch, q	ch
e	er	d	d
ei	ay	f	f
i	ir	g	g
i (in, ing)	ee (in ing)	h	h
ia	ya	k	k
ian	yen	l	l
iang	yung	m	m
iao	yao	n	n
ie (ian)	yair (yen)	ng	ng
ie, ue	yair, wair	p	p
iong	yoong	r	r
iu	yo	s, x	s
o	or	sh, x	sh
ou	o	t	t
u (un ong)	oo (oon, oong)	w	w
ü, (ün)	ew (ewn)	y	y
ua (uan, uang)	wa (wun, wung)	z	z
uai	wai	zh, j	j
uan	wen, wun		
ui	way		
uo	wor		
wai	wai		

If you go to China today you'll see Pinyin everywhere: on maps, road signs, shop signs and in brand names. Despite widespread recognition many Chinese can't read Pinyin and you'll find its use particularly limited in rural areas.

This book doesn't use Pinyin but uses instead an intuitive pronunciation system due to the fact that Pinyin can be misleading for English speakers as some letters and syllables don't correspond well to English pronunciation. Pinyin 'c', for example, is pronounced like the 'ts' in 'cats' and Pinyin 'q' is pronounced like the 'ch' in 'cheese'. Our pronunciation system is designed to allow you to read as though you were reading English aloud and be understood. The table opposite shows the correspondence between our symbols and the Pinyin system to help you match any Pinyin words you may see with our system.

You'll notice that we've used the same letter for several pairs of Pinyin letters (eg, Pinyin 'ch' and 'q' are represented by just ch in our system). This is a simplification for ease of pronunciation which won't compromise your ability to be understood.

writing system

汉字

Chinese is often described as a language of pictographs. Many of the basic Chinese characters are in fact highly stylised pictures of what they represent, but the majority of Chinese characters are compounds of a 'meaning' element and a 'sound' element. Each Chinese character represents a spoken syllable. Most Chinese words are comprised of two separate characters.

The bulkiest Chinese dictionaries have some 100,000 characters, but to be able to read a newspaper you only need to know a mere few thousand. Theoretically, all Chinese dialects use the same writing system so people from all over China should be able to read and understand the Chinese characters in the words and phrases in this book. In practice Cantonese adds about 3000 specialised characters and many dialects don't have a written form at all.

plunge in!

别怕说错！

The most important thing to keep in mind with Mandarin pronunciation is just to get out there and give it a go! Don't waste your time getting hung up on tones or anything else for that matter. Let the desire to communicate carry you along and help you make the most out of your travel experience. And remember, speaking a new language is, above all, great fun!

Beijingese

Speakers of Mandarin are spread far and wide from Manchuria in north east China to Yunan in south west China. It should come as no surprise therefore that there are many different dialects of Mandarin. These dialects differ from each other in vocabulary, grammar (subltly) and – most obviously to the foreign ear – pronunciation.

The pronunciation given in this book is based on 'Beijingese', the dialect of Mandarin that's spoken in the capital Beijing. This is because Modern Standard Chinese is based upon the Beijing dialect.

One feature of standard Mandarin that's a reflection of a peculiarly Beijing pronunciation is the addition of an 'r' sound at the end of many words. This 'r' sound is represented in this phrasebook by the character 儿. You won't expect to hear this pronunciation from Mandarin speakers in other parts of China. Also be aware that outside the capital the sibilant (hissing) sounds 's', 'z' and 'zh' may not match the patterns of the Beijing standard. Generally speaking, the greater the distance from the capital the more you should expect to hear divergent pronunciations.

With the status of official language comes a certain prestige. In following the pronunciation given in this book you may find that you are complemented on your 'correct' Mandarin. You should also find that you'll be understood throughout China as all Chinese have broad exposure to the official language.

This chapter is a basic grammar of Mandarin explained in layman's terms. It's designed to help you make your own sentences. We hope it'll encourage you to explore beyond the territory of the phrases given in this phrasebook and to create your own adventures in communication and cultural exchange. You should be all the more encouraged to do so by the fact that Mandarin grammar is really quite a simple and logical system.

a/an & the

One thing that you won't have to bother about when putting together a Mandarin sentence are the equivalents for the English articles 'a/an' and 'the'. This is because Mandarin doesn't have articles at all. In Mandarin the context indicates whether something indefinite (corresponding to 'a/an') or definite (corresponding to 'the') is meant.

adjectives see describing things

articles see a/an & the

be

Although Mandarin has an equivalent of the English verb 'to be', shì 是, it's not used in quite the same way as in English. The verb shì is only ever used with a noun, as in the sentence:

I'm a doctor.
我是医生。

wǒr shìr ēe·shērng
(lit: I am doctor)

The verb shìr is dropped altogether with adjectives – a Mandarin speaker says literally 'I thirsty' not 'I am thirsty'. (The particle ler 了 indicates that it's a temporary condition, ie, that I'm not thirsty all the time.)

I'm thirsty.
我渴了。

wór kěr·ler
(lit: I thirsty-ler)

commands

To express a command in Mandarin you place emphasis on the verb. A positive command is formed by just stating the verb in a commanding tone:

Leave!
滚！

góon
(lit: roll (away)!)

A negative command is formed by putting 'not want' bóo·yào 不要 (sometimes abbreviated to byáir 别) before a verb. There's also a polite form of a negative command – akin to saying 'needn't' in English. In this case 'not need' bóo·yòong 不用 is placed before the verb. This has an abbreviated form bérng 甭.

not want	不要	bóo·yào
not want (abbreviated form)	别	byáir
not need	不用	bóo·yòong
not need (abbreviated form)	甭	bérng

Don't shout!
不要喊！

bóo·yào hún
(lit: not-want shout)

No need for formalities!
不用客气！

bóo·yòong kèr·chee
(lit: not-need politeness)

comparing things

To compare one thing to another, you insert the word běe 比 'compare' between the two objects you wish to compare. As in English, the object being compared comes before the yard-stick of comparison.

China is bigger than Australia.
中国比
澳大利亚大。

jōong·gwór běe
ào·dà·lèe·yǎ dà
(lit: China compare
Australia big)

This one's better than that one.
这个比那个人好。

jày·ger běe này·ger hǎo
(lit: this-one compare
that-one good)

counting things

In Mandarin, when you talk about quantities of any noun, it's important to put a classifier or 'measure word' between the number and the noun. This concept is not entirely alien to English. We talk about 'two pairs of pants', 'two bunches of bananas', 'two sheets of paper', etc. The system is a bit more highly developed in Mandarin and classifiers must be used every time numbers are used with a noun. Different classifiers are used for different kinds of objects, taking into account their shape, or a general catergory (based on Chinese logic) to which they belong. The full list of classifiers is too long to give here but these are the most common ones:

generic classifier	个	ger
big things (mountains, buildings, elephants etc)	座	zwòr
chairs, knives, teapots, tools or implements with handles	把	bǎ
drinking receptacles (cups, glasses etc)	杯	bāy
flat things (tickets, stamps etc)	张	jūng
flowers (the blossoms, not the plants)	朵	dǒr
long things (fish, snakes, rivers etc)	条	tyáo
nondescript animals (dogs, cats etc)	只	jīr
people	位	wày
trees	棵	kèr
vehicles	辆	lyŭng

Don't be intimidated by this system. The good news is that you can get by just using the 'generic' (all-purpose) classifier ger 个. It may not be strictly correct, and you may find people gently correcting you, but you'll be understood.

Classifiers are used with the demonstrative pronouns 'this' (jày 这) and 'that' (này 那) and between pronouns and nouns (see also **pointing things out**).

This week.
这个星期。

jày·ger sīng·chēe
(lit: this-ger week)

That woman.
那位女士。

này wày nêw·shìr
(lit: that-wày woman)

describing things

As in English, words that describe or modify nouns, ie, adjectives come before the noun. Usually, the particle der 的 is placed between the adjective and the noun.

a big strawberry
大的草莓

dà der tsăo·máy
(lit: big der straw-berry)

expressing time

Verbs in Mandarin don't change their form according to when an action takes place, ie, they don't show tense (for more on verbs see **verbs**). The time something takes place can be, instead, conveyed by the use of adverbs of time (words that modify a verb and indicate time). So to talk about things in the past, present or future you place an adverb of time – such as 'a while ago' (yĕe·chyén 以前), 'last year' (chèw·nyén 去年), 'now' (syèn·zài 现在) 'tomorrow' (míng·tyēn 明天) or '(this) morning' (zăo·shùng 早上) – before the verb to specify when the action took place.

Tomorrow I'm going to Beijing.
我明天去
北京。

wŏr míng·tyēn chèw
bǎy·jīng
(lit: I tomorrow go Beijing)

Now she lives in Beijing.
他现在住在北京。   tā syèn·zài jòo zài bǎy·jīng
                            (lit: she now live in Beijing)

In the morning I didn't eat anything.
我早上没吃饭。   wŏr zǎo·shùng máy·chīr fùn
                            (lit: I morning not-eat meal)

past tense alternative forms

The particle ler 了 can be added to a verb to indicate that an action has been completed. In many cases this is just like the past tense in English.

He has gone to Shanghai.
他去了上海。   tā chèw·ler shùng·hǎi
                            (lit: he go-ler Shanghai)

For things that have happened some time in the unspecified past, the particle gwòr is used.

He's been to Taiwan.
我去过台湾。   tā chèw·gwor tăi·wūn
                            (lit: he go-gwòr Taiwan)

future tense alternative forms

The verb yào 要 'want', when placed before a verb, can be used to indicate the future. If you're less than certain as to what you'll do tomorrow, yào can be replaced with syŭng 想 'feel like' or dǎ·swùn 打算 'plan to' to indicate future events.

I'm going to Hong Kong.
我要去香港 。   wŏr yào chèw syūng·gŭng
                            (lit: I want go Hong-Kong)

I feel like going to Hong Kong.
我想去香港。   wór syūng chèw syūng·gŭng
                            (lit: I feel like go Hong-Kong)

I'm planning to go to Hong Kong.
我打算去   wór dǎ·swùn chèw
香港。   syūng·gŭng
                            (lit: I plan to go Hong-Kong)

have

To say that you have something in Mandarin, you use the word yŏ 有.

I have a ticket.
我有票。 wór yŏ pyào
(lit: I have ticket)

To say that you don't have something just place the particle máy 没 'not' before yŏ.

I don't have a ticket.
我没有票。 wór máy·yŏ pyào
(lit: I not-have ticket)

Joining words

To connect two words or phrases, place a joining word (or conjuction) between the two elements. The most common conjunctions are 'and' hér 和 and 'or' hái·shìr 还是.

I like rice and noodles.
我喜欢米饭和 wór sĕe·hwūn mĕe·fùn hér
面条。 myèn·tyów
(lit: I like rice and noodle)

Are you American or English?
你是美国人 nĕe shìr mǎy·gwór rérn
还是英国人。 hái·shir yīng·gwór rérn
(lit: you are American
person or English person)

location

Location is indicated by the word zài 在, which literally means 'is located'. The word zài is used with almost all prepositions of place (words such as 'opposite' or 'behind' which indicate a spatial relationship). Note that zài comes before, but not necessarily in front of, the preposition in the sentence.

The bank is opposite the hotel.
银行在酒店
对面。
yín·húng zài jyǒ·dyèn
dwày·myèn
(lit: bank is-located hotel opposite)

You're sitting behind me.
你坐在我的后边。
něe zwòr zài wǒr·der hò·byēn
(lit: you sit is-located my behind)

need

The verb 'need' is expressed by the compound word sēw·yào
需要, which includes the word yào 要 'to want'.

I need to go to the toilet.
我需要上厕所。
wǒr sēw·yào shùng tsèr·swǒr
(lit: I need mount toilet)

As with all negatives, to say you don't need something, just
place bòo 不 'not' before sēw·yào.

I don't need money.
我不需要钱。
wǒr bòo sēw·yào chyén
(lit: I not-need money)

negatives

To form negative sentences in Mandarin, you place the particle bòo 不 'not' before the verb or adjective that you wish to
negate. (Note that when bòo appears before a word with the
same tone, it changes to a rising tone).

I'm not hungry.
我不饿。 wǒr bóo èr
(lit: I not hungry)

It's not OK.
不行。 bòo síng
(lit: not passable)

The particle máy 没 is used instead of bòo to make a negative out of the word 'have' and also when the sentence refers to past events. Here máy can be thought of as the equivalent of the English 'haven't'.

I haven't eaten lunch.
我没吃午饭。 wǒr máy·chīr wǒo·fùn
(lit: I máy eat lunch)

nouns

Nouns are usually made up of two words (characters) called compounds. Nouns have only one fixed form and they don't show gender (masculine, feminine etc) or number (singular or plural).

lunch	午饭	wǒo·fùn
		(lit: noon-rice)
lunches	午饭	wǒo·fùn
		(lit: noon-rice)

particles

Mandarin makes use of a number of particles. These are 'function words' which don't necessarily have a definable meaning of their own but serve a grammatical function within a sentence. The particle ler 了, for example, when attached to a verb indicates that an action has been completed.

pointing things out

To point things out in Mandarin you can use the following expressions known as demonstrative pronouns.

that	那	này
this	这	jày

These can be combined with the generic classifier ger to give the following expressions:

that one	那个	này·ger
this one	这个	jày·ger

possession

To show possession, simply add der 的 to a personal pronoun, then follow it with the object or person that's possessed.

my passport   我的护照   wǒr·der hòo·jào
(lit: I-der passport)

your child   你的孩子   něe·der hái·zir
(lit: you-der child)

1st person (sg)	my	我的	wǒr·der
2nd person (sg)	your(s)	你的	něe·der
3rd person (sg)	his/her(s)/its	他的/她的/它的	tā·der
1st person (pl)	our(s)	我们的	wǒr·mērn·der
2nd person (pl)	your(s)	你们的	něe·mērn·der
3rd person (pl)	their(s)	他们的	tā·mērn·der

For other personal pronouns, see **pronouns** opposite.

prepositions see time and location

pronouns

Pronouns in Mandarin don't change their form according to whether they are the subject (performer of the action, eg, 'I') or object (undergoer of the action, eg, 'me') of a sentence. Note that whilst 'he/him', 'she/her' and 'it' are represented by different characters they are pronounced in exactly the same way.

1st person (sg)	**I/me**	我	wǒr
2nd person (sg)	**you**	你	něe
3rd person (sg)	**he/him**	他	
3rd person (sg)	**she/her**	她	tǎ
3rd person (sg)	**it**	它	
1st person (pl)	**we/us**	我们	wǒr·měrn
2nd person (pl)	**you (pl)**	你们	něe·měrn
3rd person (pl)	**they/them**	他们	tǎ·měrn

You'll notice that plural pronouns are formed with the simple addition of ·mern 们 to the singular forms.

questions

The most common way of forming questions in Mandarin is simply to put the particle ma 吗 at the end of a statement.

He's going to see the Great Wall.
他要去长城。 tā yào·chèw chúng·chérng
(lit: he going Great-Wall)

Is he going to see the Great Wall?
他要去长城吗? tā yào·chèw chúng·chérng ma
(lit: he going Great-Wall ma)

question words

Who?	谁	sháy
Who are you?	你是谁?	něe shìr sháy
Which?	哪个	nǎy·ger
Which place?	哪个地方?	nǎy·ger dèe·fūng
What?	什么	shérn·mer
What's this?	什么时候?	jèr shìr shérn·mer
Where?	哪	nǎr
Where's he going?	他去哪?	tā chèw nǎr
How?	怎么	zérn·mer
How do I get there?	怎么走?	zěrn·mer zǒ
When?	什么时候	shérn·mer shír·hò
When do you go?	你什么时候走?	něe shérn·mer shír·hò zǒ

time

A time relationship between a noun and another word in the sentence is reflected by the use of prepostions of time.

I watched the television before eating.

我吃饭前		wǒr chīr·fùn chyén
看了电视。		kùn·ler dyèn·shìr
		(lit: I eat-rice after watched ler television)

after	前	chyén
before	后	hò
until	到	dòw

verbs

One delightfully simple aspect of Mandarin grammar is that verbs have fixed forms. This means that they don't change their form according to who or what is the subject (the person or thing perfoming the action of the verb) as they do in English, eg, 'I am' but 'you are', 'he is' etc. Only one form of each verb exists so there's no need to memorise long lists of varying verb forms as you may have had to do when learning other languages. To see how this works, look at the table below for the verb chīr 吃 'eat'.

I eat a meal.	我吃饭。	wǒr chīr fàn
You (sg) eat a meal.	你吃饭。	něe chīr fàn
He/She eats a meal.	他/她/它吃饭。	tā chīr fàn
We eat a meal.	我们吃饭。	wǒr·mērn chīr fàn
You (pl) eat a meal.	你们吃饭。	něe·mērn chīr fàn
They eat a meal.	他们吃饭。	tā·mērn chīr fàn

Not only do Mandarin verbs not change according to who or what is performing the action of the verb, but they also remain fixed regardless of when the action took place, ie, they don't change according to tense.

Of course, no language can get by without having some way of expressing when an action takes place. See, **expressing time,** for an explanation of the devices Mandarin uses.

want

The verb 'to want' is expressed in Mandarin with the verb syúng 想.

I want to eat.
  我想吃。   wǒr syúng chīr
                                     (lit: I want eat)

As with all negatives, to say you don't want something, just place the negative particle bòo 'not' before syúng.

I don't want to eat.
  我不想吃。   wǒr bòo syúng chīr
                                       (lit: I not want eat)

word order

Word order of basic sentences in Mandarin is the same as in English, ie, subject–verb–object. This means that sentences are formed in the same order as in English – with the person or thing that performs the action of the verb coming first, followed by the verb, followed by the undergoer of the action as in the phrase below:

I eat a meal.
我吃饭。

wŏr chīr fùn
(lit: I eat rice)

yes & no

Mandarin doesn't have words that correspond directly to 'yes' and 'no' when used in isolation. To answer a question in the affirmative, you simply repeat the verb used in the question. To answer a question in the negative, place the negative particle bòo 不 'not' before the repeated verb. Remember that when bòo comes before another word with a falling tone, its tone alters to bóo. The particle ma 吗 is a question marker (see **questions** for an explanation).

Are you hungry?	你饿吗？	něe èr ma (lit: you hungry ma)
Yes.	饿。	èr (lit: hungry)
No.	不饿。	bóo èr (lit: not hungry)

You're likely to hear the word dwày 对 as an equivalent to 'yes' as well. It literally means 'correct'. In the negative, this becomes bóo dwày 不对 ('not correct').

Are you leaving tomorrow?

你明天走吗？

něe míng·tyēn zǒ ma
(lit: you tomorrow leave ma)

Yes, I am.

对, 明天走。

dwày míng·tyēn zǒ
(lit: correct tomorrow leave)

No, I'm not.

不对明天走。

bóo dwày míng·tyēn zǒ
(lit: not correct tomorrow leave)

language difficulties
语言障碍

Do you speak English?
你会说英文吗?   née hwày·shwōr yīng·wérn ma

Does anyone speak English?
有谁会说英文吗?   yǒ sháy hwày·shwōr yīng·wérn ma

Do you understand?
你明白吗?   něe míng·bái ma

I understand.
明白。   míng·bái

I don't understand.
我不明白。   wǒr bòo míng·bái

I speak a little.
我会说一点。   wǒr hwày·shwōr ēe·dyěn

Could you write that in Pinyin for me?
请用拼音写。   chǐng yòong pīn·yīn syǎir

Could you write that down for me (in Chinese characters)?
请用中文   chíng yòong jōong·wérn
写下来。   syàir·syà·lál

Please point to the phrase in this book.
请指书上的范句。   chíng jǐr shōo·shùng der fùn·jòo

What does 'syōong māo' (panda) mean?
"熊猫" 是   syōong māo shìr
什么意思?   shér·ma èe·sir

How do you ...?   怎么……?   zěr·ma ...
  pronounce this   念这个   nyèn jày·ger
  write 'panda'   写 "熊猫"   syǎir syōong māo

Could you please ...?	请你……?	chíng něe …
repeat that	再说一遍	zài shwōr ee·byen
speak more slowly	慢一点说	mùn ēe·dyěn shwōr
write it down	写下来	syǎir·syà·lái

tone deaf

Mandarin is a tonal language (for an explanation, see **tones** in **pronunciation**, page 14). While this fact can sometimes cause humiliation for the foreign visitor to China, it's also a rich source of mirth for Chinese people who happen upon outsiders. For example, foreign diplomats (wài·jyāo·gwūn 外交官) habitually introduce themselves in Mandarin as wāi·jyào·gwǔn 歪胶管 (lit: 'rubber U-bend pipes').

Fortunately, foreigners are not the butt-end of all Mandarin pronunciation jokes. Southerners, particularly Cantonese speakers, are notorious in Beijing and other bastions of 'correct' Chinese for getting their sibilants ('hissing' sounds such as 's', 'sh' and 'z') all mixed up. A bunch of tongue twisters exist to weed out Southern pretenders, such as the following:

sìr·shír·sìr jīr shír·shīr·zīr shìr sīr·der
四十四只
石狮子是死的。

Forty-four stone lions are dead.

cardinal numbers

基数

Numbers in Mandarin are easy to learn. Multiples of 10 are made by stating the multiple followed by 10 – so 20 is literally 'two ten'. Two is a tricky number, generally pronounced àr unless it's joined with a classifier, in which case it will be pronounced lyǔng (see classifiers below).

0	零	líng
1	一	ēe
2	二 / 两	àr/lyǔng
3	三	sūn
4	四	sìr
5	五	wǒo
6	六	lyò
7	七	chēe
8	八	bā
9	九	jyo
10	十	shír
11	十一	shir·ēe
12	十二	shír·àr
13	十三	shír·sūn
14	十四	shír·sìr
15	十五	shír·wǒo
16	十六	shír·lyò
17	十七	shír·chēe
18	十八	shír·bā
19	十九	shír·jyǒ
20	二十	àr·shír
21	二十一	àr·shir·ēe
22	二十二	àr·shír·àr
30	三十	sūn·shír

40	四十	sìr·shír
50	五十	wǒo·shír
60	六十	lyò·shír
70	七十	chēe·shír
80	八十	bā·shír
90	九十	jyǒ·shír
100	一百	ēe·bǎi
101	一百零一	ēe·bǎi lǐng·ēe
103	一百零三	ēe·bǎi lǐng·àr
113	一百一十三	ēe·bǎi ēe·shír·sūn
122	一百二十二	ēe·bǎi àr·shír·àr
200	两百	lyúng·bǎi
1,000	一千	ēe·chyēn
10,000	一万	ēe·wùn
1,000,000	一百万	ēe·bǎi·wùn
100,000,000	一亿	ēe·èe

ordinal numbers

序数

1st	第一	dèe·ēe
2nd	第二	dèe·àr
3rd	第三	dèe·sūn
4th	第四	dèe·sìr
5th	第五	dèe·wǒo

fractions

百分比

a quarter	四分之一	sìr·fērn·jīr·ēe
a third	三分之一	sūn·fērn·jīr·ēe
a half	一半	ēe·bùn
three-quarters	四分之三	sìr·fērn·jīr·sūn
all	所有	swór·yǒ
none	没有	máy·yǒ

classifiers

These are the most commonly used classifiers or 'counters' which are used when counting things. For an explanation of how they work, see the **phrasebuilder**, page 22.

generic classifier
个   qer

flat things (tickets, stamps etc)
张   jūng

long things (fish, snakes, rivers etc)
条   tyáo

people
位   wày

nondescript animals (dogs, chickens etc)
只   jīr

blg things (mountains, buildings, elephants etc)
座   zwòr

amounts

常用数量

China has a complete set of words for imperial weights and measures. In mainland China (though not in Hong Kong or Taiwan) these have all been recast in metric mould, so that foreign visitors are at most required to multiply by two to yield a standard international metric measure.

How much?	多少?	dōr·shǎo
How many?	几个?	jěe·ger

Finger counting is widely used in China in conjunction with the spoken number when shopping or bargaining. There are a few regional variations but you should be able to get the hang of it pretty quickly.

七
7 chēe

八
8 ba

九
9 jyŏ

十
10 shír

ALTERNATIVES

7 chēe

8 bā

10 shír

Please give me ...	请给我……	chǐng gáy wǒr ...
(50) grams	(50) 克	(wǒo·shír) kèr
1 Chinese ounce (=50 grams)	1两	ēe·lyǔng
1 Chinese pound (=half a kilo)	1斤	ēe·jīn
a bottle	一瓶	ēe·píng
a dozen	打	dá
a few	一些	ēe·syāir
a jar	一罐	ēe·gwùn
a kilo	1公斤	ēe·gōong·jīn
less	少一点	shǎo·ēe·dyěn
a little	一小块	ēe·syǎo·kwài
a lot	好多	hǎo·dōr
many	好几个	háo·jēe·ger
more	多一些	hǎo·èe·syāir
a packet	一盒	ēe·hér
a slice	一块	ēe·kwài
some	一些	ēe·syāir
a tin	一罐	ēe·gwùn

telling the time

说时间

Telling the time in Mandarin is simple. To express a time on the hour simply give the hour followed by dyěn 点 'point' and jōong 钟 'clock'. For all other times, give the hour followed by dyěn 点 and then the number of minutes past the hour followed by the word fērn 分 'minutes'. For example, the literal translation of 'five past ten' is 'ten points five minutes'.

What time is it?	现在	syèn·zài
	几点钟?	jée·dyěn jōong
It's (ten) o'clock.	(十)点钟。	(shír)·dyěn joong
Five past (ten).	(十)点	(shír)·dyěn
	五分。	wǒo·fērn
Quarter past (ten).	(十)点	(shír)·dyěn
	十五分。	shír·wǒo·fērn
Half past (ten).	(十)点	(shír)·dyěn
	三十分。	sūn·shír·fērn
Twenty to (eleven).	(十)点	(shír)·dyěn
	四十分。	sìr·shír·fērn
Quarter to (eleven).	(十)点	(shír)·dyěn
	四十五分。	sìr·shír·wǒo·fērn
am	早上	zao·shùng
pm	晚上	wǔn·shùng

At what time (does it start)?
什么时候(开始)?   shér·mer shír·hò (kāi·shír)

(It starts) At ten.
十点钟(开始)。   shír·dyěn jōong (kāi·shír)

It starts at (9:57 pm).
(晚上   (wǔn·shùng
9点57分)   jyó·dyěn wǒo·shír·chēe·fērn)
开始。   kāi·shír

days

The days of the week follow a simple pattern in Mandarin. The word 'week' (sīng·chēe 星期) comes first followed by numbers one to six (starting with Monday). Sunday is the 'day of heaven' – the day of worship in the Western world from which the seven-day week was introduced.

Monday	星期一	sīng·chēe ēe
Tuesday	星期二	sīng·chēe àr
Wednesday	星期三	sīng·chēe sūn
Thursday	星期四	sīng·chēe sìr
Friday	星期五	sīng·chēe wǒo
Saturday	星期六	sīng·chēe lyò
Sunday	星期天	sīng·chēe tyēn

months

As with numbers, the months in Mandarin follow a system of pure logic. The word 'month' (ywàir 月) is prefaced with numbers one to twelve starting with January. The Western-style calendar was only imported to China some 200 years ago and, as the new calendar was felt to be foreign enough, further complicated linguistic terms were thought best avoided.

January	一月	ēe·ywàir
February	二月	àr·ywàir
March	三月	sūn·ywàir
April	四月	sìr·ywàir
May	五月	wǒo·ywàir
June	六月	lyò·ywàir
July	七月	chēe·ywàir
August	八月	bā·ywàir
September	九月	jyǒ·ywàir
October	十月	shír·ywàir
November	十一月	shír·ēe·ywàir
December	十二月	shír·àr·ywàir

dates

What date is it today?
今天几号？   jīn·tyēn jǐe hào

It's (18 October).
（十月十八号）。   (shír·ywàir shír·bā hào)

seasons

spring	春天	chōon·tyēn
summer	夏天	syà·tyēn
autumn	秋天	chyō·tyēn
winter	冬天	dōong·tyēn

present

目前时态

now	现在	syèn·zài
this ...	这个……	jày·ger ...
afternoon	下午	syà·wǒo
month	月	ywàir
morning (after breakfast)	早上	zǎo·shùng
morning (before lunch)	上午	shùng·wǒo
week	星期	sīng·chēe
this year	今年	jīn·nyén
today	今天	jīn·tyēn
tonight	今天晚上	jīn·tyēn wǔn·shùng

past

過去時間

(three days) ago	（三天）以前	(sūn·tyēn) ěe·chyén
day before yesterday	前天	chyén·tyēn
last month	上个月	shùng·ger ywàir
last night	昨天晚上	zwór·tyēn wǔn·shùng
last week	上个星期	shùng·ger sīng·chēe
last year	去年	chèw·nyén
since (May)	从（五月）	tsóong (wǒo·ywàir)
yesterday ...	昨天……	zwór·tyēn ...
afternoon	下午	syà·wǒo
evening (after dinner)	晚上	wǔn·shùng
morning (after breakfast)	早上	zǎo·shùng
morning (before lunch)	上午	shùng·wǒo

future

將来時

day after tomorrow	后天	hò·tyēn
in (six days)	（六天）以后	(lyò·tyēn) ěe·hò
next ...	下个……	syà·ger ...
month	月	ywàir
week	星期	sīng·chēe
next year	明年	míng·nyén

tomorrow ...	明天……	míng·tyēn ...
afternoon	下午	syà·wǒo
evening	晚上	wǔn·shùng
(after dinner)		
morning	早上	zǎo·shùng
(after breakfast)		
morning	上午	shùng·wǒo
(before lunch)		
until (June)	到(六月)	dào (lyò·ywàir)

during the day

从早到晚

Time during the day is divided up slightly differently in Mandarin than it is in English. In China, eating is one of the most important activities of the day so significant units of time fall before or after meals.

afternoon	下午	syà·wǒo
dawn	早晨	zǎo·chérn
(before breakfast)		
day	白天	bái·tyēn
evening	晚上	wǔn·shùng
(after dinner)		
midday	中午	jōong·wǒo
(lunch & siesta time)		
night	深夜	shērn·yàir
(sleep time)		
early morning	早上	zǎo·shùng
(after breakfast)		
late morning	上午	shùng·wǒo
(before lunch)		
sunrise	日出	rìr·chōo
sunset	日落	rìr·lwòr

the tyranny of time

Attitudes towards time and punctuality vary from culture to culture. The Chinese tend to view punctuality as a virtue and you should find that people arrive on time for meetings and social events. They may even arrive a little ahead of time, just to be on the safe side. In business dealings, punctual attendance at appointments can be interpreted as a sign of earnestness.

Another thing to bear in mind when planning events is that the Chinese are very superstitious when it comes to numbers. When setting a date you might be wise to check with your Chinese counterparts that the numbers contained in the proposed date are favourable. The number four (sìr 四), in particular, is considered unlucky as it sounds like the word for 'death' (sǐr 死).

How much is it?
多少钱?   dōr·shǎo chyén

Please write down the price.
请写下来。   chíng syáir·syà lái

Do you accept ...?   你们收……吗?   nēe·mern shò ... ma
   credit cards   信用卡   sìn·yòong kǎ
   debit cards   借记卡   jyàir·jèe·kǎ
   travellers cheques   旅行支票   lěw·síng jīr·pyào

I'd like ..., please.   可以……吗?   kér·ěe ... ma
   my change   找零钱   jǎo líng·chyén
   a refund   退钱   twày chyén
   to return this   退还这个   twày·hwún jày·ger

I'd like to ...   我要……   wǒr yào ...
   cash a cheque   兑现一张   dwày·syèn ee·jūng
                      支票   jīr·pyào
   change a   换旅行   hwùn lěw·síng
    travellers cheque   支票   jīr·pyào
   change money   换钱   hwùn·chyén
   get a cash   现金透支   syèn·jīn tò·jīr
    advance
   withdraw money   取现金   chěw syèn·jīn

Where's ...?	······在哪？	... zài năr
an ATM	自动取款机	zìr·dòong chéw·kwŭn·jēe
a place to change foreign money	换外币的地方	hwùn wài·bèe der dèe·fung

What's the ...?	······是什么？	... shìr shér·mer
charge for that	手续费	shŏ·sèw·fày
exchange rate	兑换率	dwày·hwùn·lèw

It's ...	是······	shìr ...
(1200) RMB	(1, 200) 元	(ēe·chyēn lyúng·băi) ywén
free	免费的	myĕn·fày der

Chinese cash

RMB (Renminbi rérn·mīn·bèe**)** – 'People's Money' – the official term for the Chinese currency

yuan – the official name for the basic unit of RMB
元   ywén

kuai – commonly used colloquial term for a yuan
块   kwài

jiao – the official term; 10 jiao make up one yuan
角   jyăo

mao – commonly used colloquial term for a jiao
毛   máo

fen – the official term; 10 fen make up one jiao
分   fērn

getting around

找路

Which ... goes to (Hangzhou)?	到(杭州) 坐几号……？	dào (húng·jō) zwòr jěe·hào ...
boat	船	chwún
bus	车	chēr
plane	飞机	fāy·jēe
train	火车	hwǒr·chēr

Is this the ... to (Hangzhou)?	这个…… 到(杭州)大吗？	jày·ger ... dào (húng·jō) ma
boat	船	chwún
bus	车	chēr
train	火车	hwǒr·chēr

When's the ... (bus)?	……(车) 几点走	... (chēr) jée·dyén·zǒ
first	首趟	shǒ·tùng
last	末趟	mòr·tùng
next	下一趟	syà ēe·tùng

What time does it leave?
几点钟出发？ jée·dyěn·jōong chōo·fā

What time does it get to (Hangzhou)?
几点钟到(杭州)？ jée·dyěn·jōong dào (húng·jō)

How long will it be delayed?
推迟多久？ twāy·chǐr dōr·jyǒ

Is this seat free?
这儿有人吗？ jèr yǒ·rérn ma

That's my seat.
那是我的座。 nàr shìr wǒr·der zwòr

Can you tell me when we get to (Hangzhou)?
到了 (杭州) dào·ler (húng·jō)
请叫我, 好吗？ chíng jyào wǒr hǎo·ma

I want to get off here.
下车, 啊。 syà chēr a

How long do we stop here?
在这里停多久？ zài jèr yào tíng dōr·jyǒ

tickets

On Chinese trains there are no classes, instead the options are: hard seat (yìng·zwòr 硬座) or soft seat (rún·zwòr 软座) and hard sleeper (yìng·wōr 硬卧) or soft sleeper (rún·wōr 软卧). Classes do exist on long-distance boat services in China.

Where do I buy a ticket?
哪里买票？ ná·lee mǎi pyào

Do I need to book?
要先订票吗？ yào syēn·dìng pyào ma

A ... ticket to (Dalian).	一张到 (大连)的……票。	ēe·jung dào (dà·lyén) der ... pyào
1st-class	头等	tó·děrng
2nd-class	二等	àr·děrng
3rd-class	三等	sūn·děrng
child's	儿童	ár·tóong
one-way	单程	dūn·cherng
return	双程	shwūng·cherng
student	学生	shwáir·shērng

I want to travel by ... train.	我想走……	wór·syúng mǎi ...
direct	直快车	jír·kwài chēr
express	特快车	tèr·kwài chēr
fast	快车	kwài·chēr
local	慢车	mùn chēr
slow	普通车	pǒo·tōong chēr

I'd like a ... ticket.	我想钟……	wór·syúng zǒ ...
hard-seat	硬座票	yìng·zwòr pyào
soft-seat	软座票	rún·zwòr pyào

Buying tickets in China can be something of a nightmare for foreigners. Seemingly interminable queues snake towards small ticket windows. The Western etiquette of not pushing or cutting in simply doesn't apply. One approach to overcoming these difficulties might be to find someone who wants to practice English to help you. Ask around with these phrases:

Do you speak English?

| 你会说 | née hwày·shwŏr |
| 英文吗? | yīng·wérn ma |

Does anyone speak English?

| 有谁会说 | yŏ sháy hwày·shwŏr |
| 英文吗? | yīng·wérn ma |

Your potential helper may be able to cut to the front of the queue in effortless Chinese style to purchase your ticket for you.

To make things even easier, you could bring a pre-prepared slip of paper with your ticket details written down in Mandarin script to post through the ticket window. Use these phrases to help devise your message:

Could you write down the ticket details in Chinese characters for me?

| 请帮我写 | chíng būng·wŏr syáir |
| 详细情况。 | syŭng·sèe chíng·kwùng |

Could you write down (Dalian) in Chinese characters?

| 请帮我 | chíng būng·wŏr |
| 写下(大连)。 | syáir·syà (dà·lyén) |

Armed with such a slip of paper, you should be assured of obtaining your ticket to ride as long as you can fight your way to the front of the queue.

I'd like a ... berth.	我想钟……	wór·syŭng zŏ …
hard-sleeper	硬卧	yìng·wŏr
soft-sleeper	软卧	rún·wŏr

I'd like a/an ... berth.	我想睡……	wór·syŭng shwày …
bottom	下铺	syà·poo
middle	中铺	jŏong·poo
upper	上铺	shùng·poo

I'd like a/an ... seat.	有没有……座。	yŏ·máy·yó … zwŏr
aisle	走廊	zŏ·lúng
(non)smoking	(不)吸烟	(bòo) sēe·yēn
window	窗户	chwūng·hoo

Is there (a) ...?	有……吗？	yŏ … ma
air-conditioning	空调	kōong·tyáo
blanket	毛毯	máo·tŭn
sick bag	呕吐袋	ŏ·tòo dài
toilet	厕所	tsèr·swŏr

I'd like to ... my ticket, please.	请问, 我想……票。	chíng wèrn wór·syŭng … pyào
cancel	退	twày
change	改	gǎi
confirm	确定	chwàir dìng

How much is it?
多少钱？   dōr·shăo chyén

How much is a (soft-seat) fare to ...?
到……的 (软座票)   dào … der (rún·zwòr pyào)
多少钱？   dōr·shăo chyén

How long does the trip take?
几个小时到点？   jĕe·ger syăo·shír dào·dyĕn

Is it a direct route?
是直通的吗？   shìr jír·tōong·der ma

Can I get a stand-by ticket?
能买站台票吗？   nérng·măi jùn·tái pyào ma

What time should I check in?
几点钟登记？   jée·dyĕn·jōong dērng·jèe

luggage

行李

Where can I find ...?	……到哪里找？	... dào nár·lee jǎo
the baggage claim	取行李处	chěw síng·lee chòo
the left-luggage office	行李 寄存处	síng·lee jēe·tsǒon chòo
a luggage locker	行李 暂存箱	síng·lee zǔn·tsóon·syùng
a trolley	小推车	syǎo twāy·chēr

My luggage has been ...	我的行李 被……了。	wǒr·der síng·lee bày ... ler
damaged	摔坏	shwāi·hwài
lost	丢	dyō
stolen	偷走	tō·zǒ

That's (not) mine.
那（不）是我的   nà (bóo·)shìr wǒr·der

Can I have some coins/tokens?
我想换
一些硬币。   wór·syǔng hwùn
ēe·syāir yìng·bèe

plane

飞机

Where does flight (BJ8) arrive/depart?
(BJ八号)飞机   (bāy·jāi bā hào) fāy·jēe
在哪里起飞/进港?   zài ná·lee chěe·fāy/děe·dá

Where's ...?	……在哪?	... zài nǎr
the airport shuttle	机场巴士	jēe chǔng bā·shir
arrivals	入境口	ròo·jìng kǒ
departures	出境口	chōo·jìng kǒ
the duty-free shop	免税店	myěn·shwày dyèn
gate (8)	(八号)登机口	(ba hào) derng·jēe kǒ

listen for ...		
gwòr·jòong síng·lee	过重行李	excess baggage
shó·tee sing·lee	手提行李	carry-on ~~baggage~~
síng·lee pyào	行李票	ticket

bus & coach

公共车与长途车

How often do buses come?
这儿的车来的多吗?   jèr·der chēr lái·der dōr ma

Which number bus goes to (Harbin)?
到(哈尔滨)   dào (hā·er·bīn)
座几号车?   zwòr jěe·lòo chēr

Does it stop at (Harbin)?
在(哈尔滨)能下   zài (hā·er·bīn) nérng syà
车吗?   chēr ma

transport

What's the next stop?
下一战是哪里？　　　　　　　　syà·ger jùn shìr ná·lee

I'd like to get off at (Harbin).
我在 (哈尔滨)　　　　　　　　　wǒr zài (hā·er·bīn)
要下车。　　　　　　　　　　　yào syà chēr

Please stop pushing!
不要挤啰！　　　　　　　　　　bóo·yào jée lor

city	市内	shìr·này
city bus	大巴	dà·bā
inter-city	长途	chúng·tóo
inter-city bus	长途车	chúng·tóo chēr
local	本地	běrn·dèe
private-run bus	小巴	syǎo·bā
sleeper bus	卧铺	wōr·pòo
	长途车	chúng·tóo chēr

subway & train

地铁与火车

Which platform for the ... train?
……列火车到　　　　　　　　… lyàir hwór·chēr
哪个站台？　　　　　　　　　dào jěe·hào jùn·tái

What station is this?
这是哪个站？　　　　　　　　jèr shìr shér·mer jùn

What's the next station?
下一站是哪个？　　　　　　　syà·ee jùn shìr shér·mer

Does it stop at (Tianjin)?
在(天津)能   zài (tyēn·jīn) nérng
下车吗?   syà chēr ma

Do I need to change?
需要倒车吗?   sēw·yào líng·chyén ma

Which line goes to …?
到……座哪个线?   dào … zwòr nǎr·ger syèn

How many stops to …?
到……座几站?   dào … zwòr jěe·jùn

Is it …?	是……车吗?	shìr .., chēr ma
direct	直通	jír·tōong
express	特快	tèr·kwài
Which carrlage	……座几号	… dào jěe·hào
Is (for) …?	车厢?	chēr·syūng
dining	吃饭	chīr·fùn
soft sleeper	软卧	rárn·wòr

boat

船舶

How long is the trip to …?
几个小时到……?   jěe·ger syǎo·shír dào …

Is there a fast boat?
有快艇吗?   yǒ kwài·tǐng ma

How long will we stop here?
这里停留多久?   jèr·lee ting·lyó dōr·jyǒ

What time should we be back on board?
几点钟   jée·dyěn·jōong
再上船?   zài·shùng chwún

What's the sea like today?
今天海浪大不大?   jīn·tyēn hái·lùng dà·boo·da

I feel seasick.
我有点恶心。   wǒr yó·dyěn èr·sīn

Is/Are there ... on the boat?	船上有 ……吗？	chwún·shùng yǒ … ma
karaoke	卡拉OK	kāi·la·o·kay
life jackets	救生衣	jyò·shērng ēe
a toilet	厕所	tsèr·swǒr
cabin	船舱	chwùn·tsūng
captain	船长	chwùn·jǔng
deck	甲板	jyā·bǔn
ferry	渡船	dòo·chwùn
lifeboat	救生艇	jyò·shērng tǐng
life jacket	救生衣	jyò·shērng ēe
yacht	帆船	fún·chwùn

hire car & taxi

出租车与车租赁

I'd like a taxi ...	我要订 一个 出租车, ……	wór yào dìng ēe·ger chōo·zōo chēr …
to depart at (9am)	（早上9 点钟） 出发	(zǎo·shùng jyó· dyěn jōong) chōo·fā
now	现在	syèn·zài
tomorrow	明天	míng·tyēn

Where to?
到哪里？ dào nár·lee

(The Great Wall), if that's OK.
（长城），好吗？ (chúng·chérng) hǎo ma

Where's the taxi rank?
出租车往哪打？ chōo·zōo chēr wúng·nár·dǎ

Is this taxi free?
这出租车有人吗？   jày chōo·zōo chēr yǒ·rérn ma

Please put the meter on.
请打表。   chǐng dá·byǎo

How much is it to (the Great Wall)?
到(长城)   dào (chúng·chérng)
多少钱？   dōr·shǎo chyén

I'd like to hire a self-drive car .
我想租赁   wór·syǔng zōo·lín
一辆轿车。   ee·lyǔng jyào·chēr

I'd like to hire a car with a driver.
我想包一个车。   wór·syǔng bāo ee·ger chēr

How much to hire a car with a driver to …?
包一个车到……   bāo ee·ger chēr dào …
多少钱？   dōr·shǎo chyén

That's too expensive.
那太贵了。   nà tài gwày ler

Is it air-conditioned?
有空调吗？   yǒ kōong·tyáo ma

Is petrol included?
包括汽油吗？   bāo·kwòr chèe·yǒ ma

Are tolls included?
包括路费吗？   bāo·kwòr lòo·fày ma

Could I have a receipt for the toll?
请给我路费票   chǐng gáy·wǒr lòo·fày·pyào

Please take me to (this address).
请带我到   chǐng dài·wǒr dào
(这个地址)。   (jày·ger dèe·jǐr)

How much is it (to this address)?
多少钱到
（这个地址）？
dōr·shǎo chyén dào
(jày·ger dèe·jǐr)

Where are we going?
我们到哪去？
wǒr·mern dào nár chèw

Something's wrong with your meter.
你的表有问题。
née·der byǎo yǒ·wèrn·těe

I'll write down your licence number and report you to the PSB.
我会记下车号，
报到给
公安局。
wǒr hwày jèe·syà něe·der
chēr·hào bào gáy
gōong·ūn·jěw

Please ...	请……	chǐng ...
slow down	满点开	mùn·dyěn kāi
stop here	在这儿停	zài jèr tíng
wait here	在这儿等	zài jèr děrng

bicycle

骑自行车

Bicycles are an excellent method for getting around Chinese cities or patrolling tourist sites. In a country with more than 300 million bikes some organisation is required to prevent cycle chaos. In cities you'll be required to park your bike at a bicycle parking lot known as a tsóon·chēr·chǔng 存车场 overseen by an attendant.

I'd like ...	我想……	wór·syǔng ...
my bicycle repaired	修这辆车	syō jày·ger chēr
to buy a bicycle	买一辆车	mǎi ēe·lyǔng chēr
to hire a bicycle	租一辆 自行车	zōo ēe·lyǔng zìr·síng·chēr

I'd like a ... bike.	我要个⋯⋯车。	wǒr yào·ger ... chēr
mountain	山地	shūn·dèe
racing	赛	sài
second-hand	二手	àr·shǒ

How much is it per ...?	一⋯⋯多少钱?	ēe ... dōr·shǎo chyén
day	天	tyēn
hour	小时	syǎo·shír

Do I have to pay a deposit?
要给钱吗?   yào gáy yā·jīn ma

How much is the deposit?
押金多少?   yā·jīn dōr·shǎo

I have a puncture.
穿孔了。   chwùn·kòong ler

Could you pump up my tyres, please?
能帮我打气吗?   nérng būng·wǒr dǎr·chèe ma

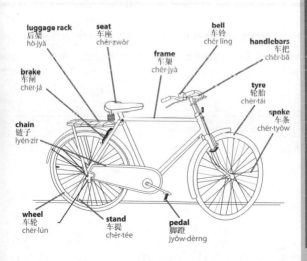

luggage rack 后架 hò·jyà

seat 车座 chēr·zwòr

bell 车铃 chēr líng

handlebars 车把 chēr·bǎ

frame 车架 chēr·jyà

brake 车闸 chēr·já

tyre 轮胎 chēr·tāi

spoke 车条 chēr·tyǒw

chain 链子 lyén·zir

wheel 车轮 chēr·lún

stand 车提 chēr·tée

pedal 脚蹬 jyǒw·dèrng

How much to have this repaired?
修这些多少钱？ syō jày·syāir dōr·shǎo chyén

That's too expensive.
那太贵了。 tài gwày ler

Where's the bicycle parking lot?
存车场在哪？ tsóon·chēr·chǔng zài nár

My bike's been stolen.
我号自行车 wǒr·der zir·síng·chēr
被偷走了。 bày tō zǒ ler

local transport

本地交通

Are you waiting for more people?
还等人吗？ hái·děrng rérn ma

Can you take us around the city please?
请带我到 chǐng dài·wǒr dào
城里转一圈。 chérng·lěe jwùn ee chwēn

How many people can ride on this?
车上能做 chēr·shùng nérng·zwòr
多少人？ dōr·shǎo rérn

border crossing

过境

I'm ...	我是······来的。	wǒr shìr ... lái·der
in transit	过境	gwòr·jìng
on business	出差	chōo·chāi
on holiday	度假	dòo·jyà
on a student visa	持学生	chír shwáir·shērng
	签证	chyēn·jèrng

I'm here for ...	我要住······	wǒr yào jòo ...
(three) days	(三)天	(sūn) tyēn
(three) months	(三)个月	(sūn)·ger ywàir
(three) weeks	(三)个星期	(sūn)·ger sing·chēe

I'm going to (Beijing).
我到(北京)去。　　　　wǒr dào (bǎy·jīng) chèw

I'm staying at (the Pujiang Hotel).
我驻　　　　　　　wǒr jòo
(浦江宾馆)。　　　　(póo·jyūng bīn·gwǔn)

The children are on this passport.
孩子在这个护照上。　　hái·zir zài jày·ger hòo·jào shùng

My visa is in order.
我的签证　　　　　　wǒr·der chyēn·jèrng
办好了。　　　　　　bùn·hǎo·ler

Do I have to pay extra for that?
这样要加钱吗?　　　　jày·yung yào jyā·chyěn ma

listen for ...		
chyēn·jèrng	签证	visa
ēe·jyā	一家	family
hòo·jào	护照	passport
twún·tēe	团体	group

at customs

I have nothing to declare.
我没有东西报。 wǒr máy·yǒ dōong·see bào

I have something to declare.
我有东西报。 wór·yǒ dōong·see bào

Do I have to declare this?
这个要报吗？ jày·ger yào bào ma

I didn't know I had to declare it.
哦，才知道这个要 ō tsái jīr·dào jày·ger yào
报关。 bào gwūn

That's (not) mine.
那(不)是我的。 này (bóo·)shìr wǒr·der

signs		
海关	hǎi·gwūn	**Customs**
免税	myěn·shwày dyèn	**Duty-Free**
入境	ròo·jìng	**Immigration**
护照检查	hòo·jào jyěn·chá	**Passport Control**
检疫	jyěn·èe	**Quarantine**

PRACTICAL

66

Where's (a bank)?
(银行) 在哪?   (yín·húng) zài năr

Excuse me, please.
请问   chǐng wèrn

How do I get there?
怎么走?   zěrn·mer zŏ

How far is it?
有多远?   yŏ dŏr ywĕn

Can you show me where I am on the map?
您认识地图吗?   nĕe rèrn·shir dèe·tŏo ma
我在哪里?   wŏr zài ná·lee

Can you show me where it is on the map?
请帮我在   chǐng būng·wŏr zài
地图上找。   dèe·tóo shùng jăo

listen for ...		
fērn·jōong	分钟	... minutes
goong·lee	公里	... kilometres
mĕe	米	... metres

It's   在……   zài ...
  behind ...   ……的后面   ... der hò·myèn
  close   离这不远   lĕe jèr bòo ywén
  here   这里   jèr·lee
  in front of ...   ……的   ... der
       前面   chyén·myèn
  near ...   ……附近   ... fòo·jìn
  next to ...   ……旁边   ... púng·byēn
  on the corner   十字路口   shír·zìr lòo·kŏ
  opposite ...   ……的对面   ... der dwày·myèn
  straight ahead   直前面   jír chyén·myèn
  there   那里   nàr

directions

north	北	bǎy
south	南	nún
east	东	dōong
west	西	sēe

Turn at ...	在……拐弯。	zài ... gwǎi·wūn
the corner	十字路口	shír·zìr lòo·kǒ
the traffic lights	红绿灯	hóong·lèw·dērng

Turn towards the ...	往……拐。	wǔng ... gwǎi
left	左	zwór
right	右	yò

By ...	……去。	... chèw
bus	坐车	zwòr·chēr
foot	走路	zǒ·lòo
subway	地铁	dèe·tyǎir
taxi	打车	dǎ·chēr
train	坐地铁	zwòr dèe·tyǎir

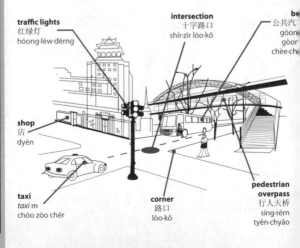

traffic lights
红绿灯
hóong·lèw·dērng

intersection
十字路口
shír·zìr lòo·kǒ

b
公共汽
gōon
gòor
chèe·ch

shop
店
dyèn

pedestrian overpass
行人天桥
síng·rérn
tyēn·chyǎo

taxi
taxi m
chōo zǒo chēr

corner
路口
lòo·kǒ

finding accommodation

找住店

Where's a ...?	哪里有……？	ná·lee yǒ ...
guesthouse	宾馆	bīn·qwǔn
hostel	招待所	jāo·dài·swǒr
hotel	酒店	jyǒ·dyèn
luxury hotel	高级酒店	gao·jee jyǒ·dyèn
university	学校	shwǎir·syào
dormitory	招待所	jāo·dài·swǒr

Can you recommend somewhere ...?	你能推荐一个……的地方住吗？	něe nérng twǎy·jyèn ēe·ger ... der dèe·fūng jòo ma
cheap	便宜	pyén·ee
good	好	hǎo
luxurious	舒服	shōo·foo
nearby	比较近	bée·jyào jìn
romantic	有情调	yǒ chíng·dyào

What's the address?
地址是多少？　　　　　dèe·jǐr shìr dōr·shǎo

Can you please show me on the map where it is?
请帮我
在地图上找。

chíng bung·wǒr
zài dèe·tóo shùng jǎo

For responses, see **directions**, page 67.

local talk		
dive	烂小屋	lùn syǎo·wōo
rat-infested	老鼠窝	láo·shǒo wōr
top spot	好地方	hǎo dèe·fūng

booking ahead & checking in

定房与登记

Can foreigners stay here?
外国人能住
这里吗？

wài·gwór rérn nérng jòo
jèr·lee ma

I'll arrange it with the PSB.
我到派出所
跟他们商量。

wŏr dào pài·chōo·swŏr
gērn tā·mern shūng·lyung

I'd like to book a room, please.
我想订房间。

wór·syŭng dìng fúng·jyēn

I have a reservation.
我有预订。

wór·yŏ yèw·dìng

My name's ...
我叫……

wŏ·jyào ...

listen for ...		
hòo·jào	护照	**passport**
jòo jĕe·tyēn	几天	**How many nights?**
jòo·mŭn	住满	**full**

For (three) nights.
住(三)天。

jòo (sūn) tyēn

For (three) weeks.
住(三)个星期。

jòo (sūn)·ger sīng·chēe

From (2 July) to (6 July).
从(7月2号)
到(7月6号)。

tsóong (chēe·ywàir àr·hào)
dào (chēe·ywàir lyò·hào)

Do I need to pay upfront?
预先付钱吗？

yèw·syēn fòo chyén ma

How much is it per ...?	每……多少钱？	**máy ... dōr·shăo chyén**
night	天	tyēn
person	人	rérn
week	星期	sīng·chēe

Can I pay	能用……	nérng·yòong …
by …?	付帐吗?	fòo·jùng ma
credit card	信用卡	sìn·yòong kǎ
travellers cheque	旅行支票	lěw·síng jīr·pyào

For other methods of payment, see **money**, page 49.

Do you have	有没有	yǒ·máy·yǒ
a … room?	……房?	… fǔng
double (suite)	套	tào
single	单人	dūn·rérn
twin	双人	shwung·rérn

Do you have a room with a bathroom?
有带浴室
的房间吗?
yǒ dài yèw·shír
der fúng·jyēn ma

Do you give student discounts?
有没有学生
折扣?
yǒ·máy·yǒ shwáir·shērng
jér·kò

Can I see it?
能看房间吗?
nérng kùn fǔng·jyēn ma

I'll take it.
好了,可以了。
hǎo ler kér·ěe ler

---

signs

We've given Pinyin romanisations of these common signs (in the fourth column) as well as our own pronunciation guides as you may see these signs in Pinyin in cities.

bathroom	厕所	tsèr·swǒr	ce suo
entry	入口	ròo·kǒ	ru kou
exit	出口	chōo·kǒ	chu kou
female	女	něw	nü
male	男	nún	nan

requests & queries

When is breakfast served?
早饭几点钟开？   zǎo·fùn jée·dyěn·jōong kāi

Where is breakfast served?
早饭在哪里开？   zǎo·fùn zài ná·lee kāi

Please wake me at (seven am).
（早上   (zǎo·shùng
七点钟）   chēe·dyěn·jōong)
请叫醒我。   chǐng jyào·síng wǒr

Is there hot water all day?
全天有热水吗？   chwén·tyēn yǒ rèr·shwǎy ma

Is there heating?
有暖气吗？   yó nwǔn·chèe ma

What times does the ... come on?	…… 几点钟开？	… jée·dyěn·jōong kāi
heating	暖气	nwǔn·chèe
hot water	热水	rèr·shwǎy

Can I use the ...?	能用一下……吗？	nérng yòong ēe·syà ... ma
kitchen	厨房	chóo·fǔng
laundry	洗衣房	sěe·ēe·fǔng
telephone	电话	dyèn·hwà

Do you have a/an ...?	有没有……？	yǒ·máy·yǒ ...
elevator	电梯	dyèn·tēe
laundry service	洗衣服务	sěe·ēe fóo·wòo
message board	通告兰	tōong·gào lún
safe	保险箱	báo·syěn syùng
swimming pool	游泳池	yó·yǒong chír

Do you ... here?	你们能……吗？	něe·mérn nérng ... ma
arrange tours	安排旅游团	ūn·pái lěw·síng twún
change money	换钱	hwùn·chyén

Could I have ..., please?	能不能给我……？	nérng·bòo·nérng gǎi·wǒr…
an extra blanket	多一个毛毯	dōr ēe·ger máo·tǔn
my key	房间钥匙	ēe·ger yào·shir
a mosquito net	一个蚊帐	ēe·ger wérn·jùng
a receipt	发票	fā·pyào
some soap	一块肥皂	ēe·kwài fáy·zào
a towel	一个毛巾	ēe·ger máo·jīn

Is there a message for me?
有人留言吗？   yǒ rérn lyó·yén ma

Can I leave a message for someone?
我能留个信条吗？   wǒr nérng lyó ger sìn·tyǎo ma

I'm locked out of my room.
我进不了房间。   wǒr jìn·boo·lyáo fũng·jyēn

complaints

投诉

The room's too ...	房间太……了。	fũng·jyēn tài ... ler
bright	亮	lyùng
cold	冷	lérng
dark	暗	ùn
expensive	贵	gwày
noisy	吵	chǎo
small	小	syǎo

accommodation

73

The ... doesn't work.	……有毛病。	... yŏ máo·bìng
air-conditioning	空调	kōong·tyáo
fan	电风扇	dyèn·fērng·shùn
light	电灯	dyèn·dērng
shower	淋浴头	lín·yèw tó
tap (faucet)	水龙头	shwăy·lóong·tó
toilet	厕所	tsèr·swŏr

I saw ... in my room.	我房间里有……	wór fŭng·jyēn·lee yŏ ...
a big rat	一个大老鼠	ēe·ger dà láo·shŏo
cockroaches	蟑螂	jūng·lúng
mice	耗子	hào·zir

Can I get an extra (blanket)?
我能多拿
一个(毛毯)吗？

wŏr nérng dōr·ná
ēe·ger (máo·tŭn) ma

This (pillow) isn't clean.
这个(枕头)有点脏。

jày·ger (jěrn·tó) yó·dyěn zūng

---

a knock at the door ...

Who is it?	是谁？	shìr sháy
Just a moment.	等一下。	děrng ēe syà
Come in.	请进。	chīng jìn
Come back later, please.	请过一会再来。	chīng gwòr·ēe·hwàr zài lái

checking out

退房

What time is checkout?
几点钟退房？

jée·dyěn·jōong twày·fŭng

Can I have a late checkout?
我能晚点
退房吗？

wŏr nérng wún·dyěn
twày·fŭng ma

Can you call a taxi for me (for 11 o'clock)?
请帮我订一个
（早上十一点的）车。
chǐng bùng wǒr dìng ēe·ger
(zǎo·shùng shír·ēe·dyěn der) chēr

I'm leaving now.
我现在走了。
wǒr syèn·zài zǒ ler

Can I leave my bags here?
能放一下行李吗？
nérng fùng·ēe·syà síng·lěe ma

There's a mistake in the bill.
帐单上有问题。
jùng·dūn shùng yǒ wern·tee

What's that charge for?
这项是什么？
jày syùng shìr shér·mer

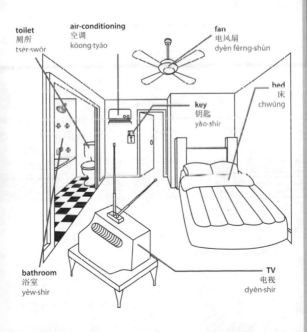

toilet
厕所
tsér·swǒr

air-conditioning
空调
kōong·tyáo

fan
电风扇
dyèn fērng·shùn

bed
床
chwǔng

key
钥匙
yào·shír

bathroom
浴室
yèw·shir

TV
电视
dyèn·shir

Could I have my deposit back, please.
请帮我退押金。　　　　　　chǐng bùng wǒr twày yā·jīn

I had a great stay, thank you.
我在这住得　　　　　　　　wǒr zài jèr jòo·der
很开心，谢谢。　　　　　　hěrn kāi·sīn syàir·syair

I'll recommend it to my friends.
我会给朋友　　　　　　　　wǒr hwày gǎy pérng·yǒ
推荐这个地方。　　　　　　twāy·jyèn jày·ger dèe·fūng

I'll be back …　　我……再回来。　　wǒr … zái hwáy·lái
　　in (three) days　过 (三) 天　　gwòr (sūn) tyēn
　　on (Tuesday)　　下个 (星期二)　syà·ger (sīng·chēe àr)

Could I have　　请帮我拿……　　chǐng bùng wǒr ná …
my …, please?
　　deposit　　押金　　　　　yā·jīn
　　passport　　护照　　　　　hòo·jào
　　valuables　　贵重物品　　　gwày·jòong wòo·pǐn

camping

野营

Where can we spend the night?
在哪里可以　　　　　　zài ná·lee kér·ěe
住下一晚上？　　　　　jòo·syà ēe wǔn·shùng

Can we camp here?
在这里能　　　　　　　zài jèr·lěe nérng·jòo
住帐篷吗？　　　　　　jùng·pérng ma

Can we light a fire here?
在这里能　　　　　　　zài jèr lěe nérng
生火吗？　　　　　　　shērng·hwór ma

Is it safe to sleep in this place?
住这里安全吗？　　　　jòo jèr·lee ūn·chwén ma

renting

租房

I'm here about the ... for rent.	我是租······来的。	wŏr shìr zoo ... lái der
Do you have a/an ... for rent?	有出租······吗?	yŏ chōo·zōo ... ma
apartment	楼房	ló·fŭng
house (basic)	平房	píng·fŭng
room	房间	fŭng·jyēn
villa (luxurious)	别墅	byáir·shòo
furnished	带家具的	dài jyā·joo der
partly furnished	带部分家具的	dài bòo·fern jyā·joo der
unfurnished	不带家具的	bóo dài jyā·joo der

staying with locals

住老百姓家里

Can I stay at your place?
我能在你家住吗?　　　wŏr·nérng zài nĕe jyā jòo ma

Is there anything I can do to help?
有什么事能帮你吗?　　yŏ shér·mer shìr nérng būng née ma

I have my own ...	我带了自己的······	wŏr dài·ler zìr·jĕe der ...
mattress	褥子	rŏo·zir
sleeping bag	睡袋	shwày·dài

Can I ...?	我能……吗？	wǒr·nérng ... ma
bring anything	带来一些	dài lái ēe·syāir
for the meal	什么	shér·mer
do the dishes	帮你洗	būng něe sée
	盘子	pǔn·zir

Thanks for your hospitality.
谢谢你的宽待。   syàir·syàir něe der kwūn·dài

the host with the most

Food has great significance in Chinese culture. If you're staying in a Chinese home or have just been invited to share a
meal, the surest way to gladden the hearts of your hosts is to
heartily express your appreciation of their culinary prowess.
Here are two handy phrases:

The food was delicious!
吃的真香！   chīr·der jērn syūng

My stomach is very happy.
吃的真饱。   chīr·der jērn bǎo

In return, you can expect to hear this constant encourage-
ment from your hosts to overindulge yourself:

Eat up!
多吃一点！   dōr chīr ēe·dyěn

For more dining-related expressions, see **eating out**,
page 163.

looking for ...

问路

Where's ...?	……在哪?	... zài nǎr
an antique	古董	góo·dǒong
shop	市场	shìr·chǎng
a market	菜市场	tsài·shìr·chǎng
a shopping centre	商场	shāng·chǎng
a supermarket	超市	chāo·shìr

Where can I buy (a padlock)?
哪里能买到
(一把锁)？   ná·lee nérng mǎi·dào
(ēe·bá swǒr)

For phrases on directions, see **directions**, page 67.

making a purchase

买货

I'm just looking.
我先看看。   wǒr syēn kùn·kun

I'd like to buy (an adaptor plug).
我想买   wòr·syúng mǎi
(一个插座)。   (ēe·ger chā·zwòr)

How much is it?
多少钱？   dōr·shǎo chyén

Can I look at it?
我能看看吗？   wǒr·nérng kùn·kun ma

Please write down the price.
请写下来。   chíng syǎir·syà lái

Do you have any others?
有没有别的？   yǒ·máy·yǒ byáir·der

Do you accept ...?	你们收……吗？	něe·mern shò … ma
credit cards	信用卡	sìn·yòong kǎ
debit cards	借记卡	jyàir·jèe·kǎ
travellers cheques	旅行支票	lěw·síng jīr·pyào

Could I have a ..., please?	请给我……	chǐng gáy·wǒr …
bag	一个袋子	ēe·ger dài·zir
receipt	开发票	kāi fā·pyào

Could I have it wrapped?
能包装一下吗？
nérng bāo·jwūng ee·syà ma

Does it have a guarantee?
有保修期吗？
yó bǎo·syō·chēe ma

Can I have it sent overseas?
你能寄到
国外吗？
něe nérng jèe·dào
gwór·wài ma

Will I be allowed to take this out of the country?
我能带出境吗？
wǒr nérng dài chōo·jìng ma

Can you order one for me?
能买进一个吗？
nérng mǎi·jìn·lǎi ēe·ger ma

Can I pick it up later?
过一会来拿, 好吗？
gwòr ee·hwàr lái ná hǎo ma

It's faulty.
有毛病。
yǒ máo·bìng

This item is a fake.
这是假货。
jèr·shìr jyǎ·hwòr

local talk		
a bargain	实惠	shír·hwày
grand sale	大甩卖	dà·shwāi·mài
on special	打折扣	dǎ jér·ko
a rip-off	真灾人	jèrn zāi·rérn
to bargain	砍价	kǔn·jyà

I'd like …, please.	可以……吗？	kér·ĕe … ma
my change	找零钱	jăo líng·chyén
a refund	退钱	twày chyén
to return this	退还这个	twày·hwún jày·ger

playing it cool

Whether you're wheeling and dealing in China, or just trying to get a few yuan knocked off the price of a portrait of Mao, there are a few points to keep in mind to help your negotiations go smoothly.

The concept of 'saving face' (myèn·zir 面子) is important in Chinese culture. Essentially it's about avoiding being made to look stupid or to back down in front of others – a concept which isn't limited to the Chinese of course. Negotiated settlements that provide benefits to both parties are preferable to confrontation. A desire to save face may lead people to disguise uncomfortable truths.

Chinese men and women are generally reserved with hand and facial movements. The animated gesticulating of Westerners can seem undignified and even comical to them.

A smile doesn't necessarily mean happiness. Chinese people may also smile when they're embarrassed or worried.

For more on body language, see **romance**, page 138.

bargaining

谈价

You're kidding!
开什么玩笑！
kāi shér·mer wún·syào

That's too expensive!
太贵了！
tài·gwày ler

Can you lower the price?
能便宜一点吗？
nérng pyén·èe ee·dyĕn ma

Do you have something cheaper?
有便宜一点的吗？
yŏ pyén·èe ee·dyĕn der ma

I'll give you (five kuai).
给你(五块)钱。　　　gáy·něe (wǒo·kwày) chyěn

That's my final offer.
就给这么多。　　　jyò gǎy jèr·mer dōr

clothes

衣服

My size is …	我穿……号。	wǒr chwūn … hào
(40)	(40)	(sìr·shír)
large	大	dà
medium	中	joong
small	小	syǎo
extra large	X 大	ài·ker·sìr dà

Can I try it on?
能试试　　　　　　nérng shung shìr·shir
穿吗?　　　　　　chwūn ma

Is there a mirror?
有镜子吗?　　　　yǒ jìng·zir ma

It doesn't fit.
穿得不合身。　　　chwun·der bòo hér·shērn

Where can I find a tailor?
哪里能找个　　　　ná·lee nérng·jǎo·ger
裁缝?　　　　　　tsǎi·fèrng

For clothing items, see the **dictionary**.

repairs

修东西

Can I have my	你能修	něe nérng·syō
… repaired here?	我的……吗?	wǒr·der … ma
When will	……什么时候	… shér·mer shír·hò
my … be ready?	来拿?	lái·ná
backpack	背包	bày·bāo
camera	照相机	jào·syùng·jēe
glasses	眼镜	yén·jìng
shoes	鞋子	syáir·zir
sunglasses	墨镜	mòr·jìng

hairdressing

理发

I'd like (a) ...	我想……	wór·syǔng ...
blow wave	烫发	tùng·fà
colour	染色	rǔn·sèr
haircut	剪发	jyěn·fà
my beard trimmed	整理胡子	jérng·lee hóo·zir
shave	剃胡子	tèe hóo·zir
trim	剪 点	jyèn·ee·dyěn

Don't cut it too short.
不要剪得太短。   bóo·yào jyěn·der tài dwǔn

Please use a new blade.
请用一个   chǐng yòong ēe·ger
新的刀片。   sīn·der dāo·pyèn

Shave It all off!
剃光了吧！   tèe·gwūng lèr ba

I should never have let you near me!
(lit: How can I explain this to my parents?)
哎哟，我怎么跟   ai·yo wor zér·me gěrn
父母交待？   fòo·mǒo jyāo·dài

For colours, see the **dictionary**.

books & reading

文化世界

Do you have ...?	有没有……？	yǒ·máy·yǒ ...
a book by (Jin Yong)	（金庸） 的书	(jin·yōong) der shōo
an entertainment guide	娱乐指南	yěw·lèr jír·nún

Is there an English-language ...?	附近有 英文……吗？	fòo·jìn yǒ yīng·wērn ... ma
bookshop	书店	shōo·dyèn
section	书兰	shōo·lún

I'd like a …	我想	wór·syŭng
	买一个……	măi·ee·ger …
copy of the *China Daily*	中国日报	jūng·gwór rìr·bào
dictionary	词典	tsír·dyěn
newspaper (in English)	(英文)报纸	(yīng·wěrn) bào·jīr
notepad	笔记本	běe·jèe·běrn

Can you recommend a book to me?

你能推荐一个
好书吗？

něe nérng twāy·jyèn ee·ger
hǎo shōo ma

Do you have Lonely Planet guidebooks?

有没有
Lonely Planet
的旅行指南书？

yŏ·máy·yŏ
lór·ne·lěe pŏo·lā·nái·tèr
der lěw·yó jír·nún shōo

PRACTICAL

music

音乐

I'd like a ... | 我想买 | wór·syúng mǎi
 | 一个…… | ēe·ger ...
   blank tape | 空磁带 | kōong tsǐr·dài
   CD | CD | sēe·dèe
   DVD | DVD | dēe·wǎy·dèe

I'm looking for something by (Zhou Huajian).
我在找(周华健) | wǒr zài jǎo (jō hwá jyèn)
的曲了。 | der chēw·zir

What's his/her best recording?
他/她最好的CD是 | tā zwày hǎo der CD shìr
哪个? | nǎr·ger

Can I listen to this?
我能听一下吗? | wǒr·nérng tīng ee·syà ma

photography

摄影

Can you ...? | 能……吗? | nérng ... ma
   develop this | 洗这个 | sēe jày·ger
     film | 胶卷 | jyāo·jwěn
   load my | 安装这个 | ùn·Jwūng Jày·ger
     film | 胶卷 | jyāo·jwěn

I need ... film | 我想买 | wór·syúng mǎi
for this camera. | 这个机子的…… | jày·ger jēe·zir der ...
 | 胶卷。 | jyāo·jwěn

   APS | APS | āi·pēe·ai·sir
   B&W | 黑白 | hāy·bái
   colour | 彩色 | tsǎi·sèr
   slide | 幻灯 | hwùn·dērng
   ... speed | ……感 | ... gǔn·
 | 光度 | gwūng·dòo

shopping

85

How much is it?
多少钱?   dōr·shǎo chyén

When will it be ready?
什么时候来取?   shér·mer shír·hò lái chěw

I need a passport photo taken.
我想照一幅   wór·syǔng jào ee·foo
一寸的照片。   ēe·tsōon der jào·pyèn

I'm not happy with these photos.
这卷洗的不好。   jày jwèn sěe·der bòo·hǎ

I don't want to pay the full price.
请帮我打   chǐng būng·wór
个折扣。   dǎ ger jér·kò

souvenirs		
antique	古董	góo·dǒng
bronze	铜器	tóong·chèe
calligraphy	书法	shōo·fǎ
ceramics	陶瓷	táo·tsír
coins	钱币	chyén·bèe
ink painting	笔画	bée·hwà
jade	宝玉	bǎo·yèw
oil painting	油画	yó·hwà
scroll	国画	gwór·hwà
silk	丝绸	sīr·chǒ
stamps	邮票	yǒ·pyào
statue	塑像	sòo·syùng
tea	茶叶	chá·yàir
woodblock print	木刻	mòo·ker

通讯

post office

在邮局

I want to send a ...	找想寄 一个……	wŏr·syúng jèe ēe·ger ...
fax	传真	chwún·jèrn
letter	信	sìn
parcel	包裹	bāo·gwŏr
postcard	明信片	míng·sìn·pyèn
I want to buy a/an ...	我想买 一个……	wŏr·syúng mǎi ēe·ger ...
aerogram	带有票的 信封	dài yŏ·pyào der sìn·fērng
envelope	信封	sìn·fêrng
stamp	邮票	yŏ·pyào
customs	海关	hăi·gwūn
declaration	报税	bào·shwày
domestic	国内	gwór·này
fragile	易碎	èe·swày
international	国际	gwór·jèe
mailbox	信箱	sìn·syūng
postal service	信件	sìn·jyèn
postcode	邮编号码	yŏ·byēn hào·mă
to send	寄信	jèe·sìn

snail mail

air	航运	húng·yèwn
express	特快	tèr·kwài
registered	挂号	gwā·hào
surface (land)	陆运	lòo·yèwn
surface (sea)	海运	hăi·yèwn

Please send it by airmail/surface mail to (Australia).

请寄航运/   chǐng jèe húng·yèwn/
海运到(澳大利亚)。   hǎi·yèwn dào (ào·dà·lee·ya)

It contains (souvenirs).

里面有(纪念品)。   lěe·myèn yǒ (jèe·nyèn·pǐn)

Where's the poste restante section?

领取指示写   líng·chěw jǐr·shìr syǎir
在哪里?   zài ná·lee

Is there any mail for me?

有没有我的来信?   yǒ·máy·yǒ wǒ·der lái·sìn

phone

打电话

What's your phone number?

您的电话   nǐn der dyèn·hwà
号码是多少?   hào·mǎ shìr dōr·shǎo

Where's the nearest public phone?

这附近有公用   jèr fòo·jin yǒ gōong·yòong
电话吗?   dyèn·hwà ma

Can you help me find the number for …?

请帮我找一下……   chǐng būng·wor jǒw·ee·syà …
的号码。   der hào·mǎ

I want to …	我想……	wór·syǔng …
buy a phonecard	买一个	mǎi ēe·ger
	电话卡	dyèn·hwà kǎ
call (Singapore)	打电话给	dǎ dyèn·hwà gǎy
	(新加坡)	(sīn·jyā·pōr)
make a (local) call	打(市内)	dǎ (shìr·này)
	电话	dyèn·hwà
reverse the charges	打对方	dǎ dwày·fūng
	付款	fòo·kwǔn
	的电话	der dyèn·hwà
speak for (three) minutes	用	yòong
	(三)分钟	(sūn)·fērn·jōong

How much does it cost per minute?
打一分钟   dǎ ēe·fērn·jōong
多少钱?   dōr·shǎo chyén

The number is ...
号码是……   hào·mǎ shìr ...

What's the area code for (New Zealand)?
(新西兰) 的区号   (sīn·sēe·lún) der chēw·hào
是多少?   shìr dōr·shǎo

It's engaged.
占线了。   jùn·syèn ler

I've been cut off.
断掉了。   dwùn·dyào ler

The connection's bad.
电话线不好。   dyèn·hwà·syèn bòo·hǒw

Hello.
喂。   wày

Can I speak to ...?
我找……   wó jǒw ...

It's ...
这是……   jèr shìr ...

Is ... there?
……在吗?   ... zài ma

Please tell him/her I called.
请告诉他/她   chǐng gào·soo tā
我打来了。   wór dǎ·lái ler

Can I leave a message?
我能留言吗?   wǒ nérng lyó yén ma

My number is ...
我的号码是……   wǒr·der hào·mǎ shìr ...

I don't have a contact number.
我在这儿没有   wǒr zài jèr máy·yǒ
电话。   dyèn·hwà

I'll call back later.
我晚点在打过来。   wǒr wún·dyěn zài dǎ·gwòr·lái

mobile/cell phone

手机

I'd like a ...	我想买 一个……	wór·syúng mǎi ēe·ger ...
charger for my phone	充电器	chǒng·dyèn chèe
mobile/cell phone	手机	shǒ·jēe
(100 yuan) prepaid card	（一百块的） 预付卡	(ēe·bǎi kwài der) yèw·fòo·kǎ
SIM card	SIM卡	sīm·kǎ

What are the rates?
电话费怎么算？   dyèn·hwà·fày zěr·mer swùn

(30 fen) per minute.
每分钟
（三毛钱）。   máy·fērn·jōong
(sūn·máo·chyén)

the internet

上网

Where's the local Internet café?
附近有网吧吗?   fòo·jìn yó wǔng·bā ma

Can I get an account with a local Internet provider?
我能开一个   wǒr nérng kāi·ee·ger
IP账户吗?   ai·pèe jùnq·hoo ma

I'd like to ...	我想……	wór·syǔng …
check my email	看一下电子信箱	kùn ee·syà dyèn·zir sìn·syǔng
get Internet access	上网	shùng·wǔng
use a printer	打印	dǎ·yìn
use a scanner	扫描	sǎo·myáo

Do you have ...?	有……吗?	yǒ … ma
PCs	IBM	ài·bēe·àr·moo
a Zip drive	ZIP盘	zíp pún
How much per ...?	每……多少钱?	máy … dōr·shǎo chyén
hour	小时	syǎo·shír
(five) minutes	(五)分钟	(wǒo)·fērn·jōong
page	页	yàir

How do I log on?

我怎么登入？　　　　　　　wǒr zér·mer dērng·ròo

Please change it to English-language preference.

请帮找换成　　　　　　　　chǐng bǔng·wǒr
换成英文　　　　　　　　　hwùn·chérng yīng·wérn
格式。　　　　　　　　　　gěr·shìr

This connection's really slow.

网速太慢了。　　　　　　　wǔng·sòo tài mùn ler

It's crashed.

死机了。　　　　　　　　　sǐr·jēe ler

I've finished.

上完了。　　　　　　　　　shùng wún ler

bank

银行

With the rapid development of China's electronic banking network over recent years, you can generally avoid queueing up in Chinese banks. Withdrawals can instead be made at automated teller machines (zìr·dòong chéw·kwǔn·jēe 自动取款机) dotted across all major cities.

What time does the bank open?

银行什么 时候开门?	yín·húng shér·mer shír·hò kāi·mern

Where can I ...?	我在哪里 能……?	wǒr zài ná·lee nérng ...
I'd like to ...	我要……	wǒr yào ...
cash a cheque	兑现 一张支票	dwày·syèn ee·jūng jīr·pyào
change a travellers cheque	换旅行 支票	hwǔn lěw·síng jīr·pyào
change money	换钱	hwùn·chyén
get a cash advance	现金透支	syèn·jīn tò·jīr
withdraw money	取现金	chěw syèn·jīn

Where's ...?	……在哪?	... zài nǎr
an ATM	自动 取款机	zìr·dòong chéw·kwǔn·jēe
a place to change foreign money	换外币 的地方	hwùn wài·bèe der dèe·fūng

The ATM took my card.

取款机
吃了我的卡。

chéw·kwǔn·jēe
chīr·ler wǒr·der kǎ

I've forgotten my PIN.

我忘了我的
密码。

wǒr wùng·ler wǒr·der
mèe·mǎ

Can I use my credit card to withdraw money?

能用信用卡
取现金吗？

něrng yòong sìn·yòong·ká
chěw syèn·jīn ma

Has my money arrived yet?

我的汇款
到了没有？

wǒr·der hwày·kwǔn
dào·ler máy·yǒ

How long will it take to arrive?

还要等多久？

hái·yào·děrng dōr·jyǒ

What's the ...?	……是什么？	... shìr shér·mer
charge for that	手续费	shǒ·sèw·fày
exchange rate	兑换率	dwày·hwùn·lèw

For other useful phrases see **money**, page 49.

I'd like a/an ...	我想买 一个……	wór·syúng mǎi ēe·ger ...
audio set	录音向导	lòo·yīn syùng·dǎo
catalogue	画册	hwà·tsèr
guide	指南书	jír·nún shoo
guidebook in English	英文指南 书	yīng·wérn Jír·nún shōo
(local) map	(本地)地图	(běrn·dèe) dèe·tǒo

Do you have information on local...?	有没有关于 ……的资料？	yǒ·máy·yǒ gwūn·yóo ... der zīr·lyào
culture	地方 文化	dèe·fūng wérn·hwà
history	地方史	dèe·fūng shǐr
religion	地方 宗教	dèc fūng zōong·jyào

I'd like to see ... 我想看……	wór·syǔng kùn ...
What's that? 那是什么？	nà shìr shér·mer
Who made it? 是谁做的？	shìr sháy zwòr·der
How old is it? 有多老？	yǒ dōr lǎo

Can I take photos?
可以照相吗？   kér·ĕe jào·jao·syùng ma

Could you take a photo of me?
你能帮我   nĕe nérng būng wŏr
照相吗？   jào·syùng ma

Can I take a photo (of you)?
我能照（你的）   wŏr nérng jào (nĕe·der)
像吗？   syùng ma

I'll send you the photograph.
我会把照片   wŏr hwày bǎ jào·pyèn
寄给你。   jèe·gay nĕe

Please write down your name and address.
请记下你的   chǐng jèe·syà nĕe·der
地址。   dèe·jĭr

---

you haven't seen anything yet

On your travels around China, local people are likely to be curious to find out which of China's many attractions are on your itinerary. To help you communicate on this score, here are the Mandarin names of some of China's tourist drawcards. You could introduce them by using the first two phrases:

I've been to …
我去过……   wŏr chèw·gwòr …

I'm planning to go to …
我打算去……   wór dǎ·swùn … chèw

Army of Terracotta Warriors in Xi'an	兵马俑	bīng·má·yŏong
Forbidden City	故宫	gòo·gōong
Great Wall	长城	cháng·chérng
Guilin	桂林	gwāy·lín
Pingyao	平遥	píng·yów
Tai Shan	泰山	tài·shūn
West Lake of Hangzhou	西湖	sēe·hóo

getting in

What time does it open?
几点关门？ jée·dyěn gwūn·mérn

What time does it close?
几点开门？ jée·dyěn kāi·mérn

What's the admission charge?
门票多少钱？ mérn·pyào dōr·shǎo chyén

Is there a 有……折扣吗？ yǒ … jér·kò ma
discount for …?

children	儿童	ár·tóong
families	家庭	jyā·tíng
groups	团体	twún·těe
older people	老年	lǎo·nyén
students	学生	shwáir·shěrng

tours

Can you 你能推荐 něe nérng twāy·jyèn
recommend a …? 一个……吗？ ēe·ger … ma
When's the 下一个……是 syà·ee·ger … shìr
next …? 什么时候？ shér·mer shír·hò

boat-trip	船游	chwún·yó
day trip	一日游	ēe·rìr·yó
tour	向导游	syùng·dǎo·yó

Is ... included?	包括……吗?	bāo·kwòr ... ma
accommodation	住宿	jòo·sōo
the admission price	票价	pyào·jyà
food	饮食	yǐn·shír
transport	交通	jyāo·tōong

The guide will pay.
向导员
会付钱。

syùng·dǎo·ywén
hwày fòo·chyén

The guide has paid.
向导员
已经付了钱。

syùng·dǎo·ywén
ěe·jīng fòo·ler chyén

How long is the tour?
向导游要
多长时间?

syùng·dǎo·yó yào
dōr·chéng shír·jyēn

Chinese dynasties

The abbreviations BCE and CE stand for Before Common Era and Common Era and are equivalent to the terms BC and AD.

Xia dynasty (2070–1600BCE)
夏朝　　　　　　　　　syà·cháo

Shang dynasty (1600–1046BCE)
上朝　　　　　　　　　shùng·cháo

Zhou dynasty (1046–256BCE)
周朝　　　　　　　　　jō·cháo

Spring and Autumn period (770–476BCE)
春秋时期　　　　　　　chōon·chyō shír·chēe

Warring States period (475–221BCE)
战国时期　　　　　　　jùn·gwór shìr·chēe

Qin dynasty (221–207BCE)
秦朝　　　　　　　　　chín·cháo

Han dynasty (206BCE–220CE)
汉朝　　　　　　　　　hùn·cháo

Tang dynasty (618–907CE)
唐朝　　　　　　　　　túng·cháo

Song dynasty (960–1279CE)
宋朝　　　　　　　　　sòong·cháo

Yuan dynasty (1279–1368)
元朝　　　　　　　　　ywén·cháo

Ming dynasty (1368–1644)
明朝　　　　　　　　　míng·cháo

Qing dynasty (1644–1911)
清朝　　　　　　　　　chīng·cháo

Republic of China (1911–1949)
民国时期　　　　　　　mín·gwór shír·chēe

People's Republic (lit: Liberated Era) (1949–present)
解放时期　　　　　　　jyáir·fùng shír·chēe

What time should we be back?

几点要回来？   jée·dyěn yào hwáy·lái

I'm with them.

我跟他们在一块。   wǒr gērn tā·mern zài ee·kwàr

I've lost my group.

我找不到   wór jǎo·boo·dào
我的团体。   wǒr·der twún·těe

---

hello stranger

One of the mild annoyances you're likely to face on the road if you venture outside the cosmopolitan centres is the incessant exclamation 老外 lǎo·wài. Or alternatively 'Hello lǎo·wài hello!'. The first character means 'old' and is a mark of respect in Chinese. The second character literally means 'outside'.

Used in this context, however, the expression is not exactly polite but nor is it cause for offence either. You could think of it as akin to 'Hey Old Whitey!' or something of that nature. It's certainly a lot better than outmoded forms of address such as 'Foreign Devil' or 'American Spy'. If you answer by saying hello be prepared for your audience to break into hysterical laughter.

I'm attending a ...	我来参加 一个……	wǒr lái tsūn·jyā ee·ger ...
conference	研讨会	yèrn·tǎo·hwày
course	培训班	páy·sèwn·būn
meeting	会议	hwày·ee
trade fair	洽谈会	chyǎ·tún·hwày
I'm with ...	我跟…… 一块来的。	wǒr gērn ... ee·kwàr·lǎi ler
(China Travel Co.)	(中旅 公司)	(jūng·lěw gōong·sīr)
my colleague(s)	(几个)同事	(jěe·ger) tóng·shìr
(two) others	(两个)人	(lyǔng·ger) rérn

I'm alone.
我一个人来的。 wǒr ēe·ger·rérn lái ler

I have an appointment with ...
我跟……有约。 wǒr gērn ... yǒ·ywǎir

I'm staying at ..., room ...
我驻在……, wǒr jòo zài ...
……房间。 ... hào fūng·jyēn

I'm here for (two) days.
我要呆(两)天。 wǒr yào dāi (lyǔng)·tyēn

I'm here for (two) weeks.
我要呆(两)个 wǒr yào dāi (lyǔng)·ger
星期。 sīng·chēe

That went very well.
刚才开得很好。 gūng·tsǎi kāi·der hérn·hǎo

Thank you for your time.
谢谢你们的 syàir·syair něe·men·der
关照。 gwūn·jào

Shall we go for a drink?
我们是不是要
出去喝杯酒？

zǔn·men shìr·boo·shir yào
chōo·chew hēr·bāy·jyǒ

Shall we go for a meal?
我们是不是要
出去吃饭？

zǔn·men shìr·boo·shir yào
chōo·chew chīr·fùn

It's on me.
我请客。

wór chǐng kèr

Where's the …?
  business
    centre
  conference
  meeting

……在哪？
商务
中心
研讨会
会议

… zài nǎr
shūng·wòo
jōong·sīn
yérn·tǎo·hwày
hwày·ee

I need …
  a computer
  an Internet
    connection
  an interpreter
  to send a fax

我需要……
一个电脑
联上
网络
一位翻译
发一个
传真

wǒr sēw·yào …
ee·ger dyèn·nǎo
lyén·shùng
wǔng·lwòr
ee·wày fūn·èe
fā ee·ger
chwén·jērn

---

clinching the deal Chinese style

The notion of guanxi gwūn·see 关系 (connections) is central to doing business in China. In a country where people often have to compete for goods and services in short supply, a network of advantageous reciprocal connnections in places of power is all important. Obtaining goods and services through such channels is colloquially known as 'going through the back door' (zǒ·hò·mér 走后门). Typical displays of guanxi are lavish banquets fuelled with Chinese spirit (bái·jyǒ 白酒). If you want to cut any deals while in China, you may be wise to adopt the local custom in this regard.

残疾旅行者年迈旅行者

In China older people are revered. To be called an 'old man'
(dà·yair 大爷 lit: grand father) or an 'old woman' (dà·mā 大妈
lit: great mother) is a compliment, a tribute to your maturity
and wisdom. Disabled people, on the other hand, will not find
China easy as there are precious few facilities for the disabled.

I have a disability.
我活动有障碍。 wŏr hwór·dòong yŏ jùng·ai

I need assistance.
我需要帮助。 wŏr sēw·yào bùng·joo

Is there wheelchair access?
轮车能走进 lóon·chēr nérng zŏ·jìn
门口吗? mérn·kŏ ma

How wide is the entrance?
门口有多宽? mérn·kŏ yŏ dōr·kwūn

I'm deaf.
我耳朵聋了。 wór ăr·dōr lóong ler

I have a hearing aid.
我带有助听器。 wŏr dài·yŏ jòo·tīng·chèe

How many steps are there?
有几个台阶? yó jĕe·ger tái·jyāir

Is there a lift?
有电梯吗? yŏ dyèn·tēe ma

Are there rails in the bathroom?
浴室里有扶手吗? yèw·shir lee yŏ fóo·shŏ ma

Could you help me cross the street safely?
请问, 能帮我 chĭng·wèrn nérng bùng·wŏr
过马路吗? gwòr mă·lòo ma

Is there somewhere I can sit down?
哪里可以座一下 ná·lee kér·ĕe zwòr·ēe·syà
休息? syō·see

older person	老年人	lǎo·nyén·rérn
person with a disability	残疾人	tsǔn·jée rérn
ramp	坡道	pōr·dào
walking frame	拐杖架子	gwǎi·jùng jyā·zir
walking stick	拐杖	gwǎi·jùng
wheelchair	轮车	lóon·chēr

spelling it out

Most Chinese are familiar with the Latin alphabet through their knowledge of Pinyin and English. If you want to spell out your name in hotels etc, you should follow the Chinese pronunciation of the alphabet in the chart below as you probably won't be understood if you say the letters as in English. Latin letters can be represented with characters representing the sounds.

A	阿	a	N	恩	ērn
B	悲	bāy	O	呕	ō
C	西	sēe	P	披	pēe
D	弟	dèe	Q	酷	kòo
E	衣	ēe	R	耳	ǎr
F	饿夫	èr·foo	S	饿死	èr·sǐr
G	鸡	jēe	T	踢	tēe
H	爱耻	ài·chǐr	U	忧	yō
I	挨	āi	V	维	wáy
J	宅	jāi	W	大波伟	dà·bō·wǎy
K	开	kāi	X	哎渴死	ai·kér·sǐr
L	饿罗	èr·lwór	Y	歪	wāi
M	饿母	èr·mǒo	Z	自得	zìr·dér

children

Chinese people think foreign children are fascinating. You may find that travelling with children greatly facilitates striking up conversations with locals and getting to know them.

Is there a ...?	这儿	jèr
	有没有……?	yǒ máy·yǒ …
child discount	儿童折扣	ár·tóong jér·kò
child-minding service	保姆服务	báo·mǒo fóo·wòo
child's portion	儿童	ár·tóong
	分量	fèrn·lyùng
crèche	幼儿园	yò·ár·ywèn
family ticket	家庭票	jyā·tíng pyào

I need a/an ...	我在找	wǒr zài jǎo
	一个……	ēe·ger …
baby seat	婴儿座	yīng·ár zwòr
(English-speaking) babysitter	（会讲	(hwày shwōr
	英文的）	yìng·wérn der)
	保姆	báo·mǒo
cot	婴儿床	yīng·ár chwúng
highchair	高凳子	gāo·dèrng·zir
plastic bag	塑料袋子	sòo·lyào dài·zir
plastic sheet	塑料布	sòo·lyào bòo
potty	婴儿马桶	yīng·ár má·tǒng
pram	小推车	syǎo·twāy·chēr
sick bag	呕吐袋	ǒ·tòo dài
stroller	婴儿推车	yīng·ár twāy·chēr

Do you hire prams/strollers?

这儿能租用　　　　　jèr nérng zoo·yòong
婴儿推车吗?　　　　yīng·ár twāy·chēr ma

Are children allowed?

能带小孩去吗?　　　nérng dài hái·zir chèw ma

Are there any good places to take children around here?

附近有孩子   jèr·lee yŏ hái·zir
玩的地方吗?   wár·der dèe·fūng ma

Is there space for a pram/stroller?

有地方放推车吗?   yŏ dèe·fūng fùng twāy·chēr ma

Do you mind if I breast-feed here?

喂孩子你不介意吗?   wày hái·zir nĕe boo·jyàir·èe ma

Could I have some paper and pencils, please?

能借用纸笔吗?   nérng jyàir·yòong jír·bĕe ma

Is this suitable for …-year-old children?

对……岁孩子合适吗?   dwày … swày hái·zir hér·shìr ma

Do you know a dentist who's good with children?

哪个牙科看   năr·ger yá·kēr kùn
孩子看得比较好?   hái·zir kùn·der bĕe·jyào hăo

Do you know a doctor who's good with children?

哪个大夫看   năr·ger dài·foo kùn
孩子看得比较好?   hái·zir kùn·der bĕe·jyào hăo

Where's the nearest …?	这儿附近有 ……吗?	jèr fòo·jìn yŏ … ma
park	公园	gōong·ywén
playground	孩子 活动 地方	hái·zir hwór·dòong dèe·fūng
swimming pool	游泳池	yó·yŏong chír
tap	水龙头	shwăy·lóong·tó
theme park	游乐园	yó·lèr·ywén
toyshop	玩具店	wár·jùo dyèn

Do you sell …?	你们卖……吗?	nĕe·mern mài … ma
baby painkillers	孩子止痛药	hái·zir jĭr·tòong yào
baby wipes	婴儿纸巾	yīng·ár jír·jīn
disposable nappies	一次性 尿裤	ēe·tsìr·sìng nyào·kòo
tissues	纸巾	jír·jīn

For health issues, see **health**, page 191.

basics

开头

Note that in Mandarin, the word 'please' (chǐng 请) always precedes a request. You're likely to become familiar with the last two phrases below as Chinese people use them a lot.

Yes.	是。	shìr
No.	不是。	bóo·shìr
Please ...	请……	chǐng ...
Thank you (very much).	多谢 (谢您)。	dōr·syàir (syàir nín)
You're welcome.	不客气。	boo kèr·chee
Excuse me. (to get attention)	劳驾。	láo·jyà
Excuse me. (to get past)	借光。	jyàir·gwūng
Sorry.	对不起。	dwày·boo·chěe
As you please.	随便。	swáy·byèn
No problem.	没关系。	may·gwun·see

greetings & goodbyes

打招呼

In common parlance, née 你 ('you' singular) can have the polite form nín 您. This polite form is particularly common in Beijing. You'll encounter it as part of some common greetings.

Greetings all.	大家好。	dà·jyā hǎo
Hello. (general)	你好。	née·hǎo
Hello. (Beijing)	您好。	nín·hǎo
Hi. (lit: Have you eaten?)	吃饭了吗？	chǐr·fùn ler ma

Good …	……好。	… hǎo
afternoon	下午	syà·wóo
evening	晚上	wǔn·shùng
morning (after breakfast)	早上	zǎo·shùng

How are you? (general)
你好吗？ · née·hǎo ma

How are you? (Beijing)
您好吗。 · nín·hǎo·ma

Fine. And you?
好。你呢？ · hǎo. něe ner

What's your name?
你叫什么名字？ · něe jyào shér·mer míng·zir

My name is …
我叫…… · wǒr jyào …

I'd like to introduce you to …
给你介绍…… · gáy něe jyǎir·shào …

I'm pleased to meet you.
幸会。 · sìng·hwày

This is my …	这是我的……	jèr shìr wǒr·der …
child	孩子	hái·zir
colleague	同事	tóong·shìr
friend	朋友	pérng·yǒ
husband	丈夫	jùng·foo
partner (intimate)	对象	dwày·syùng
wife	太太	tài·tài

For other family members, see **family**, page 114.

SOCIAL

Goodbye.	再见。	zài·jyèn
Bye.	拜拜。	bài·bai
See you later.	回头见。	hwáy·tó jyèn
Good night.	晚安。	wǔn·ūn

titles & addressing people

尊称与称呼人

China is host to a wealth of titles and terms of address, reflecting the richness of China's feudal past. Travellers to China can get by using the three titles given below. The last term syáo·jyǎir 小姐 is becoming the generic term for women of unspecified marital status. Be aware that it can carry a derogatory overtone of 'prostitute' but only if used in sexually suggestive contexts.

Mr/Sir (lit: first born)
先生   syēn·sherng

Mrs/Madam
小姐/女士   něw·shìr

Ms/Miss (lit: little sister)
小姐   syáo·jyǎir

on friendly terms

In China, the friendliest way to address people is by bringing them into your family. You can call a woman of an older generation ā·ée 阿姨 (auntie). It's polite to give people the benefit of the doubt on the upwards side when guessing their age.

In Beijing, gēr·mer 哥们儿 (buddy) and jyǎir·mer 姐们儿 (sis) are popular for men and women respectively, reflecting Beijing's laid-back youth culture. Elsewhere, the terms dà·gēr 大哥 (big brother) and jyǎir·jyair 姐姐 (big sister) are commonly used. On the less friendly side, to call one of your peers sōon·zir 孙子 (grandchild) – a rank two full generations below yours – is a popular insult.

making conversation

聊天

Here are some common greetings and conversation starters that you may encounter or that may help you to break the ice.

Have you eaten?
吃饭了吗？
chīr·fùn ler ma

Stepping out?
出去吗？
chōo·chèw ma

You've arrived!
你来啰！
něe lái lor

(You're) Off to the market?
买菜去！
mǎi·tsài chèw

Do you live here?
你住这儿吗？
něe jòo jèr·lee ma

Where are you going?
上哪儿去？
shùng·nǎr chèw

What are you doing?
干吗啦？
gūn·mǎ la

Do you like it here?
喜欢这儿吗？
sěe·hwūn jèr·lee ma

I love it here.
我很喜欢这里。
wǒr hérn sěe·hwūn jèr·lee

Are you here on holiday?
你来这儿旅游吗？
něe lái·jìr lěw·yó ma

listen for ...

People are often curious to know how foreigners get over their initial culture shock. You may well have curious locals address this question to you.

něe zài jèr·lee sěe·gwùn ler ma
你在这儿习
惯了吗？ **Are you accustomed to life here?**

I'm here ... 我来这儿…… wŏr lái·jìr ...
  for a holiday 旅游 lĕw·yó
  on business 出差 chōo·chāi
  to study 留学 lyó·shwáir

How long are you here for?
你在这儿住多久? nĕe zài jèr·lee jòo dōr·jyŏ

I'm here for (four) weeks.
我驻(四)个星期。 wŏr jòo (sìr)·ger sīng·chēe

Can I take a photo (of you)?
我可以照(你得) wŏr kĕr·ĕe jào (nĕe·der)
相吗? syùng ma

That's (beautiful), isn't it?
哇,太(好看)了! wā tài (hăo·kùn) ler

Just joking.
开坑笑。 kāi·wún·syào

What's this called?
这个叫什么? jày·ger jyào shér·mer

Great!	太棒!	tài·bùng
Hey!	劳驾!	láo·jyà
It's OK.	还行。	hái·síng
Just a minute.	等一下,啊。	dĕrng·ee·syà a
Maybe.	有可能。	yó kĕr·nérng
No problem.	没事。	máy·shìr
No way!	不可能!	bòo kĕr·nérng
Sure, whatever.	行,行,行。	síng síng síng
That's enough!	行了,行了!	síng·ler síng·ler

nationalities

Where are you from?
你从哪儿来？   něe tsóong·năr lái

I'm from ...	我从⋯⋯来。	wŏr tsóong ... lái
Australia	澳大利亚	ào·dà·lèe·ya
Canada	加拿大	jyā·nā·dà
Singapore	新加坡	sīn·jyā·pō

For more nationalities, see the **dictionary**.

conversation starters

When trying to start up a conversation in China, never be afraid to ask, or state, the obvious. If a friend is coming out of a restaurant with red-fried pork smeared all over their face, best check to see whether they've eaten by asking chīr·fùn ler ma 吃饭了吗？ ('Have you eaten?'). If you can't think of an obvious question to ask, try stating the obvious. It's as easy as talking about the weather. If a friend has just arrived at your house, let them know they've arrived with a gleeful něe lái lor 你来啰! ('You've arrived!').

age

Try not to be too ruffled if everyone asks how many years you've managed to pack on over your life's journey. They don't mean to cause offence, but are simply curious to know how old you are – age is an indication of status and wealth in traditional China.

How old ...?	⋯⋯多大了？	... dōr·dà ler
are you	你	něe
is your daughter	你的女儿	něe·der něw·ár
is your son	你的儿子	něe·der ár·zir

I'm ... years old.
我……岁。 wǒr ... swày

He/She is ... years old.
他/她……岁。 tā ... swày

Too old!
快报废了。 kwài bào·fày ler

I'm younger than I look.
我还小了。 wǒr hái syǎo ler

For your age, see **numbers & amounts**, page 37.

occupations & studies

Expect curious Chinese people to ask 'How much do you earn?'
(něe jèrng dōr·shǎo chyén 你挣多少钱) as it's one of the top
ten questions asked of foreigners. This curiosity is probably
explained by the rise of the free market and free-market jobs in
China – a new and exciting phenomenon.

What's your occupation?

| 你做什么 | něe zwòr shér·mer |
| 工作？ | gōong·zwòr |

I'm a/an ...	我当……	wǒr dūng ...
accountant	会计	kwài·jèe
chef	厨师	chóo·shīr
engineer	工程师	gōong·chérng·shīr
journalist	记者	jèe·jǐr
teacher	老师	lǎo·shīr

I ...	我……	wǒr ...
do business	做生意	zwòr shērng·èe
do casual work	打工	dǎ·gōong

I work in ...	我做……	wǒr zwòr ...
	工作。	gōong·zwòr
administration	秘书	mèe·shoo
health	卫生	wày·shērng
sales & marketing	推广	twāy·gwúng

I'm ...	我……了。	wǒr ... ler
retired	退休	twày·syō
self-employed	下海	syà·hǎi
unemployed	下岗	syà·gǔng

I'm studying ...	我学……	wór seewǎir ...
humanities	文科	wérn·kēr
(Mandarin) Chinese	中文	jōong·wérn
science	理科	lěe·kēr

What are you studying?

你学习什么？   něe shwáir·sěe shér·mer

For more occupations and studies, see the **dictionary**.

family

家庭

Mandarin kinship terms can get very complicated as there are different titles according to age hierarchy and whether the relationship is maternal or paternal. Included here are the terms for immediate family members and a selection of extended-family terms.

I'm ...	我……了。	wǒr ... ler
single	单身	dūn·shērn
married	结婚	jyáir·hōon
separated	分手	fērn·shǒ
divorced	离婚	lée·hōon
in a relationship	有伴	yǒ·bàr

Are you married?

你结婚了吗？   něe jyáir·hōon ler ma

Do you have a family of your own?
你成家了吗？   něe chérng·jyā ler ma

I live with someone.
我有伴儿。   wór yǒ bàr

Do you have a/an …?	你有……吗？	née yǒ … ma
I (don't) have a/an …	我（没）有……	wǒr (máy) yǒ …
aunt (mat.)	阿姨	ā·ée
brother	兄弟	syūng dee
brother (elder)	哥哥	gēr·ger
brother (younger)	弟弟	dèe·dee
daughter	女儿	něw·ár
father	父亲	fòo·chīn
grandchildren	孙子女	sōon·zír·něw
granddaughter	孙女	sōon·něw
grandfather (mat.)	外公	wài·gōong
grandfather (pat.)	爷爷	yǎir·yair
grandmother (mat.)	外婆	wài·pór
grandmother (pat.)	奶奶	nǎi·nai
grandson	孙子	sōon·zir
husband	丈夫	jùng·foo
mother	母亲	mǒo·chīn
partner (intimate)	对象	dwày·syùng
sister	姐妹	jyǎir·mày
sister (elder)	姐姐	jyǎir·jyair
sister (younger)	妹妹	mày·may
son	儿子	ár·zir
uncle (father's younger brother)	叔叔	shōo·shoo
wife	太太	tài·tai

farewells

Tomorrow is my last day here.
明天我要走了。 míng·tyēn wǒr yào zǒ ler

If you come to (Scotland) you can stay with me.
有机会来（苏克兰）， yǒ jēe·hwày lái (sōo·kèr·lún)
可以来找我。 kér·ěe jáo·wǒr

Keep in touch!
保持联系！ bǎo·chír lyén·see

It's been great meeting you.
认识你实在 rèrn·shìr něe shír·zài
很高兴。 hěrn gāo·sìng

Here's my ...	给你我的……	gáy·née wǒr·der ...
What's your ...?	你的……是	něe·der ... shìr
	什么？	shér·mer
address	地址	dèe·jǐr
email address	网址	wúng·jǐr
phone number	电话号码	dyèn·hwà hào·mǎ

well wishing

Bon voyage!
一路平安。 ēe·lòo píng·ūn

Congratulations!
恭喜，恭喜。 gōong·see gōong·see

Good luck!
祝你好运。 jòo née hǎo·yèwn

Happy birthday!
生日快乐。 shērng·rìr kwài·lèr

Happy (Chinese) New Year!
新年好。 sīn·nyén hǎo

Congratulations! May you make lots of money!
(Chinese New Year greeting; especially in southern China.)
恭喜发财 gōong·see fā·tsái

common interests

共同兴趣

What do you do in your spare time?
你有什么爱好吗？　　　　　　nǐ yǒ shér·mer ài·hao ma

Do you like ...?	你喜欢……吗？	nǐe sěe·hwūn ... ma
I (don't)	我(不)	wǒr (bòo)
like ...	喜欢……	sěe·hwūn ...
calligraphy	书法	shōo·fǎ
climbing mountains	爬山	pǎ·shūn
computer games	电子游戏	dyèn·zir yó·sèe
cooking	做饭	zwòr·fùn
dancing	跳舞	tyào·wǒo
drawing	画画	hwà·hwàr
drinking	喝酒	hēr·jyǒ
eating	吃饭	chīr·fun
films	看电影	kùn dyèn·yǐng
gardening	养花	yúng·hwǎ
music	听音乐	tīng·yīn·ywàir
photography	拍照	pǎi·jào
reading	看书	kùn·shōo
sport	体育	těe·yèw
surfing the Internet	冲网	chōong·wǔng
talking	聊天	lyáo·tyàr
travelling	旅游	lěw·yó
walking	散步	sùn·bòo
watching TV	看电视	kùn dyèn·shìr
window shopping	逛商店	gwùng·jyāir

For sporting activities, see **sport**, page 143.

music

音乐

Do you …?	你爱……吗？	něe ài … ma
dance	跳舞	tyào·wǒo
go to concerts	参加	tsūn·jyā
	音乐会	yīn·ywàir·hwày
listen to music	听音乐	tīng·yīn·ywàir
play an instrument	弹乐器	tún ywàir·chee
sing	唱歌	chùng·gēr

What … do you like?	你喜欢 什么……？	née sěe·hwūn shér·mer …
bands	音乐队	yīn·ywàir dwày
music	音乐	yīn·ywàir
singers	歌手	gēr·shǒ

alternative music	非主流音乐	fāy·jǒo·lyó yīn·ywàir
blues	布鲁斯音乐	bòo·lòo·sīr yīn·ywàir
Chinese	中国传统	jōong·gwór
traditional music	音乐	chwún·tǒong yīn·ywàir
classical music	古典	góo·dyěn yīn·ywàir
easy listening	轻音乐	chīng yīn·ywàir
electronic music	电子音乐	dyèn·zir yīn·ywàir
folk music	民谣音乐	mín·yáo yīn·ywàir
heavy metal	重金属音乐	jòong·jīn·shǒo yīn·ywàir
hip hop	说唱音乐	shwōr·chùng yīn·ywàir
jazz	爵士	jwàir·shìr yīn·ywàir
Peking opera	京剧	jīng·jòo
pop	流行音乐	lyó·síng yīn·ywàir
rock	摇滚	yāo·gǒon
world music	国际民谣	gwór·jèe mín·yáo
	音乐	yīn·ywàir

Planning to go to a concert? See **tickets**, page 53 and **going out**, page 127.

the main games

In China you won't go far without seeing groups of people (often retired men) in public places such as teahouses or parks playing either board games or cards. The most popular game is Mahjong má·jyùng 麻将. The shuffling of Mahjong tiles is often accompanied by the hum of conversation which sometimes becomes animated as money is won or lost on the game.

Some claim that the game of chess was invented in China. While this claim is hard to prove it is true that both Chinese chess syùng·chée 象棋 and international chess gwór·jèe syùng·chée 国际象棋 are very popular. The Chinese love of gambling extends to numerous forms of card games póo·kèr pái 扑克牌 with bridge being very popular.

cinema & theatre

电影与戏剧

I feel like going to a ...	我想去 看……	wór syǔng·chèw kùn ...
Did you like the ...?	这个…… 好看吗?	jày·ger ... hǎo·kùn ma
ballet	芭蕾	ba·lày
film	电影	dyèn·yíng
play	戏剧	sèe·jèw

What's showing at the cinema/theatre tonight?

今晚可以去看
什么节目?

jīn·wǔn kér·èe chèw·kùn
shér·mer jyáir·mòo

Is it in English?

是英文版吗?

shìr yīng·wérn bǔn ma

Does it have (English) subtitles?

有(英文)字母吗?

yǒ (yīng·wérn) zìr·mǒo ma

Is this seat taken?

这座有人吗?

jèr yǒ rérn ma

Have you seen …?
你看过……吗？   něe kùn·gwor … ma

Who's in it?
是谁演的？   shìr sháy yěn·der

It stars …
主角是……   jóo·jyǎo shìr …

I thought it was …   我觉得……   wór jwǎir·der …
    excellent   很好看   hérn·hǎo kùn
    long   有点长   yó dyěn chúng
    OK   还行   hái·síng

I (don't)   我（不）   wǒr (bòo)
like …   喜欢……   sěe·hwūn…
    action movies   动作片   dòong·zwòr pyēn
    animated films   动画片   dòong·hwà pyēn
    Chinese cinema   中国   jōong·gwór
                        电影   dyèn·yīng
    comedies   喜剧片   sěe·jòo pyēn
    documentaries   纪实片   jèe·shír pyēn
    drama   戏剧片   sèe·jèw pyēn
    Hong Kong   香港   syūng·gǔng
      cinema   电影   dyèn·yīng
    horror movies   恐怖片   kǒong·bòo pyēn
    kung fu movies   武打片   wóo·dǎ pyēn
    sci-fi movies   科幻片   kèr·hwùn pyēn
    short films   短篇   dwǔn·pyēn
                        电影   dyèn·yīng
    thrillers   刺激片   tsìr·jee pyēn
    war movies   战争片   jùn·jērng pyēn

feelings

感觉

Physical sensations (hot, hungry, etc) are expressed in the form 'I am ...', while sentiments (depressed, disappointed, etc) are expressed in the form 'I feel ...'. These phrases could come in handy as in China friendliness is often expressed through an exaggerated concern for the welfare of others.

I'm (not) ...	我 (不) ……吗	wǒr (bòo) ... ma
Are you ...?	你……吗？	něe ... ma
cold	冷	lěrng
hot	热	rèr
hungry	饿	èr
thirsty	渴	kěr
tired	累	làiy

I (don't)	我 (不)	wǒr (bòo)
feel ...	感到……	gǔn·dào...
Do you feel ...?	你感到……吗？	něe gǔn·dào ... ma
annoyed	生气	shērng·chèe
depressed	郁闷	yèw·mern
disappointed	遗憾	ée·hùn
embarrassed	不好意思	bòo·hǎo èe·sīr
happy	高兴	gāo·sìng
in a hurry	忙	múng
sad	不高兴	bòo·gāo·sìng
surprised	惊讶	jīng·yà
worried	着急	jáo·jée

If feeling unwell, see **health**, page 191.

opinions

见解

Did you like it?
你觉得好吗？　　　　　　　　née jwǎir·der hǎo ma

What do you think of it?
你觉得怎么样？　　　　　　　née jwǎir·der zěr·mer yùng

I thought it was …	我觉得……	wór jwǎir·der …
It's …	它……	tā …
awful	很差劲	hěrn chā·jìn
beautiful	好美	háo·mǎy
boring	很无聊	hěrn wóo·lyáo
great	很棒	hěrn bùng
interesting	很有意思	hérn yǒ èe·sir
OK	还行	hái·síng
strange	奇怪	chěe·gwài

mixed emotions	
a little	
有一点	yó ēe·dyěn
I'm a little sad.	
我有一点不高兴。	wór yǒ ēe·dyěn bòo·gāo·sìng
very	
很	hěrn
I'm very surprised.	
我很惊讶。	wór hěrn jīng·yà
extremely	
非常	fāy·chúng
I'm extremely happy.	
我非常高兴。	wǒr fāy·chúng gāo·sìng

politics & social issues

When talking about social, political and environmental issues, keep in mind that certain issues are too politically sensitive to discuss with strangers. In addition, your status as a rich foreigner may affect how your questions are understood. Unqualified criticism of things Chinese is not likely to win you any friends.

Who do you vote for?
你投哪个党？   něe·tó năy·ger dǔng

I support the … party.
我支持……党。   wǒr jǐr·chǐr … dǔng

I'm a member of the … party.
我是……党员。   wǒr shìr … dǔng·ywén

communist party	共产党	gōong·chún·dǔng
conservative	保守派	báo·shǒ pài
democratic forces	民主党派	mín·joo dǔng·pài
green activists	环保分子	hwún·bǎo fērn·zir
leftist	左翼	zwǒr·jèe
reformist	改革派	gǎi·gér pài
rightist	右翼	yò·jèe
social democratic party	社会民主党	shèr·hwày mín·joo dǔng
socialist	社会主义党	shèr·hwày jǒo·èe dǔng

Did you hear about …?
你听说过……吗？   něe tīng·shwōr·gwor … ma

Do you agree?
你同意吗？   něe tóong·èe ma

I (don't) agree with …
我（不）同意……   wǒr (bòo) tóong·èe …

How do people feel about …?
你觉得……
怎么样？   née jwāir·der …
zěr·mer·yùng

How can we protest against …?

我们该怎么
对抗……？

wǒr·mern gāi zěr·mer
dwày·kùng …

How can we support …?

我们该怎么
支持……？

wǒr·mern gāi zěr·mer
jīr·chǐr …

abortion	堕胎	dwòr·tái
animal rights	动物权	dòong·wòo·chwén
crime	犯罪	fùn·zwày
	活动	hwór·dòong
democracy	民主主义	mín·joo jǒo·èe
discrimination	歧视	chée·shìr
drugs	毒品	dóo·pǐn
the economy	经济	jīng·jèe
education	教育	jyào·yew
the environment	环境	hwún·jìng
equal opportunity	平等待遇	píng·děrng dài·yew
euthanasia	安乐死	ūn·lèr·sǐr
Falun Gong	法轮功	fǎ·lóon·gōong
family planning	计划生育	jēe·hwa shērng·yèw
foreign investment	境外投资	jìng·wài tó·zīr
globalisation	全球化	chwén·chyó·hwà
government policies	边疆	byēn·jyūng
in Xinjiang/Tibet	政策	jèrng·tsir
human rights	人权	rérn·chwén
indigenous issues	土著人	tǒo·jōo·rérn
	问题	wèrn·těe
inequality	不平等	bòo píng·děrng
party politics	党派斗争	dǔng·pài dò·jērng

privatisation	私有化	sīr·yŏ·hwà
racism	种族	jŏong·zóo
	歧视	chée·shìr
relations with Taiwan	海峡两岸关系	hăi·syá lyŭng·ùn gwun·see
sexism	大男人主义	dà nún·rérn jŏo·èe
social welfare	社会福利	shèr·hwày fóo·lèe
the war in …	……战争	… jùn·jērng
terrorism	恐怖主义	kŏong·bòu jŏo·èe
unemployment	下岗问题	syà·gŭng wèrn·tĕe
US foreign policy	美国对外政策	măy·gwór dwày·wài jèrng·tsir

the environment

环保

You may find that concern about many issues, including environmental ones, is very far removed from the minds of most Chinese who contend with more pressing issues of local importance.

Is there a … problem here?

本地有……问题吗?   jèr·lee yŏ … wèrn·tĕe ma

What should be done about ...?
……应该怎么处理。 ... yīng·gǎi zěr·mer chòo·lee

conservation	环保	hwún·bǎo
deforestation	乱砍乱伐	lwùn·kǔn lwǔn fá
drought	干旱	gūn·hùn
ecosystem	生态	shērng·tài
	环境	hwún·jìng
endangered species	临危物种	lín·wāy wòo·jŏong
genetically modified food	转基因食品	jwǔn·jēe·yīn shír·pǐn
hunting	狩猎	shŏ·lyàir
hydroelectricity	水发电	shwǎy·fā·dyèn
irrigation	农业水利	nóong·yàir shwǎy·lèe
nuclear energy	核发电	hěr fā·dyèn
nuclear testing	核试验	hér shìr·yèn
ozone layer	臭氧层	chò·yúng·tsérng
pesticides	农药	nóong·yào
pollution	污染	wōo·rún
poverty	贫困问题	pín·kùn wèrn·těe
recycling programme	回收措施	hwáy·sho tswòr·shīr
the Three Gorges Project	三峡 工程	sūn·syá gōong·chérng
toxic waste	有毒废物	yŏ·dóo fày·wòo
water supply	水资源	shwǎy zīr·ywén

Is this a protected ...?	这个是被保护……吗？	jèr shìr bày·bǎo·hòo der ... ma
forest	森林	sērn·lín
park	公园	gōong·ywén
species	物种	wòo·jŏong

where to go

向哪去

What's there to do in the evenings?
晚上有什么
好玩的吗？
wǎn·shùng yǒ shér·mer
hǎo·wár der ma

What's on ...? ……有什么
活动？
... yǒ shér·mer
hwór·dòong

  locally 这儿附近 jèr fòo jìn
  this weekend 这个周末 jày·ger jō·mòr
  today 今天 jīn·tyēn
  tonight 今天晚上 jīn·tyēn wǔn·shùng

Where can I find ...? ……怎么找？ ... zěr·mer jǎo
  clubs 夜总会 yàir·zǒong·hwày
  gay venues 同志吧 tóong·jìr·bā
  places to eat 吃饭的
地方
chīr·fùn der
dèe·fāng
  pubs 酒吧 jyǒ·bā

Is there a 本地有没有 běrn·dèe yǒ·máy·yǒ
local ... guide? ……指南？ ... jǐr·nún
  entertainment 娱乐 yéw·lèr
  film 电影 dyèn·yǐng
  music 音乐 yīn·ywàir

I feel like going to a ...	我想 到……去。	wór·syŭng dào … chèw
bar/pub	酒吧	jyŏ·bā
café	咖啡屋	kā·fāy·wōo
nightclub	夜总会	yàir·zŏong·hwày
party	趴提	pā·tee
restaurant	饭馆	fùn·gwŭn

I feel like going to ...	我想去……	wór·syŭng chèw …
listen to a concert	听音乐会	tīng yīn·ywàir hwày
the Peking opera	看京剧	kùn jīng·jòo
see a film	看电影	kùn dyèn·yĭng
see a show	看演出	kùn yĕn·chōo
see some acrobats	看杂技	kùn ză·jèe
sing karaoke	唱卡拉OK	chùng kā·lā·ō·kày
watch a ballet	看芭蕾	kùn bā·lăy

For more on bars and drinks, see **romance**, page 133, and **eating out**, page 157.

street beat

In China's crowded cities, a lot of life – particularly in summer – is lived out on the streets and in the precious open spaces and parks. An evening's entertainment might consist of activities such as kite flying (fùng·fērng·jèrng 放风筝) or playing pool (dǎ·tái·chyó 打台球). In the warmer months, young people indulge in open-air dancing to rock music (bēng·dèe 蹦迪) while older people gather in the parks for ballroom dancing sessions (tyào jyāo·ee wǒo 跳交谊舞).

invitations

What are you doing …?	你……有事吗？	něe … yǒ shìr mạ
now	现在	syèn·zài
this weekend	这个周末	jày·ger jō·mòr
tonight	今天晚上	jīn·tyēn wǔn·shùng

Would you like to go (for a) …?	你想去……吗？	něe syung chew … mạ
I feel like going (for a) …	我想去……	wór syǔng chèw …
banquet	大吃大喝	dà·chīr dà·hēr
coffee	喝咖啡	hēr kā·fāy
dancing	跳舞	tyào·wǒo
drink	喝酒	hēr·jyo
meal	吃饭	chīr·fùn
out somewhere	外面玩	chōo·chèw wár
walk	散散步	sùn·sun bòo

The drinks are on me.
这回我来请。　jày hwáy wǒr lái chīng

Do you know a good restaurant?
你认识一个
好饭馆吗？　něe rèrn·shir ee·ger
hǎo fùn·gwǔn ma

Do you want to come to the concert with me?
你想跟我去
音乐会吗？　née syǔng gērn·wǒr chèw
yīn·ywàir hwày ma

We're having a party/banquet.
我们要开
趴提/饭局。　wǒr·mern yào·kāi
pā·tee/fùn·jǒo

You should come.
你应该来。　něe yīng·gāi lái

129

responding to invitations

答复

Sure!
好！
hǎo

Yes, I'd love to.
好，我愿意。
hǎo wǒr ywèn·èe

That's very kind of you.
你太客气了。
něe tài kèr·chee ler

Where shall we go?
我们到哪儿去？
wǒr·mern dào·nǎr chèw

No, I'm afraid I can't.
不行，我不能来。
bòo·síng wǒr bòo·nérng lái

Sorry, I can't sing/dance.
不好意思，我不会
唱歌/跳舞。
bòo·hǎo èe·sīr wǒr boo·hwày
chùng·gēr/tyào·wǒo

What about tomorrow?
明天行吗？
míng·tyēn síng ma

arranging to meet

约人

What time will we meet?
几点钟碰头？
jée·dyěn·jōong pērng·tó

Where will we meet?
在哪里碰头？
zài ná·lee pērng·tó

Let's meet at ... 我们在…… wǒr·mern zài ...
见面。 jyèn·myèn

    (eight) o'clock （八）点钟 (bā)·dyěn jōong
    the entrance 门口 mérn·kǒ

I'll pick you up.
我来接你。 wŏr lái jyāir nĕe

Are you ready?
准备好了吗？ jŏon·bày hào ler ma

I'm ready.
准备好了。 jŏon·bày hào ler

I'll be coming later.
我里晚一点来。 wŏr yào wŭn·ēe·dyĕn lái

Where will you be?
我在哪里找你？ wŏr zài ná·lee jáo nĕe

If I'm not there by (nine) o'clock, don't wait for me.
如果到了（九）点 róo·gwŏr dào·ler (jyó)·dyĕn
钟还没来，就 jōong hăi·máy lái jyò
不要等我。 bóo·yào dérng·wŏr

OK!
好了！ hăo ler

I'll see you then.
不见不散。 bóo·jyèn bóo·sùn

See you later/tomorrow.
明天/以后见。 míng·tyēn/ĕe·hò jyèn

I'm looking forward to it.
我期待他的到来。 wŏr chēe·dài tă·der dào·lái

Sorry I'm late.
不好意思，来晚了。 bòo·hăo èe·sīr lái·wún ler

Never mind.
没事。 máy·shìr

drugs

毒品

I don't take drugs.
我不吃毒。

wŏr bòo·chīr dóo

I take ... occasionally.
我偶尔吃……

wŏr ó·ăr chīr ...

Do you want to have a smoke?
想抽一点吗？

syŭng chō·ee·dyĕn ma

Do you have a light?
有火吗？

yó hwŏr ma

I'm high.
起飞了。

chĕe·fāy ler

This drug is for personal use.
这个药品是
私用的。

jày·ger yào·pĭn shīr
sīr·yòong·der

asking someone out

培人出去玩

Where would you like to go (tonight)?
(今天晚上) (jīn·tyēn wǔn·shùng)
想到哪里玩？ syǔng dào·nà·lee wár

Would you like to do something (tomorrow)?
(明天)想 (míng·tyēn) syǔng
出去玩吗？ chōo·chew wár ma

Yes, I'd love to.
好啊，很想去。 hǎo a hérn syǔng·chèw

I'm busy.
对不起，我有事。 dwày·boo·chée wór·yo·shir

He's ...	他真是个……	tā jērn·shir ger ...
a bastard	混仗子	hòon·zǎi·zir
hot	帅哥	shwài·gēr
She's ...	她真是个……	ta jern·shir ger ...
a bitch	婊子	byǎo·zir
cute	靓妹	lyùng·mày
What a babe!	哇，真可爱！	wa jěrn kěr·ài
He/She gets around.	他/她心不专一。	tā sīn bòo jwūn·ēe

pick-up lines

调情

Would you like a drink?
请你喝点   chíng·něe hēr·dyěn
什么吗?   shér·mer ma

You look like some cousin of mine.
你长得像   née jǔng·der syùng
我的表妹。   wǒr·der byǎo mày

You're a fantastic dancer.
你跳得真好。   něe tyào·der jērn·hǎo

Can I …?   我能   wǒr nérng
    培你……吗?   páy·něe … ma
  be with you   一起到老   ēe·chēe dào·lǎo
   forever
  dance with you   跳个舞   tyào·ger·wǒo
  sit here   座一会   zwòr·ee·sya

rejections

被拒绝

I'm here with my boyfriend/girlfriend.
我同男朋友/   wǒr tóong nún·pérng·yo/
女朋友一起来了。   něw·pérng·yo ēe·chee lái ler

Excuse me, I have to go now.
对不起,我要走。   dwày·boo·chēe wǒr yào zǒ

I'd rather not.
我不想。   wǒr bòo syǔng

No, thank you.
谢谢,下一次吧。   syàir·syair syà·ee·tsir ba

getting closer

I like you very much.
我很喜欢你。 wǒr hérn sěe·hwūn něe

You're great.
你真棒。 něe jērn bùng

Let's kiss!
咱们亲一下吧! zŭn·mern chīn·ee·sya ba

Do you want to come inside for a while?
想进来坐坐吗? syŭng jìn·lái zwòr·zwor ma

Do you want a massage?
你喜欢被 něe sěe·hwūn bày
按摩吗? ùn·mór ma

local talk		
Go and play (somewhere else)!	玩去!	wár·chèw
Leave me alone!	别烦我!	byáir fún wǒr
Piss off!	滚开!	gŏon·kāi

sex

Do you have a (condom)?
你带了 něe dài·ler
(避孕套)吗? (bèe·yèwn·tào) ma

Let's use a (condom).
咱们用一个 zŭn·mern yòong·ee·ger
(避孕套)吧。 (bèe·yèwn·tào) ba

I won't do it without protection.
没有防备, máy·yó fūng·bày
我不来玩。 wǒr bòo lái·wár

romance

135

Kiss me.
快点儿亲我！
kwài·dyǎr chīn wǒr

I want you.
我想你了。
wǒr·syúng něe ler

I want to make love to you.
我想跟你在
一起。
wór·syǔng gērn·něe zài
ēe·chěe

It's my first time.
是我的第一次。
shìr wǒr·der dèe·ēe·tsìr

Don't worry, I'll do it myself.
没事，我自己来。
máy·shìr wǒr zìr·jee lái

How about going to bed?
咱们上床，
好吗？
zǔn·mern shùng·chwún
hǎo ma

Touch me here.
摸我这儿。
mōr wǒr jèr

Do you like this?
喜欢这样吗？
sěe·hwūn jày·yung ma

I (don't) like that.
我（不）喜欢
这样。
wǒr (bòr) sěe·hwūn
jày·yung

I think we should stop now.
该结束吧！
gāi jyáir·shòo ma

Oh yeah!	真是！	jērn shìr
That's great	真棒。	jērn·bùng
Easy tiger!	慢点来！	mùn·dyěn lái

faster	快点	kwài·dyǎr
harder	用劲	yòong·jìn
slower	慢点	mùn·dyǎr
softer	轻点	chīng·dyǎr

That was ...	刚才真……	gūng·tsái jērn ...
amazing	不可思议	bòo·kěr sìr·èe
weird	有点奇怪	yó·dyěn chěe·gwài
wild	好玩	hǎo·wár

Can I ...?	我可以……吗?	wŏr kér·ĕe ... ma
call you	给你打电话	gáy nĕe dă·dyèn hwà
see you	见你	jyèn·nĕe
stay over	在这儿过夜	zài jèr gwòr·yàir

love

爱情

I love you.
我爱你。 wŏr ài nĕe

I think we're good together.
我觉得我们
俩挺配合。 wŏr jwáir·der wŏr·mern lyúng tĭng pày·hér

Will you ...?	你能同我一起……吗?	nĕe nérng tóong wŏr èe·chĕe ... ma
go out with me	谈朋友	tún pérng·yo
live with me	住下来	jòo·syà·lái
marry me	结婚	jyáir·hōon

---

yesterday's comrade

Following the Communist Revolution, the officially sanctioned term of address for both men and women was 'comrade' (tóong·jìr 同志). In today's China this word isn't commonly used as a term of address and has undergone a shift in meaning – yesterday's 'comrade' is now a slang word for 'gay'.

This is a kind of play on words, as the literal meaning of 'comrade' in Chinese is 'of the same mindset'. While in revolutionary circles this mindset entailed a vision of a new society, today's mindset is a particular vision of sexuality. The self-appellation of tóong·jìr as used by China's gay community can be seen as a subversive means of self-empowerment, challenging the more official tag of 'homosexual' (tóong·sìng lyèn 同性恋 lit: same sex love).

problems

出问题

Are you seeing someone else?
你有别的朋友吗？
née yǒ byáir·der pérng·yǒ ma

He/She is just a friend.
他/她是普通朋友。
tā shìr pǒo·tōong pérng·yo

You're just using me for sex.
你只是用我放
情欲。
née jǐr shìr yòong·wǒr lái fā
chīng·yèw

I never want to see you again.
我再也不想
见到你。
wǒr zài·yǎir bòo·syǔng
jyèn·dào něe

I don't think it's working out.
咱们谈得有点
不大对头了。
zǔn·mern tún·der yó·dyǎr
bóo·dà dwày·tó ler

We'll work it out.
我们可以找出路。
wǒr·mern kér·ěe jáo chōo·lòo

body language

Beware of inadvertently sending the wrong signals with your body language while in China. Squeezing hard on people's hands when shaking hands is known to be an attribute of scary, hairy foreigners. Chinese handshakes are soft – more of a gentle clasp really. Foreigners staring at locals while speaking to them is also off-putting as the norm in China is not to look people in the eye when talking to them. When someone is addressing you, however, it's alright to look at them.

Don't be put off by people gesturing at their noses as if they have an itch. The nose, as opposed to the heart, is the symbolic centre of the self in China. Don't kiss anyone by way of greeting unless you want to frighten or titillate as it's not socially acceptable.

religion

信仰

What's your religion?
你信什么叫？   née sìn shér·mer jyào

Are you religious?
你信教吗?   nĕe sìn·jyào ma

I'm ...	我信……	wŏr sìn ...
agnostic	也没什么信	yăir máy·shér mer sìn
an atheist	无神论	wŏo·shérn·lòon
Buddhist	佛教	fór·jyào
Catholic	天主教	tyēn·jŏo·jyào
Christian	基督教	jēe·dŏo·jyào
Hindu	印度教	yìn·doo·jyào
Jewish	犹太教	yó·tài·jyào
Muslim	伊斯兰教	ee·sìr·lún·jyào

I (don't) believe in ...	我(不)信……	wŏr (bòo) sìn ...
astrology	星象	sīng·syùng
fate	命运	mìng·yèwn
fengshui	风水	fērng·shwăy
God	上帝	shùng·dèe

Confucianism	儒教	róo·jyào
Daoism	道教	dào·jyào
Falun Gong	法轮功	fă·lóon·gōong

Can I ... here?	我能……在这里吗？	wǒr nérng ... zài jèr·lee ma
Where can I ...?	我在哪里可以……？	wǒr zài ná·lee kér·ěe ...
attend a service	参加礼拜	tsūn·jyā lěe·bài
pray	祈祷	chée·dǎo
meditate	静坐	jìng·zwòr

cultural differences

文化差异

Is this a local or national custom?
这是地方风俗吗？ jèr shìr dèe·fūng fērng·sóo ma

I don't want to offend you.
我不想得罪你们。 wǒr bòo syǔng dér·zwày něe·mern

I'm not used to this.
我没有这个习惯。 wǒr máy·yǒ jày·ger sěe·gwùn

I'd rather not join in.
我最好不参加。 wǒr zwày·hǎo bòo tsūn·jyā

I'll try it.
我可以试试。 wǒr kér·ěe shìr·shir

I didn't mean to do anything wrong.
我没想走错。 wǒr máy·syǔng zǒ·tswòr

I'm sorry, it's against my ...	不好意思，是违背我的……的。	bòo·hǎo èe·sīr shìr wǎy·bày wǒr·der ... der
beliefs	信仰	sìn·yǔng
religion	宗教	zōong·jyào

This is ...	这有点……	jày yó·dyěn ...
different	与众不同	yěw·jòong bòo·tóong
fun	好玩	hǎo·wár
interesting	意思	èe·sīr

When does the gallery open?

| 艺术馆 | èe·shoo·gwǔn |
| 几点开门? | jée·dyěn kāi·mérn |

When does the museum open?

| 博物馆 | bóo·wòo·gwǔn |
| 几点开门? | jée·dyěn kāi·mérn |

What kind of art are you interested in?

你喜欢	née sěe·hwūn
什么样	shér·mer·yùng
的艺术?	der èe·shoo

What's in the collection?

| 这儿收藏了 | jèr·lee shò·tsúng·ler |
| 什么? | shér·mer |

What do you think of ...?

| 你觉得…… | něe jwáir·der ... |
| 怎么样? | zěr·mer·yùng |

It's a/an ... exhibition.

| 是一个……展览。 | shìr ēe·ger ... jún·lǔn |

I'm interested in ...

| 我对…… | wǒr dwày ... |
| 感兴趣。 | gǔn·sìng·chew |

I like the works of ...

| 我喜欢…… | wór sěe·hwūn ... |
| 的作品。 | der zwòr·pǐn |

It reminds me of ...

| 让我想到…… | rùng wór·syǔng dào ... |

... art	......艺术	... èe·shoo
comic	漫画	mùn·hwà
graphic	版画	bǔn·hwà
modern	现代派	syèn·dai pài
postmodern	后现代	hò·syèn·dai
realist	现实主义	syèn·shír jǒo·èe
performance	演示	yěn·shìr
Western	西方	sēe·fūng
artwork	艺术品	èe·shoo pǐn
bronze	铜器	tóong·chèe
calligraphy	书法	shōo·fǎ
ceramics	陶瓷	táo·tsír
Cultural	文华	wérn·hwà
Revolution	大革命	dà·gěr·mìng
curator	策划者	tsèr·hwà jěr
design	设计	shèr·jee
dynasty	皇朝	hwúng·cháo
etching	刻板	kèr·bǔn
exhibit	展出	jún·lùn
exhibition hall	展览馆	jún·lún·gwǔn
jade	玉器	yèw·chèe
installation	多媒体	dōr·máy·těe
opening	开幕	kāi·mòo
painter	画家	hwà·jyā
painting	画儿	hwàr
period	时代	shír·dài
permanent	普通展览	pǒo·tōong jún·lùn
collection		
print	印刷	yìn·shwā
scriptures	经书	jīng·shōo
scroll	国画	gwór·hwà
sculptor	雕塑家	dyāo·sòo jyā
sculpture	雕塑	dyāo·sòo
statue	塑像	sòo·syùng
studio	工作室	gōong·zwor·shǐr
style	风格	fērng·gér
technique	方法	fūng·fǎ
woodblock print	木刻	mòo·kèr

sporting interests

体育活动

In Mandarin any sport can be 'played' using the verb wár 玩 but generally this has light-hearted connotations, as in 'to have a kick of the ball'. If you want to express such a playful interest in sport then use these two phrases below:

I play/do ...
我喜欢玩……   wór sĕe·hwūn wár ...

What sport do you play?
你喜欢玩什么   née sĕe·hwūn wár shér·mer
体育？   tĕe·yèw

To say that you really play a sport, you need to use an appropriate verb such as 'hit' (dǎ 打) or 'kick' (tēe 踢). Some sports (such as gymnastics and martial arts) are identified not by hits or kicks but by the rigorous 'repetitive training' (lyèn 练) required of the practitioner. The verb 'do' (gǎo 搞) can be used when you're not sure whether you should hit, kick or train harder (as in cycling or athletics).

sports that take dǎ 打 (hit)

I play/do ...	我喜欢打……	wór sĕe·hwūn dǎ ...
I follow ...	我喜欢看……	wór sĕe·hwūn kùn ...
(beach) volleyball	(沙滩)排球	(shā·tūn) pái·chyó
badminton	羽毛球	yĕw·máo·chyó
basketball	篮球	lún·chyó
handball	手球	shŏ·chyó
hockey	曲棍球	chĕw·gùn·chyó
table tennis	乒乓球。	pīng·pūng chyó
tennis	网球	wŭng·chyó
water polo	水球	shwǎy·chyó

sports that take tēe 踢 (kick)

I play/do ...	我喜欢踢……	wór sěe·hwūn tēe ...
I follow ...	我喜欢看……	wór sěe·hwūn kùn ...
American football	美式 橄榄球	máy·shìr gún·lǔn·chyó
Australian Rules football	澳式 橄榄球	ào·shìr gún·lǔn chyó
football (soccer)	足球	zóo·chyó
rugby	英式 橄榄球	yīng·shìr gún·lǔn chyó

sports that take gǎo 搞 (do)

I play/do ...	我喜欢搞……	wór sěe·hwūn gǎo ...
I follow ...	我喜欢看……	wór sěe·hwūn kùn ...
archery	射箭	shèr·jyèn
fencing	剑术	jyèn·shòo
long distance running	长跑	chúng·pǎo
rowing	划船	hwǎ·chwún
sailing	帆船	fūn·chwún
scuba diving	潜水游	chyén·shwǎy yǒ
shooting	射击	shèr·jēe
swimming	游泳	yó·yǒong
track & field	田径	tyěn·jìng
weightlifting	举重	jěw·jòong

sports that take lyèn 练 (rigorous training)

I play/do ...	我喜欢练……	wór sěe·hwūn lyèn ...
I follow ...	我喜欢看……	wór sěe·hwūn kùn ...
gymnastics	体操	těe·tsāo
judo	柔道	ró·dào
karate	空手道	kōong·shǒ·dào
martial arts	武术	wǒo·shòo
taekwondo	太空道	tài·kōong·dào
tai chi	太极拳	tài·jée·chwén

In Mandarin, the many styles of martial arts are collectively known as wǒo·shòo 武术. Each style embodies its own particular spirit and philosophy (drawing on Confucianism, Taoism, Buddhism and Zen). Here are a few styles that travellers to China may see:

Bagua Zhang　八卦掌　bā·gwā jùng
(Eight Trigram Boxing)
The characteristics of this martial art style, in which practitioners wheel around in circles kicking and landing palm strikes, are the skills of subterfuge, evasion, speed and unpredictability.

Shaolin Boxing　沙林拳　shào·lín chwén
Originating at Shaolin monastery and still practised there today, this major martial art form draws on Zen Buddhist beliefs and bases its forms on five animals: dragon, snake, tiger, leopard and crane.

Taijiquan　太极拳　tài·jée·chwén
Known in the West as tai chi, this graceful centuries-old Chinese system promotes flexibility, circulation, strength, balance, meditation and relaxation. Based on Taoist beliefs, it's traditionally practiced as a form of self-defence without the use of force.

Xingyi Quan　形意拳　síng·èe chwén
(Body-Mind Boxing)
Often mentioned in the same breath as taijiquan this martial art is more dynamic and powerful. The movements of this – perhaps the oldest form of martial art still practised in China – are performed in a relaxed state but quickly and directly.

I ...	我喜欢……	wór sěe·hwūn ...
cycle	骑自行车	chée zìr·síng·chēr
run	跑步	pǎo·bòo
walk	散散步	sùn·sun·bòo

Who's your favourite ...?	你最喜欢的……是谁?	née zwày sěe·hwūn der ... shìr sháy
sportsperson	球星	chyó·sīng
team	球队	chyó·dwày

Do you like (table tennis)?
你喜欢打
(乒乓球)吗?

née sěe·hwūn dǎ
(pīng·pūng·chyó) ma

Yes, very much.
很喜欢。

hěrn sěe·hwūn

Not really.
不太喜欢。

bóo·tài sěe·hwūn

I like watching it.
我喜欢看。

wór sěe·hwūn kùn

---

scoring

What's the score?	几比几?	jěe·bée·jěe
draw/even	打平	dǎ píng
love/zero	零	líng
match-point	赛点	sài·dyěn

going to a game

看球

Would you like to go to a game?
你想跟我去
看球吗?

née syǔng gērn·wǒr·chèw
kùn·chyó ma

Who are you supporting?
你支持哪个队?

něe jīr·chǐr nǎy·ger dwày

Who's ...?	谁……?	sháy ...
playing	在打	zài dǎ
winning	占上风	jùn·shùng·fêrng
That was a	比赛打得	běe·sài dǎ·der
... game!	真……!	jêrn ...
bad	差劲	chā·jìn
boring	无聊	wóo·lyáo
great	精彩	jīng·tsǎi

sports talk

Come on!	加油!	jyā·yó
What a goal!	进门!	jìn·mérn
What a hit!	好球!	hǎo·chyó
What a kick!	踢得好!	têe·der hǎo
What a pass!	传得好!	chwún·der hǎo
What a performance!	演得真 精彩!	yén·der jêrn jīng·tsǎi

playing sport

玩球

Do you want to play?
你想玩吗?　　　　　née syǔn wár ma

Can I join in?
我可以跟你们　　　　wǒr kér·ěe gêrn něe·mern
一起玩吗?　　　　　èe·chěe wár ma

That would be great.
好。　　　　　　　　hǎo

I can't.
我不能。　　　　　　wǒr bòo nérng

I have an injury.
我受伤了。　　　　　wǒr shò·shùng ler

sport

147

Your/My point.
你/我得分。   něe/wǒr dér fērn

Kick/Pass it to me!
踢/传给我！   tēe/chwún gáy wǒr

You're a good player.
你打得很好。   née dǎ·der hérn·hǎo

Thanks for the game.
多谢你，我打得   dōr·syàir něe wór dǎ der
很高兴   hěrn kāi·sīn

Do I have to be a member to attend?
只对会员   jīr dwày hwày·ywén
开放吗？   kāi·fùng ma

Is there a women-only session?
有女子班吗？   yó něw·zir būn ma

Where are the changing rooms?
更衣室在哪？   gērng·ēe·shǐr zài nár

Where's the nearest …?	附近哪里有……？	fòo·jìn ná·lee yǒ …
golf course	高尔夫场	gāo·er·foo chǔng
gym	健美中心	jyèn·mǎy jōong·sīn
swimming pool	游泳池	yó·yǒong chír
tennis court	网球场	wǔng·chyó chǔng

What's the charge per …?	每……要花多少钱？	máy … yào·hwā dōr·shǎo chyén
day	天	tyēn
game	场	chǔng
hour	小时	syǎo·shír
visit	次	tsìr

Can I hire a …?	我可以租一个……吗？	wǒr kér·ěe zōo·ee·ger… ma
ball	球	chyó
bicycle	自行车	zìr·síng·chēr
court	场	chǔng
racquet	拍子	pái·zir

extreme sports

刺激运动

I'd like to go ...	我想去……	wór·syŭng chĕw ...
get some kicks	找刺激	jăo tsìr·jee
rock-climbing	攀岩	pūn·yén
skydiving	跳伞	tyào·sŭn
snowboarding	滑雪板	hwā shwáir·bŭn

The rope will hold, won't it?
绳子没事吧？ shérng·zir máy·shìr ba

This is insane.
疯了！ ferng·ler

fishing

钓鱼

Where are the good spots?
到哪里钓鱼 dào·ná·lee dyào·yĕw
比较好？ bĕe·jyào hăo

Do I need a fishing permit?
需要执照吗？ sēw·yào jír·jào ma

What's the best bait?
最好的鱼饵是 zwày·hăo·der yéw·ăr shir
什么？ shér·mer

Are they biting?
有人钓到鱼了吗？ yŏ rérn dyào·dào yĕw ler ma

golf

高尔夫球

How much ...?	打……多少钱？	dă ... dōr·shăo chyén
for a round	一场	ēe·chŭng
to play 9/	9洞/	jyŏ·dòong/
18 holes	18洞	shír·bā·dòong

Can I hire golf clubs?
能租到球棍吗？　　　　　nérng zōo·dào chyó·gòon ma

What's the dress code?
要注意穿衣服吗？　　　　yào jòo·èe chwūn·ēe·foo ma

Do I need golf shoes?
需要高尔夫　　　　　　　sōo·yào gāo·er·foo
球鞋吗？　　　　　　　　chyó·syáir ma

Do I need to hire a golf cart/caddie?
需要请一个　　　　　　　sōo·yào chǐng·ee·ger
球车/球童吗？　　　　　 chyó·chēr/chyó·tóng ma

Fore!
看球！　　　　　　　　　kùn·chyó

bunker	沙坑	shā·kērng
flag	旗子	chée·zir
golf cart	球车	chyó·chēr
golf course	高尔夫场	gāo·er·foo chǔng
golf ball	高尔夫球	gāo·er·foo chyó
green	草坪	tsǎo·píng
hole	球洞	chyó·dòong
hole in one	一杆进洞	ēe·gùn jìn·dòong
iron	铁杆	tyáir·gùn
putter	推杆	twāy·gùn
tee	球座	chyó·zwòr
teeing ground	发球台	fā·chyó·tái
wood	木杆	mòo·gùn

soccer

足球

Who plays for (Beijing Guo An)?
(北京国安)有哪些　　　 (bǎy·jīng gwór·ūn) yó nǎ·syáir
球星？　　　　　　　　　chyó·sīng

He plays well.
他踢得很棒。　　　　　　tā tēe·der hěrn bùng

He played brilliantly in the match against (Italy).

他在(意大利)那场　　　tā zài (èe·dà·lèe) nà·chǔng
踢得很精彩。　　　　　tēe·der hěrn jīng·tsǎi

Which team is at the top of the league?

哪个队占第一名？　　　nǎ·ger dwày jùn dèe·ēe·míng

What a great/terrible team!

这个队真棒/臭。　　　jày·ger dwày jěrn bùng/chò

ball	球	chyó
coach	教练	jyào·lyèn
corner	角球	jyǎo·chyó
expulsion	开除场	kāi·chóo·chǔng
fan	球迷	chyó·mée
foul	犯规	fùn·gwāy
free kick	任意球	rèrn·èe chyó
goal	进门	jìn·mérn
goalkeeper	守门	shǒ·mérn
manager	经理	jīng·lěe
offside	裁位	ywàir wày
penalty	点球	dyěn·chyó
player	球员	chyó·ywén
red card	红牌	hóong·pái
referee	裁判	tsǎi·pùn
striker	前锋	chyén·fērng
throw in	边球	byēn·chyó
yellow card	黄牌	hwúng·pái

table tennis

与乒乓球

I'd like to play table tennis.

我想打乒乓球。　　　　wǒr·syúng dǎ pīng·pūng chyó

Do you know where a table tennis table is?

哪里有乒乓球桌？　　　ná·lee yǒ pīng·pūng chyó jwōr

Can I book a table?

我可以预订一个　　　　wǒr kér·ēe yèw·dìng ēe·ger
乒乓球桌吗？　　　　　pīng·pūng chyó jwōr ma?

bat	拍子	pái·zir
net	网	wǔng
serve	发球	fā·chyó
table	球桌	chyó·jwōr
table tennis ball	乒乓球	pīng·pūng chyó

tennis

网球

I'd like to play tennis.
我想打网球。 wór·syǔng dá wǔng· chyó

Can we play at night?
今天晚上可以 jīn·tyēn wún·shùng kér·ée
打吗? dǎ ma

I need my racquet restrung.
我牌子要换线。 wǒr pái·zir yào hwùn·syèn

ace	爱司球	ài·sīr chyó
advantage	领先	líng·syēn
clay	土场	tóo·chǔng
fault	失误	shīr·woo
game, set, match	局, 盘, 赛	jóo pún sài
grass	草场	tsǎo·chúng
net	擦网	tsā·wǔng
racquet	拍子	pái·zir
serve	发球	fā·chyó
set	`盘	pún
tennis	网球	wǔng·chyó
tennis court	网球场	wǔng·chyó chǔng

hiking

步行

Where can I ...?	在哪里能……?	zài ná·lee nérng …
buy supplies	买到	mǎi·dào
	预备品	yèw·bày·pīn
find someone who knows this area	找路熟的人	jǎo lòo·shǒ der rérn
get a map	买地图	mài dèe·tóo
Do we need to take ...?	需要带上……吗?	sēw·yào dài·shùng … ma
bedding	被褥	bày·rǒo
food	食品	shír·pīn
water	饮用水	yīn·yòong·shwǎy

How high is the climb?
爬山有多高? pǎ·shūn yǒ dōr gāo

How long is the trail?
步行有多远? bòo·síng yǒ dōr ywén

Do we need a guide?
需要向导吗? sēw·yào syùng·dǎo ma

Are there guided treks?
有人开向导
步行团吗? yǒ rérn kāi syùng·dǎo bòo·síng twún ma

Is it safe?
觉得安全吗? jwáir·der ūn·chwén ma

Is the track …?	路……吗？	lòo … ma
easy to follow	好找	háo·jǎo
open	开通	kāi·tòong
scenic	边风景好	byēn fērng·jíng hǎo

Which is the	哪条路径	ná·tyǎo lòo·jìng
… route?	最……？	zwày …
easiest	容易	róong·ee
most interesting	有意思	yǒ èe·sir
shortest	短	dwǔn

Is there somewhere to spend the night?
有地方住吗？   yǒ dèe·fūng jòo ma

When does it get dark?
天什么时候   tyēn shér·mer shír·hò
变黑？   byèn·hāy

Where's the nearest village?
在哪里能找   zài ná·lee nérng·jǎo
一个村子？   ēe·ger tsōon·zir

Where have you come from?
你从哪边   něe tsóong nǎ·byēn
过来了？   gwòr·lái ler

How long did it take?
走了有多久？   zǒ·ler yǒ dōr·jyǒ

Does this path go to …?
这条路到……吗？   jày·tyǎo·lòr dào … ma

Can I go through here?
我能从这儿   wǒr nérng tsōong jèr·lee
穿过吗？   chwūn·gwòr ma

Is the water OK to drink?
这儿的水   jèr·lee der shwǎy
能喝吗？   nérng·hēr ma

I'm lost.
我迷路了。   wór mée·lòo ler

beach

沙滩

Where's the ... beach?	……沙滩怎么走？	... shā·tūn zěr·mer zǒ
best	最好的	zwày·hǎo der
nearest	最近的	zwày·jìn der
public	公开的	gōong·kāi der

Is it safe to swim here?
这里游泳安全吗？   jèr·lee yó·yǒong ūn·chwén ma

What time is high/low tide?
高/低潮是   gāo/dēe cháo shìr
几点钟？   jée·dyěn·jōong

Do we have to pay?
要买票吗？   yào mǎi·pyào ma

weather

气候

What's the weather like?
天气怎么样？   tyen·chee zěr·mer·yung

What will the weather be like tomorrow?
明天天气   míng·tyēn tyēn·chee
会怎么样？   hwày zěr·mer·yùng

It's ...	天气……	tyēn·chee ...
cloudy	有云	yǒ yéwn
cold	冷	lěrng
fine	晴	chíng
freezing	很冷	hérn·lěrng
hot	热	rèr
raining	下雨	syà·yěw
snowing	下雪	syà·shwǎir
sunny	很晒	hěrn·shài
warm	暖和	nwǔn·hwór
windy	刮风	gwā·fērng

Where can I buy …?	在哪里能买到……?	zài ná·lee nérng mǎi·dào …
a rain jacket	雨衣	yéw·ēe
an umbrella	雨伞	yéw·sǔn

dry season	旱季	hùn·jèe
monsoon season	台风季	tái·fêng jèe
wet season	雨季	yěw·jèe

flora & fauna

动物与植物

What … is that?	那个……是什么?	nà·ger … shìr shér·mer
animal	动物	dòong·woo
flower	花	hwā
plant	植物	jír·wòo
tree	树	shòo

Is it …?	是……的吗?	shìr … der ma
common	常见	chǔng·jyèn
dangerous	危险	wāy·syen
endangered	临危	lín·wày
protected	受保护	shò bǎo·hòo

What's it used for?
它用来做什么? — tā yòong·lái zwòr shér·mer

Can you eat the fruit?
能吃它的果子吗? — nérng·chīr tā·der gwór·zir ma

local plants & animals		
giant panda	大熊猫	dà syóong māo
lotus	荷花	hér·hwā
peony	牡丹花	mòo·dún hwā
red-necked crane	丹领鹤	dùn·líng hèr
red panda	小熊猫	syǎo syóong·māo
Siberian tiger	东北虎	dōong·báy hǒo

key language

要点

Chinese meals come earlier than you may be used to, so get ready to wind your stomach clock back a couple of hours. Lunch is the main meal of the day and often includes a selection of stir-fried dishes and rice. Dinner is much the same as lunch but often with beer taking the place of rice. All meals are served hot – as hot food is believed to be better for the digestion.

breakfast	早饭	zǎo·fùn
lunch	午饭	wǒo·fùn
dinner	晚饭	wún·fùn
snack	小吃	syǎo·chīr
to eat	吃	chīr
to drink	喝	hēr
I'm starving!	我怪饿了！	wǒr gwài·èr ler

finding a place to eat

寻香味

Can you recommend a ...?	你可以推荐一个……吗？	něe nérng twāy·jyèn ee·ger ... ma
bar	酒吧	jyǒ·bǎ
café	咖啡屋	kā·fāy·wōo
noodle house	面摊	myèn·tūn
restaurant	饭馆	fùn·gwǔn
snack shop	夜宵店	yàir·syāo dyèn
(won ton) stall	(混沌) 摊	(hóon·dòon) tūn
street vendor	街头小吃	jyāir·tó syǎo·chīr
teahouse	茶馆	chā·gwǔn

Where would you go for …?	……该到哪里去？	… gāi dào·ná·lee chèw
a banquet	办宴会	bùn yèn·hwày
a celebration	开饭局	kāi fùn·jŏo
a cheap meal	吃得便宜一点的	chīr pyén·ee ēe·dyěn der
local specialities	地方小吃	dèe·fūng syǎo·chīr
yum cha	吃饮茶	chīr yǐn·chá
I'd like to reserve a table for …	我想预订一桌, ……的。	wór·syǔng yèw·dìng ee·jwōr … der
(two) people	(两)位	(lyǔng) wày
(eight) o'clock	(八)点钟	(bā)·dyěn jōong

Chinese cuisine

Chinese cuisine can be divided into four main schools. The character of these regional cuisines is encapsulated by the saying 'The East is sour, the West is spicy, the South is sweet and the North is salty.' (dōong swūn, sēe là, nún syén, bǎy tyén 东酸, 西辣, 南咸, 北甜).

A number of provincial cooking styles are recognised too including the ones given below.

Eastern (Shanghai) cuisine	浙菜	jèr·tsài
Western (Sichuan) cuisine	川菜	chwūn·tsài
Southern (Cantonese) cuisine	粤菜	ywàir·tsài
Northern (Shandong) cuisine	鲁菜	lŏo·tsài
Anhui cuisine	皖菜	wǔn·tsài
Chaozhou cuisine	闽菜	mǐn·tsài
Hunan cuisine	湘菜	syūng·tsài
Jiangsu cuisine	苏菜	sōo·tsài

Are you still serving food?
你们还开饭吗？ něe·mern hái kāi·fùn ma

How long is the wait?
吃饭要等多久？ chīr·fùn yào·děrng dōr·jyǒ

I'd like ..., please. 请拿来…… chǐng ná lái ...
the drink list 酒料单 jyǒ·lyào dūn
a half portion 半分 bùn·fernr
the menu 菜单 tsài·dūn
a menu in English 英文菜单 yīng wérn tsài dūn
a nonsmoking 不吸烟的 bòo·sēe·yēn der
  table 桌了 jwāo·zir
a smoking table 吸烟的 sēe·yēn der
  桌了 jwāo·zir
a table for (five) （五）位桌子 (wǒo) wày jwōr·zir

listen for ...

chíng děrng·ee·syà
请等一下。 One moment.

gwūn·mérn ler
关门了。 We're closed.

kér·ěe twǎy·jyèn ...
可以推荐…… I suggest the ...

née sēe·hwūn ... ma
你喜欢……吗？ Do you like ...?

shùng tsài ler
上菜了！ Here you go!

syǔng dyén shér·mer ner
想点什么呢？ What can I get
for you?

zwòr mǔn ler
座满了。 We're full.

zwòr ná·lee
坐哪里？ Where would
you like to sit?

eating out

159

at the restaurant

The Chinese have a word, rèr·nào 热闹 (lit: hot and noisy, ie, 'bustling') that typifies the atmosphere of their restaurants. When the Chinese eat out they like to have raucous, lip-smacking fun. The Western style of whispering couples sipping expensive wine by candlelight is not for them.

What would you recommend?
可以推荐什么呢？   kér·ĕe twāy·jyèn shér·mer ner

What's in that dish?
这道菜怎么做？   jày dào·tsài zĕr·mer zwòr

I'll have that.
来一个吧。   lái·ee·ger ba

Is it self-serve?
这里是自助的吗？   fóo·wòr shìr zìr·jòo der ma

Is service included in the bill?
单子包括服务费吗？   dūn·zir bāo·kwor fóo·wòo fày ma

Are these complimentary?
这是赠送的吗？   jày shìr zèrng·sòong der ma

communal chow

Meals in Chinese restaurants typically come not in individual servings but in communal plates (dà·pún 大盘) and diners eat directly from these. This style of eating contributes to the fun, social atmosphere of dining in China. It also contributes to the high rates of hepatitis B infection in China, so make sure you're immunised before you go.

I'd like ...	我想吃……	wór·syǔng chīr ...
the beef	牛肉面	nyó·rò myèn
noodle soup		
a local speciality	一个地方菜	ee·ger dèe·fūng·tsài
a meal fit	得像皇	der syùng hwúng
for a king	上似的	shùng sir·der

I'd like it with ...	多放一点……	dōr·jyā ēe·dyěn ...
I'd like it without ...	不要放……	bóo·yào·fùng ...
chilli	辣椒	là·jyāo
garlic	大蒜	dà·swùn
nuts	果仁	gwǒr·rérn
oil	油	yó
MSG	味精	wày·jīng

For other specific meal requests, see **vegetarian & special meals**, page 175.

look for ...		
凉菜	lyúng·tsài	appetisers (cold)
主菜	jōo tsài	main courses (usually meat dishes)
海鲜	hǎi·syēn	seafood dishes
汤类	tung·lày	soups
蔬菜	shòo·tsài	vegetable dishes (may contain meat)
主食	jōo·shír	staples
甜品	tyén·pǐn	desserts
啤酒	pée·jyǒ	beer
果汁	gwǒr·jīr	fruit juice
汽水	chèe·shwǎy	soft drinks
香槟	syūng·bīn	sparkling wines
白酒	bái·jyǒ	spirits
白兰地	bái·lún·dèe	cognac
加饭酒	Jyā·fùn·jyǒ	digestifs

For more words you might see on a menu, see the **culinary reader**, page 177.

at the table

请哪一个······

Please bring ...	请哪一个······	chíng ná·ee·ger ...
a cloth	擦布	tsā·bòo
a knife and fork	刀叉	dāo·chā
a serviette	餐巾	tsūn·jìn
a glass	杯子	bāy·zir
a wineglass	葡萄酒杯	póo·tào jyǒ·bāy

Bill, please!
买单！
mǎi·dūn

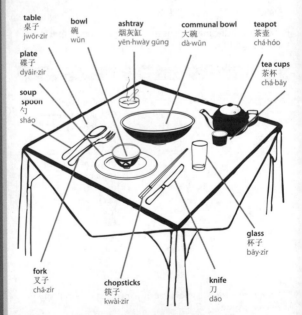

table
桌子
jwòr·zir

bowl
碗
wǔn

ashtray
烟灰缸
yēn·hwày gūng

communal bowl
大碗
dà·wǔn

teapot
茶壶
chá·hóo

plate
碟子
dyāir·zir

tea cups
茶杯
chá·bāy

soup spoon
勺
sháo

glass
杯子
bāy·zir

fork
叉子
chā·zir

chopsticks
筷子
kwài·zir

knife
刀
dāo

hái yào byáir·der ma
还要别的吗？   **Anything else?**

kér·ëe bŭng nĕe ma
我能帮你吗？   **Can I help you?**

mái·yŏ
没有。   **No, we don't have any.**

talking food

说美食

I love this dish.
这道菜真香。   jày dào tsài jērn·syūng

I love the local cuisine.
这个地方的菜   jày·ger dèe·fŭng der tsài
真好吃。   jērn hăo·chīr

That was delicious!
吃的真香！   chīr·der jērn syūng

I'm full.
吃饱了。   chīr·bǎo ler

This dish is ...	这个菜……	jày·ger tsài ... ler
(too) cold	(太)凉	(tài) lyúng
(too) spicy	(太)辣	(tài) là
superb	真香	jērn·syūng

A favourite Chinese sport is fighting over the bill in restaurants. It's considered polite in China to offer to pay the bill once or even twice, even if you're clearly the guest. A protest along the following lines may be made loudly, to show sincerity, even when it's a bluff:

You were tonight's host, but I'll pay the bill.

是你请的客,	shìr née chǐng·der kèr
我不过	wǒr boo·gwòr
是买单的。	shìr mǎi·dūn der

breakfast

早饭

A standard breakfast consists of some type of porridge, typically made from rice in the South and corn in the North, along with a selection of side dishes such as pickles, deep-fried doughsticks, or tea-eggs (hard-boiled eggs marbled with tea and star anise). Western breakfast options could be hard to come by.

What do you normally eat for breakfast?

| 早饭一般吃 | zǎo·fùn èe·būn chǐr |
| 什么? | shér·mer |

bacon	培根	páy·gērn
bread	面包	myèn·bāo
butter	黄油	hwúng·yó
cereal	烤麦片	kǎo mài·pyèn
corn porridge	玉米粥	yèw·měe jō
deep-fried dough sticks	油条	yó·tyáo
egg(s)	蛋	dùn
duck egg(s)	鸭蛋	yà dùn
fried egg(s)	炸蛋	jā dùn
hard-boiled egg(s)	煮鸡蛋	jǒo·jēe dùn
pickled duck egg(s)	咸鸭蛋	syén·yā dùn
poached egg(s)	泡蛋	pāo dùn

scrambled eggs	牛奶炒蛋	nyó·nái chǎo dùn
soft-boiled egg(s)	半煮鸡蛋	bùn·jǒo jēe·dùn
tea egg(s)	茶叶蛋	chá·yàir dùn
fresh soy milk	豆浆	dò·jyūng
milk	牛奶	nyó·nǎi
muesli	姆斯里	mǒo·sīr·lee
noodle soup	汤面	tūng·myèn
omelette	炒鸡蛋	chǎo jēe·dùn
pickled vegetables	咸菜	syén·tsài
rice porridge	白米粥	mě·jō
savoury ...	咸……	syén ...
sesame-seed pancake	芝麻煎饼	jīr·ma jyěn·bǐng
steamed buns	馒头	mún·to
sweet ...	甜……	tyén ...
sweet steamed bean-paste bun	豆沙包	dò·shā bāo
toast	烤面包	kǎo myèn·bāo
won ton soup	混沌	hún·dùn

light meals

小吃

What's that called?
那个叫什么？　　　　　　　nà·ger jyào shér·mer

I'd like ..., please.	请给我……	chǐng gáy·wǒr ...
one slice	一块	ēe·kwài
a piece	一分	ēe·fèrn
a sandwich	一个三明治	ee·ger sūn·míng·jìr
that one	那一个	nà·ee·ger
two	两个	lyǔng·ger

condiments

加饭

Do you have ...?	有没有……?	yŏ·máy·yŏ ...
chilli sauce	辣椒酱	là·jyāo jyùng
dipping sauce	黄酱	hwúng·jyùng
garlic	大蒜	dà·swùn
soy sauce	酱油	jyùng·yŏ
vinegar	醋	tsòo

For additional items, see the **culinary reader**, page 177.

methods of preparation

菜做法

I (don't) want it ...	我(不)要……的。	wŏr bóo·yào ... der
barbecued	烧烤	shāo·kăo
boiled	煮	jōo
braised	煎	jyēn
deep-fried	油炸	yó·jā
grilled	铁板烤	tyáir·bún kăo
medium	半熟半生	bùn·shērng bùn·shŏ
rare	半生	shērng
re-heated	重热	chóong·rèr
roasted	烤	kăo
steamed	蒸	jērng
stir-fried	炒	chăo
well-done	熟	shŏ
without ...	不加……	bóo·jyā ...

in the bar

酒文化

Excuse me!	劳驾!	láo·jyà
I'll have ...	我来一个……	wŏr lái ee·ger ...

Same again, please.
请再来一个。 chǐng zài lái ee·ger …

No ice, thanks.
不要加冰块啦。 bóo·yào jyā bīng·kwàr la

I'll buy you a drink.
喝什么？我请客。 hēr shér·mer wór chǐng kèr

What would you like?
你想喝什么？ née syǔng hēr shér·mer

How much is that?
总共多少钱？ zǒong·qòong dōr·shǎo chyén

Do you serve meals here?
你们有菜可点吗？ něe·mern yǒ tsài dyěn ma

listen for ...

hēr·dōr·ler něe
喝多了，你。 **I think you've had enough.**

něe hēr shér·mer
你吃什么？ **What are you having?**

nonalcoholic drinks

饮料

... water	······水	... shwǎy
boiled	开	kāi·
cold	凉开	lyǔng kāi·
still mineral	矿泉	kwùng·chwén
sparkling mineral	矿泉气	kwùng·chwén chèe
fresh drinking yogurt	酸奶	swūn·nǎi
(orange) juice	(橙)汁	(chérng) jìr
lychee-flavoured soft drink	荔枝汁	lèe·jīr jìr
soft drink	汽水	chèe·shwǎy
sour plum drink	酸梅汤	swūn·máy·tūng

(cup of) coffee	(一杯)咖啡	(ēe·bay) kā·fāy
(cup of) tea	(一杯)茶	(ēe·bāy) chá
... with (milk)	……加(牛奶)	... jyā (nyó·nǎi)
... without (sugar)	……不加(糖)	... bóo jyā (tǔng)
... coffee	……咖啡	... kā·fāy
black	黑	hāy
decaffeinated	低咖啡因	dēe kā·fāy·yīn
espresso	浓缩	nóong·swōr
iced	冰	bīng
strong	特浓	tèr·nóong
weak	淡	dùn
white	奶	bái

all the tea in China

Generally speaking, the Chinese are tea rather than coffee drinkers. Though the major cities have a nascent coffee culture, coffee can be hard to find outside the major cities. The good news is that China has many delicious teas. Try sipping some of these:

black tea	红茶	hóong·chá
chrysanthemum tea	菊花茶	jēw·hwā·chá
green tea	绿茶	lòo·chá
jasmine tea	花茶	hwā·chá
oolong tea	乌龙茶	wōo·lóong·chá

alcoholic drinks

酒类

Keep an eye out for people tapping their fingers on the table-cloth as their glass is filled – a new affectation that conquered China from the south in the early 1990s. It indicates a nonverbal appreciation of the service being rendered.

beer	啤酒	pée·jyǒ
brandy	白兰地	bái·lūn·dèe
champagne	香槟	syūng·bīn

Chinese spirit	白酒	bái·jyǒ
cocktail	鸡尾酒	jēe·wáy jyǒ
maotai	茅台酒	máo·tái jyǒ
(Chinese vodka)		
rice wine	黄酒	hwúng·jyó

a shot of ...	一樽……	ēe·zōon ...
gin	金酒	jīn·jyǒ
rum	朗姆酒	lùng·moo·jyǒ
tequila	特吉拉	tèr·jée·lā
vodka	伏特加	fóo·tèr·jyā
whisky	威士忌	way·shìr·jèe

a bottle/glass	一瓶/一杯……	ēe·píng/ēe·bāy ...
of ... wine	葡萄酒	pǒo·táo jyǒ
dessert	甜	tyén
red	红	hóong
sparkling	香槟	syūng·bīn
white	白	bái

a ... of beer	一……啤酒	ēe· ... pée·jyǒ
glass	杯	bāy
large bottle	瓶	píng
small bottle	小瓶	syǎo·píng

drinking up

喝起来

Cheers!
干杯! gūn·bāy

This is hitting the spot.
太顺口了。 tài shùn·kǒ ler

I feel fantastic!
感觉真爽! gǔn·jwáir jērn·shwǔng

I think I've had one too many.
我是不是喝多了。 wǒr shìr·boo·shìr hēr·dōr ler

I'm feeling drunk.
我有点醉。 wǒ yó·dyěn zwày

I'm pissed.
我醉了。 wǒr zwày ler

I feel ill.
我要呕。 wǒr yàò ǒ

Where's the toilet?
哪里有厕所？ ná·lee yǒ tsèr·swǒr

I'm tired, I'd better go home.
我捆了，该回家。 wǒr kòon ler gāi hwáy·jyā

Can you call a taxi for me?
你能帮我叫个
车吗？ něe nérng būng·wǒr jyào ger
chēr ma

street eats

China's bustling towns and cities teem with street vendors
(jyāir·tó syǎo·chīr 街头小吃) selling delicious snacks (syǎo·chīr
小吃) to eat on the go. Choose from among this array of
popular treats:

cold clear bean-flour noodles	凉粉	lyúng·fěrn
corn on the cob	玉米棒	yèw·mée bùng
dumpling (boiled)	饺子	jyǎo·zir
dumpling (fried)	锅贴	gwōr·tyāir
dumpling (steamed)	包子	bāo·zir
egg and spring onion pancake	煎饼	jyēn·bǐng
flat bread topped with sesame seeds	烧餅	shāo·bǐng
pork pie (large)	肉饼	rò·bǐng
pork pie (small)	馅饼	syèn·bǐng
steamed dumpling with pork, prawn, water chestnut and bamboo shoot filling	烧卖	shāo·mài
sticky rice wrapped in bamboo leaves	粽字	zòong·zir
won ton soup	混沌	hún·dùn

key language

要点

cooked	熟	shó
cured	咸	syén
dried	干	gūn
fresh	鲜	syēn
frozen	冰冻	bīng·dòong
raw	生	shērng
smoked	熏	sēwn

buying food

平苹

What's the local speciality?
有什么地方
特产?
yǒ shér·mer dèe·fūng
tèr·chǔn

What's that?
那是什么?
nà shir shér·mer

Can I taste it?
能尝一下吗?
nérng chǔng·ee·syà ma

Can I have a bag, please?
我买一包吧。
wór mǎi ēe·bao ba

How much?
多少?
dōr·shǎo

How much is (half a kilo of apples)?
(一斤苹果)
多少钱?
(ēe·jīn píng·gwǒr)
dōr·shǎo chyén

I'd like ...	我要……	wǒr·yào ...
(50) grams	(50)克	(wǒo·shír) kèr
(two) jin	(两)斤	(lyǔng) jīn
half a kilo (= one jin)	一斤	ēe·jīn
a kilo	一公斤	ēe·gōong·jīn
(two) kilos	(两)公斤	(lyǔng) gōong·jīn
a bottle	一瓶	ēe·píng
a dozen	一打	ēe·dá
half a dozen	半打	bùn·dá
a jar	一罐	ēe·gwùn
a litre	一公升	ēe·gōong·shērng
a packet	一盒	ēe·hér
a piece	一块	ēe·kwài
(three) pieces	(三)块	(sūn) kwài
a slice	一份	ēe·fèrn
(six) slices	(六)份	(lyò) fèrn
a tin	一罐	ēe·gwùn
(just) a little	(少)一些	(shǎo·)ēe·dyěn
more	多	dōr
some ...	一些……	ēe·syāir ...
that one	那个	này·ger
this one	这个	jày·ger

listen for ...

hái·yào byáir·der ma
还要别的吗？

Would you like anything else?

née syǔng yào shér·mer
你想要什么？

What would you like?

syǔng dyén shér·mer ner
想点什么呢？

What can I get for you?

wǒr nérng būng něe ma
我能帮你吗？

Can I help you?

zǒong·gòong (wǒo kwài) chyén
总共(五块)钱。

That's (five kuai).

Less.	少一点。	shǎo ēe·dyěn
A bit more.	多一点。	dōr ēe·dyěn
Enough!	够了, 够了!	gò ler gò ler

Do you have ...?	你有……吗?	nee yǒ ... ma
anything cheaper	便宜	pyén·ee
	一点的	èe·dyěn der
other kinds	别的	byáir·de

Where can I find	哪里有	ná·lee yǒ mài ... der
the ... section?	卖……的?	
dairy	奶制品	nǎi·jìr·pǐn
frozen goods	冰冻	bīng·dòong
	食品	shír·pǐn
fruit and	菜	tsài
vegetable		
meat	肉	rò
poultry	鸡	jēe
seafood	海鲜	hǎi·syēn

cooking utensils

Could I please borrow a/an ...?	我能借一个 ……吗?	wǒr nérng jyàir ēe·ger ... ma
I need a/an ...	我想要 一个……	wór·syǔng yào ēe·ger ...
bottle opener	开瓶器	kāi·píng chèe
bowl	碗	wǔn
can opener	开罐器	kāi·gwùn chèe
chopping board	菜板	tsài·bǔn
chopsticks	筷子	kwài·zir
corkscrew	螺丝开瓶器	lwór·sīr kāi·píng chèe
cup	杯子	bāy·zir
fork	叉子	chā·zir
fridge	冰箱	bīng·syūng
frying pan	炸锅	jà·gwōr
glass	杯子	bāy·zir
knife	刀	dāo
meat cleaver	菜刀	tsài·dāo
microwave	微波炉	wāy·bōr lóo
plate	盘子	pún·zir
rice cooker	电饭锅	dyèn·fùn·gwōr
saucepan	小锅	syǎo·gwōr
spoon	茶勺	chá·sháo
steamer	蒸笼	jērng·lóong
stove	炉子	lóo·zir
toaster	烤面包机	kǎo·myèn·bāo jēe
wok	锅	gwōr

vegetarian & special meals
素食与特殊食品

ordering food

Do you have ...	有没有……	yǒ·máy·yo ...
food?	食品？	shír·pín
halal	清真	chīng·jērn
kosher	犹太	yó·tài
vegetarian	素食	sòo·shír

Is there a (vegetarian) restaurant near here?
这儿附近有没有 jèr fòo·jin yǒ·máy·yo
（素食）饭馆？ (sòo·shír) fùn·gwún

I don't eat (pork).
我不吃（猪肉）。 wǒr bòo·chīr (jōo·rò)

Is it cooked in/with (meat stock)?
是用（肉汤） shìr yèwng (rò·tūng)
做的吗？ zwòr·der ma

Could you prepare	能不能	nérng·bòo·nérng
a meal without ...?	做一个不放	zwòr·ee·ger bóo·fùng
	……的菜？	... der tsài
eggs	鸡蛋	jēe·dùn
fish	鱼酱	yěw·jyùng
fish stock	鱼汤	yěw·tūng
MSG	味精	wày·jīng
poultry	家禽	jyā·chín
red meat	牛羊肉	nyó·yúng·rò

Is this ...?	这个是……的吗？	jày·ger shìr ... der ma
free of animal produce	没有动物原料	máy·yǒ dòong·woo ywén·lyào
free-range	新鲜	sīn·syēn
genetically modified	转基因	jwǔn jēe·yīn
gluten-free	无筋面粉	wó·jìn myèn·fěrn
halal	清真	chīng·jērn
kosher	犹太	yó·tài
low sugar/fat	低糖/低脂肪	dēe·túng/ dēe jír·fúng
organic	有机	yǒ·jēe
salt-free	不加盐	bòo·jyā yén

special diets & allergies

特殊膳食与过敏症

I'm on a special diet.		
我在节食。		wǒr zài jyáir·shír

I'm allergic to ...	我对……过敏。	wǒr dwày ... gwòr·mín
butter	黄油	hwúng·yó
chilli	辣椒	là·jyāo
dairy produce	奶制品	nǎi·jìr·pín
eggs	鸡蛋	jēe·dùn
gelatine	明胶	míng·jyāo
gluten	面筋	myèn·jìn
honey	蜂蜜	fērng·mèe
MSG	味精	wày·jīng
nuts	果仁	gwǒr·rérn
peanuts	花生	hwā·shērng
seafood	海鲜	hái·syēn
shellfish	贝壳	bày·kér

To explain your dietary restrictions with reference to religious beliefs, see **beliefs & cultural differences**, page 139.

culinary reader
饭食词表

These Chinese dishes and ingredients are listed in alphabetical order according to their pronunciation to enable you to easily understand what's on offer and to ask for what takes your fancy when eating out in China.

The following abbreviations identify the cuisine to which individual dishes belong:

NC – Northern Cuisine   **SC** – Southern Cuisine
EC – Eastern Cuisine   **WC** – Western Cuisine

B

bā·bǎo fùn 八宝饭 'eight treasure rice' – sweet rice dish traditionally eaten at Chinese New Year containing colourful sugary fruits, nuts & seeds

bā·bǎo là jyùng 八寶辣醬 (EC) 'eight treasure hot sauce' – made from pressed tofu & chilli

bái hóo·jyāo 白胡椒 white pepper

bái·mǐee·fùn 白米饭 rice – the staple & imbued with an almost spiritual significance to the Chinese people

bái póo·tao jyǒ 白葡萄酒 white wine

bái·jwór·syā 白灼虾 (SC) fresh whole prawns poached then simmered & served with a peanut-oil & soy sauce dip

bái·jyàir mòr 白芥末 white mustard

bái·jyǒ 白酒 Chinese vodka-like spirit

bái·lǔn·dèe 白兰地 brandy

bái·mǐee 白米 plain rice

bái·tsài 大白菜 Chinese white cabbage

bai·tsoo 白醋 white rice vinegar

bā·jyāo 八角 star anise

bā·jyǎo fěrn 八角粉 weihison powder made from ground star anise

bào 爆 'exploded' – stir-fried in super-hot oil

bào·cháo myèn 爆炒面 (WC) 'hot-wok noodles' – pan-fried crispy egg noodles often served with meat & vegetables

bāo·yéw 鲍鱼 abalone

bāo·zir 包子 steamed dumpling

bāo·zir fùn 煲仔饭 'claypot rice' – braised rice cooked in a claypot with Chinese sausage, salted fish, vegetables & mushrooms

bā·sīr píng·gwǒr 拔丝蘋果 apple pieces dipped in batter then deep-fried & coated in toffee

bǎy·jīng káo·yā 北京烤鸭 (NC) Peking duck – slices of spice-imbued roast duck often served with pancakes, shallots & plum sauce

bīng·dòong 冰冻 frozen

bīng·gǔn 饼十 Western-style biscuit

bīng·jēe·lín 冰激淋 ice cream

bīng·kwàr 冰块 ice cubes

bó·hér 薄荷 mint

bòo·dīng 布丁 (SC) Western-style pudding

bōr·lór 菠萝 pineapple

bōr·tsài 菠菜 spinach

bùn·bun jēe 拌拌鸡 (WC) 'bang bang chicken' – cold dish featuring cooked shredded chicken, cucumber & cellophane (bean thread) noodles with a sesame paste, sesame oil, garlic, ginger & chilli sauce dressing

bùn·gzir 蚌子 clam • mussel

bùn·shěrng bùn·shō 半熟半生 medium

byēn·dò 扁豆 green bean

C

chá 茶 tea

chǎo 炒 stir-fried

chǎo shùng·tsòo 炒上素 **(SC)** vegetarian stir-fried dish of mushrooms, lotus root, ginkgo nuts & fresh vegetables

cháo·fěrn 炒粉 fried rice noodles

cháo·fùn 炒飯 fried rice

cháo·jō ēe·myèn 潮州伊面 **(SC)** thin egg noodles pan-fried until crunchy & served with chives, sugar & vinegar

cháo·jo lóo·shwǎy ér 潮州卤水鹅 **(SC)** goose stewed in a rich sauce & served with a garlic & vinegar dip

cháo·jō yéw·tūng 潮州鱼汤 **(SC)** soup made from sliced fish (usually pomfret), squid, celery, mushrooms & rice cooked in chicken stock & sprinkled with dried fish pieces

cháo·jò·tsài 潮州菜 Chaozhou cuisine

cháo·myèn 炒面 fried rice noodles

chá·shǎ 叉烧 **(SC)** barbecued sweet roast pork

chā·shā·bāo 叉烧包 **(SC)** steamed barbecued pork bun

chá·yàir dùn 茶叶蛋 'tea egg' – marbled hard-boiled egg flavoured with black tea & star anise

chèe·shwǎy 汽水 soft drink • soda

chěrng jīr 橙汁 orange juice

chérng·jyùng 橙酱 marmalade

chérng·zir 橙子 orange

chérn·pée 陈皮 **(SC)** mandarin or tangerine peel used as a flavouring

chérn·tsòo 陈醋 dark vinegar

chīng·jěrn 清真 halal

chīng·jěrng dà·já·syàir 清蒸大闸蟹 **(EC)** stir-fried crab with ginger & shallots

chīng·jyáo 青椒 capsicum • bell pepper

chīng·tsài 青菜 green leafy vegetables

chīng·tūng 清汤 light broth

chín·tsài 芹菜 celery

chò dò·foo 臭豆腐 **(EC)** 'stinky tofu' – tofu fermented in cabbage juice with a pungent result

chóong·chìng hwór·gwōr 重庆火锅 **(WC)** 'Chongqing hotpot' – cook-it-yourself meal requiring diners to dip various meats & vegetables into a pot of boiling spicy stock

chóong·rèr 重热 re-heated

chōon·jwǎr 春卷 **(NC)** 'spring roll' – deep-fried pancake stuffed with a mixture that can include vegetables, chicken, pork, prawns, mushrooms, sprouts & noodles

chōw jēe·dùn 番茄炒鸡蛋 stir-fried tomato & egg

chúng·fěrn 肠粉 **(SC)** steamed rice-noodle roll stuffed with shrimp pork or beef & served with soy sauce & sesame oil

chwén·jyá·bǎo 全家宝 **(EC)** 'family happiness seafood spectacular' – seafood braised with mushrooms & pig tendon

chwén·mài myèn·bāo 全麦面包 wholemeal bread

chwūn·tsài 川菜 Western (Sichuan) cuisine – renowned for its use of the red chilli and fiery peppercorns; pork, poultry, legumes & soybeans are the main staples

chyáir·zir 茄子 aubergine • eggplant

chyáo·kěr·lèe 巧克力 chocolate

chyáo·kěr·lèe fěrn 热巧克力 hot chocolate

chyèn·bíng 签饼 **(SC)** fortune cookies

D

dà tsōong 大蔥 oversized spring onions

dà·swùn 大蒜 garlic

dà·syā 大虾 prawn

dà·já·syàir 大闸蟹 **(SC)** 'hairy crab' – so called for the hair-like growths on their legs & underbellies, these crabs are a Shanghainese delicacy

dèe·gwā 地瓜 sweet potato

dīng 丁 cubed beef, chicken or pork

dīng·syūng 丁香 clove

dò·fěrn 豆粉 bean noodles

dò·fōo 豆腐 tofu (soybean curd)

dò·foo nǎo 豆腐脑 **(NC)** salty bean-curd soup

dò·foo pèe 豆腐皮 dried bean curd

dò·foo tūng 豆腐汤 **(WC)** casserole of bean curd with bamboo shoots, ham, scallions, Chinese cabbage, ginger & shrimps

dò·jyǎo 豆角 chopped green beans

dò·jyūng 豆浆 fresh soy milk

dò·myáo 豆苗 pea shoots

dò·nǎi fěrn 豆奶粉 powdered soy milk

doon 炖 stewed

dōong·gwā 冬瓜 winter melon – type of melon with thick white flesh used in soups & other dishes

dōong·tsài 冬菜 **(NC)** Tianjin pickled cabbage

dōr·shìr (kǎo myèn·bāo) 多士 (烤面包) toast

dò·shā bāo 豆沙包 sweet steamed red bean-paste bun

dò·yá 豆芽 beansprout

dò·zir 豆子 bean

dùn 蛋 egg

dùn·bái 蛋白 egg white

dùn·dā 蛋挞 **(SC)** baked puff pastry with an egg custard filling

dūn·dūn myèn 担担面 **(WC)** 'dan dan noodles' – thin wheat noodles served with pork, scallions & a red hot chilli oil, soy sauce, sesame paste, garlic, ginger & Sichuan roasted peppercorn sauce

dùn·gāo 蛋糕 cake

dùn·hwúng 蛋黄 egg yolk

dùn·myèn 蛋面 **(SC)** egg noodles – sold dried or fresh

dùn·tūng 蛋汤 **(SC)** 'egg drop soup' – soup based on chicken broth into which raw eggs are whisked & cooked

dyěn·sīn 点心 **(SC)** dim sum – an umbrella term for the vast array of steamed & fried dumplings & small delicacies served at a yǐn chá

E

èe·dà·lèe myèn 意大利面 'Italian noodles' – pasta

ēe·myèn 伊面 **(SC)** deep-fried egg noodles

ér 鹅 goose

èr·lée· 鳄梨 avocado

F

fày 肺 lung

fáy·chúng 肥肠 large intestines of the pig

fày chúng kěr·lèr 菲帝可乐 'extreme cola' – Chinese version of Coca-Cola

fáy·rò 肥肉 fatty meat

fěrn·sīr 粉丝 vermicelli

fóo·jōo 腐竹 dried yellow soymilk sticks

fōo róo 腐乳 fermented tofu cubes, dried, steamed then bottled with wine & possessing a curiously Camembert-like taste & texture

fóo·tèr·jyā 伏特加 vodka

fó·shǒ 佛手 Buddha's hand – fragrant citrus fruit also known as the fingered citron

fūn·chyáir jyùng 番茄酱 ketchup · tomato sauce

fūng·byèn myèn 方便面 instant noodles

fùng·wǔn 饭馆 restaurant

G

gāo·dyǎn wōo 糕点屋 cake shop

gēr·zir 鸽子 pigeon

gŏ·chée·zir 枸杞子 box thorn – similar in
texture & nutritional value to spinach

gōong·bào jēe·dīng 宫爆雞丁 (NC)
marinated chicken cubes stir-fried with
chillies & peanuts & seasoned with a
sweet bean sauce

gōong·foo chá 工夫茶 (SC) congou
tea – very strong short black tea

gǒo·swáy 骨髓 bone marrow

gǒu·ròu 狗肉 dog

gùn 肝 liver

gūn 干 dried

gūn·byén 干煸 'dry-fried' – fried with
a minimum of liquids which are then
boiled away to leave the food coated
in sauce

gūn·byén nyŏ·ròu 干煸牛肉 (WC)
shredded beef, deep-fried then tossed
with chillies

gūn·byén sìr·jèe dò (WC) 干煸四季豆
deep-fried snake beans stir-fried with
garlic, ginger & shrimps & served with
soy sauce, wine, vinegar & sesame oil

gūn·jér 甘蔗 sugar cane

gún·lūn yó 橄榄油 olive oil

gwā 瓜 melon • vegetable marrow

gwày·pēe 桂皮 cinnamon bark

gwā·zir 瓜子 sunflower seeds •
pumpkin seeds

gwŏr·gūn 果干 dried fruit

gwŏr·jìr 果汁 juice

gwŏr·jyùng 果酱 jam

gwŏr·rérn 果仁 nuts

gwŏr·tyàr 锅贴 fried dumpling

H

hái·dài 海带 kelp

hǎi·jér 海蜇 jellyfish – sold in sheets &
packed in salt & served shredded

hǎi·shērn 海参 sea cucumber

hǎi·syēn 海鲜 seafood

hǎo·yó 蠔油 (SC) oyster sauce

hǎo·yó jyāir·lún 耗油芥兰 (SC)
dish of jyāir·lún (also known as gai lan,
Chinese broccoli or Chinese kale) with
oyster sauce

háo·zir 蚝子 oyster

hér·fěrn 河粉 thin round or flat
slippery rice noodles

hér·fùn 盒饭 rice & vegetable
takeaway box

hér·lŭn dò 荷兰豆 snow pea

hér·tao 核桃 walnut

hŏo·jyāo fērn 胡椒粉 pepper
(condiment)

hóo·lwór·bor 胡萝卜 carrot

hóon·dòon tún 混沌摊 won ton stall

hóong póo·tao jyŏ 红葡萄酒 red wine

hóong·chá 红茶 black tea

hóong·dò 红豆 red mung bean

hóong·shāo 红烧 (WC)
'red stew' – braised in a sweet star
anise sauce

hóong·shāo pái·góo 红烧排骨 (WC)
red-fried pork spareribs

hóong·shāo ròu 红烧肉 (WC) red-fried
pork

hóong·tsòo 红醋 red rice vinegar

hùn·bāo·bao 漢堡包 hamburger

hún·dùn hóon·dòon tún 混沌 won ton soup –
dumplings stuffed with pork & shrimp
served in chicken broth

hwā·chá 花茶 jasmine tea

hwái·yúng tsài 淮扬菜
East Coast cuisine – relatively vegetar-
ian-friendly cuisine that makes use of
a wide variety of condiments & fresh
ingredients; also home of the red stew
(meat simmered in dark soy sauce,
sugar & spices)

hwā·shērng 花生 peanut

hwā·shērng yó 花生油 peanut oil

hwā·shērng·jyùng 花生醬
peanut butter

hwáy·gwōr ròu 回锅肉 **(NC)** *sweet &
sour pork*

hwōr twǎy 火腿 *ham*

hwǒr·jēe 火鸡 *turkey*

hwǒr·twǎy 火腿 *reconstituted pig
by-product sausage*

hwúng·dòu 黄豆 *soy bean*

hwúng gwā 黄瓜 *cucumber*

hwúng·jyǒ 黄酒 *'yellow wine' –
rice wine similar in taste to sherry & best
served warm*

hwúng·jyìng 黄酱 *dipping sauce*

hwúng·jyùng 黄酱 **(NC)** *blackbean
dipping sauce*

hwúng·shùn 黄鳝 *paddy eel*

hwúng·yǒ 黄油 *butter*

J

jà ūn·chún 炸鹌鹑 *fried quail*

jēe·chìr 鸡翅 *chicken wing*

jēe dùn 鸡蛋 *chicken egg*

jēe·jwǎ (fèrng·jyǎo) 凤爪（鸡脚）
'phoenix claws' – chicken feet

jēe·ròu 鸡肉 *chicken*

jēe·tūng 鸡汤 *chicken stock*

jēe·twǎy 鸡腿 *drumstick*

jēe·wáy jyǒ 鸡尾酒 *cocktail*

jērng 蒸 *steamed*

jērn·zir 榛子 *hazelnut*

jèr·tsài 浙菜 *Eastern (Shanghai)
cuisine – the cuisine of this region is
generally richer, sweeter and more oily
than other Chinese cuisines & preserved
vegetables & pickles & salted meats are
common ingredients.*

jéw·hwā 菊花 *chrysanthemum –
flowering plant with a taste similar to
lettuce used as an accompaniment
to dishes*

jéw·hwā·chá 菊花茶
chrysanthemum tea

jěw·zir 橘子 *mandarin*

jīn·jèrn·gōo 金针菇 *golden needle
mushroom (also known as enoki mushroom in English)*

jīn·sīr·myèn 金丝面 *fried Beijing egg
noodles – similar to Japanese udon
noodles* **(NC)**

jī·ma jyùng 芝麻酱 *sesame paste*

jō 粥 *porridge*

jǒo 煮 *boiled*

jǒo·jēe 煮鸡 *hard-boiled*

jōo ròu 猪肉 *pork*

jōo·yó 猪油 *pork lard*

jò·zir 肘子 *hock (fatty pork elbow)*

jyāir·lún 芥兰 *gai lan (also known in
English as Chinese broccoli or
Chinese kale)*

jyāir·tó syǎo·chīr 街头小吃
street food vendor

jyào·bái 茭白 **(EC)** *wild rice root*

jyào·hwa 叫化鸡 **(EC)** *'beggar's
chicken' – whole, deboned chicken
stuffed with pork, vegetables, mushrooms ginger & other seasonings
wrapped in lotus leaves & wet clay or
pastry & baked for several hours*

jyǎo·zir 饺子 *boiled dumpling*

jyǎ·yéw 甲鱼 *tortoise*

jyēn 煎 *braised*

jyēn·bing 薄饼 *egg & spring onion
pancake*

jyǒ·bā 酒吧 *bar*

jyǒ·lày 酒类 *alcoholic drinks*

jyǒ·tsài 韭菜 *chinese chives*

jyūng 姜 *ginger*

jyùng·jyó pái·góo 酱炙排骨 **(EC)**
*barbecued pork ribs – a speciality of the
city of Wuxi*

jyūng·yǒ 酱油 *soy sauce*

K

kā·fāy 咖啡 *coffee*

kā·fāy·wōo 咖啡屋 *café*

kāi·shwáy 开水 *boiling water*

kāi·sìn·gwǒr 开心果 *pistachio*

kǎo 烤 *roasted*

kǎo yúng·rò chwàr 烤羊肉串 **(WC)**
char-grilled lamb kebab – a Uyghur speciality

kǒo·gwā 苦瓜 *bitter melon – resembles a knobbly cucumber & has a strong bitter taste*

kwùng·chwēn·shwáy 矿泉水 *mineral water*

L

là 辣 *hot chilli*

là·jyāo 辣椒 *chilli pepper*

làj·yáo jyùng 辣椒酱 *chilli sauce*

là·zir jēe·dīng 辣子鸡丁 **(WC)**
tender braised chilli chicken

lēe 梨 *pear*

lèe·jir jîr 荔枝汁 *lychee-flavoured soft drink*

lěe·yóo 鲤鱼 *carp*

lèe·zir 栗子 *chestnut*

lèw·chá 绿茶 *green tea*

lèw·dòu 绿豆 *green mung bean*

lēw·rò 驴肉 *donkey*

lóong·syā 龙虾 *rock lobster*

lōo·tsài 鲁菜 *Northern (Shandong) cuisine – typical ingredients are wheat pancakes, spring onions & fermented bean paste*

lór·bor 萝卜 *radish*

lún·jō myèn 兰州面 **(WC)** *Lanzhou beef noodles*

lwór·bor gāo 萝卜糕 **(SC)** *fried radish cake containing grated turnip, Chinese sausage, dried shrimp, mushrooms, spring onion & seasonings*

lwór·hùn jāi 罗汉斋 **(SC)**
vegetarian stew (with many variations) which classically includes woodear fungus & lily bud stems

lyó·lyén 榴莲 *durian – spiky fruit prized by the Chinese as the 'king of fruits' & posessing a repellant smelly-sock aroma & a dense creamy flesh* **(SC)**

lyǔng kāi·shwáy 凉开水
chilled boiled water

lyúng·fěrn 凉粉
cold bean-flour noodles

lyúng·tsài 凉菜 *appetiser*

M

má·ée shùng·shòo 蚂蚁上树 **(NC)**
'ants climbing a tree' – cellophane noodles braised with minced pork seasoned with soy sauce & served sprinkled with chopped spring onions

má·hwā 麻花 **(NC)** *Tianjin Muslim-style bread twist*

má·là tūng 麻辣烫 **(WC)** *'numblingly hot soup' – the standard cooking broth that goes with* chóong·chìng hwór·gwōr *with liberal doses of mouth-scorching Sichuan pepper & chilli oil*

máo·dò 毛豆 *fresh soy beans*

máo·tái jyō 茅台酒 *Chinese-style vodka made from millet*

má·pōr dò·foo 麻婆豆腐 *'Ma Po bean curd' – fresh bean curd marinated in spices then deep-fried in chili oil & garnished with shredded pork & fiery peppercorns* **(NC)**

máy·tsài kò·rò 梅菜扣肉 *double-cooked steamed pork with pickled salted cabbage*

máy·zir 梅子 *plum*

mée·fěrn 米粉 *rice noodles*

mèe·fērng 蜂蜜 *honey*

mīn·tsài 闽菜 *Hokkien cuisine*

mó·gōo 蘑菇 *mushroom*

mòo·gwā 木瓜 *papaya • pawpaw*

mòr·lee hwā·chá 茉莉花茶 *jasmine tea*

múng·gwǒr 芒果 *mango*

mún·tó 馒头 *steamed bun*

mùn·yéw 鳗鱼 *river eel*

mòo·sēw·rò 木须肉 **(NC)** *stir-fried pork with woodear fungus*

myèn·bāo 面包 *bread*

myèn·fěrn 面粉 *flour*

myèn·jīn chyó 面筋球 *meaty-textured gluten ball made from dough that is washed so only gluten remains – used in vegetarian dishes*

myèn·tūn 面摊 *noodle house*

myèn·tyǒw 面条 *noodles*

N

nǎi·jìrpīn 奶制品 *dairy*

nǎi·lào 奶酪 *cheese*

née·hǒ·táo 猕猴桃 *kiwifruit*

níng·měrng 柠檬 *lemon*

níng·měrng jēe 柠檬鸡 **(SC)** *lemon chicken*

nòr·měe 糯米 *glutinous rice (also known as sticky rice or sweet rice)*

nún·gwā 南瓜 *pumpkin*

nyén·gāo 黏糕 *rice cake*

nyén·gāo 年糕 *Chinese New Year sweets*

nyó·rò 牛肉 *beef*

nyó·rò tūng 牛肉汤 *beef stock*

O

ǒ·pyèn 莲藕 *lotus root – the tuber stem of the water lily which can be stuffed with rice & steamed, stir-fried, or used in soups & stews*

ǒ·shìr zǎo·tsūn 欧式早餐 *continental breakfast*

P

pái·góo 排骨 *spare ribs*

páy·gērn 培根 *bacon*

pěe·dùn shò·rò jō 皮蛋瘦肉粥 **(SC)** *preserved duck egg & pork congee*

pée·jyǒ 啤酒 *beer*

píng·gwǒr 苹果 *apple*

pòo·ér chá 普洱茶 *Pu-erh tea – aged black jasmine tea purported to have medicinal qualities & possesing a distinctive aroma & taste*

póo·tao 葡萄 *grapes*

póo·tào jyǒ 葡萄酒 *wine*

póo·tào·gūn 葡萄干 *raisins*

pyèn 片 *slice*

R

rém·shērn 人参 *ginseng – prized as a tonic & aphrodisiac*

rò 肉 *meat (pork unless otherwise stated)*

rò·bǐng 肉饼 *large pork pie*

rò·dyèn 肉店 *butcher's shop*

rò·jya·mór 肉夹馍 **(NC)** *finely chopped braised pork & coriander stuffed into a pocket of flat bread*

rò·làry 大菜 *main course*

rò·pái 肉排 *steak (beef)*

rò·syèn 肉馅 *mince*

S

sēe hóo·loo 西葫芦 *courgette • zucchini*

sēe yó·zir 西柚子 *grapefruit*

sēe·dōr 西多 **(SC)** *Cantonese French toast – French toast with peanut butter sandwiched between two slices of white bread before cooking*

sēe·gwār 西瓜 *watermelon*

sēe·hóong·shìr 西红柿 *tomato*

sēe·lūn·hwā 西兰花 *broccoli*

see·ūn hóo·loo jēe 西安葫芦鸡 *Xi'an casseroled griddled chicken* **(NC)**

sēwn 熏 *smoked*

shā·dyāir 沙嗲 *satay – originally a South East Asian dish but now a popular dim sum item*

shā·gwōr 砂锅豆腐 **(EC)** *beancurd in a claypot with dried bamboo & vermicelli*

shà·lā 沙拉 *salad*

shāo 烧 *spit-roasted meat with a sweet sauce*

shāo·bǐng 烧饼 *flat bread topped with sesame seeds*

shāo·kǎo 烧烤 *barbecued*

shāo·mài 烧買 *won ton wrappers filled with pork, prawns, water chestnuts & bamboo shoots then steamed*

shā·tūng 砂糖 *sugar*

shērng 生 *raw*

bùn shērng 半生 *rare*

shērng·tsài 生菜 *lettuce*

shér·rò 蛇肉 *snake*

shìr·zir 柿子 *persimmon*

shǒ 熟 *cooked • well-done*

shòo·tsài 蔬菜 *vegetable dishes – not usually vegetarian but featuring a specific vegetable*

shò·rò 瘦肉 *lean meat*

shūn·máy 山梅 *raspberry*

shwā yúng·rò 涮羊肉 **(NC)** *'Mongolian lamb hotpot' – sliced meat is dipped into a flame-heated hotpot of hot broth brought to the table & cabbage & noodles are later added to make a soup*

shwáy·gwōr 水果 *fruit*

shwáy·jīng sēe·rò 水晶肴肉 **(EC)** *pig's trotter jelly*

shwáy·jò jǒo·zá 水煮猪杂 **(WC)** *stewed pig intestines in a fiery blend of chilli powder, chilli paste & fresh mountain chillies*

sìng·rérn 杏仁 *almond*

sìng·táo 杏桃 *apricot*

sìr·chwārn jēe 四川鸡 **(WC)** *Sichuan chicken*

sìr·jèe pái·góo 四季排骨 **(SC)** *braised spare ribs*

sòng·rérn 松仁 *pine nut*

sǒon 筍 *bamboo shoot*

sōo·tsài 苏菜 *Jiangsu cuisine*

sūn·míng·jìr 三明治 *sandwich*

sūn·wérn yěw 三文鱼 *salmon*

swāir dò·foo 血豆腐 *bean curd soaked in pig's blood – often made into a soup*

swūn 酸 *sour*

swūn·là 酸辣 *'sour & hot' – usually a soupy style of cooking with plenty of Chinese vinegar & chilli oil*

swūn·là tūng 酸辣汤 *'hot & sour soup' – warming Sichuanese winter soup that traditionally included solidified chicken blood & is made with pepper, chillies & vinegar*

swūn·máy 酸梅 *dried sour plum*

swūn·mǎy·tūng 酸梅汤 *sour plum drink*

swūn·myáo 蒜苗 *garlic chives*

swūn·nái 酸奶 *fresh drinking yogurt*

swūn·née 蒜泥 *'garlic-fried' – cooked with a liberal dose of crushed garlic & oil*

syā·jyǎo 蝦餃 **(SC)** *bonnet-shaped prawn dumpling with translucent dough*

syā·mēe 虾米 *dried shrimp*

syāo bái·tsài 小白菜 *bok choy (cabbage-like vegetable)*

syāo tsōong 小葱 *shallot • spring onion*

syāo·chīr 小吃 *snack*

syāo·mēe 小米 *millet – the Chinese staple until it was supplanted by rice during the Han dynasty*

syáo·mōo 酵母 *yeast*

syàr bǐng 馅饼 **(NC)** *Beijing-style meat pie*

syà·rérn gwōr·ba 虾仁锅巴 **(EC)** *crisped rice with shrimp*

syā·zir 虾子 *prawn • shrimp*

syén 咸 *cured • salty • savoury*

syēn 鲜 *fresh*

syèn·bĭng 馅饼 *small pork pie*

syén·bĭng·gūn 咸餅乾 *cracker*

syén·tsài 咸菜 *pickled vegetables*

syèn·tsài 咸菜 *pickles*

syén·yā 咸鸭 *pickled duck*

syēn·yéw 咸鱼 *sardine*

syăo·mài·bòo 小卖部 *convenience store*

syũng·chāng 香肠 *pork sausage*

syūng·bĭn 香槟 *champagne*

syūng·jyāo 香蕉 *banana*

syūng·lyào 香料 *culinary herbs • spices*

syūng·māo ròu 熊猫肉 *panda – unfortunately this endangered animal sometimes appears as a menu item*

syūng·tsài 湘菜 *Hunan cuisine*

syūng·tsăo 香草 *vanilla*

T

tăo·zir 桃子 *peach*

tŏo·dòu 土豆 *potato*

tŏo·ná yéw 土拿鱼 *tuna*

tòo·zir 兔肉 *rabbit*

tsài·dūn 菜单 *menu*

tsài·hwā 菜花 *cauliflower*

tsài shìr 菜市 *fresh food market*

tsài·sīn 菜心 *Chinese flowering cabbage – sometimes known as 'choi sum' or 'choy sum' in English*

tsài·tūn 菜摊 *greengrocer*

tsài·yó 菜油 *vegetable oil*

tsăo·máy 草莓 *strawberry*

tsòo 醋 *vinegar*

tsōng·bào yúng·ròu 葱爆羊肉 **(NC)** *hot-wok lamb with shallots*

tsōong·yó·bĭng 蔥油餅 **(NC)** 'onion cakes' – fried pastries filled with spring onion

tsũng·wún 餐館 *restaurant*

tswày 脆 *crisp*

tswày·pēe 脆皮 *pork crackling*

túng hér·tao 糖核桃 *candied walnut*

tũng·chao lee·zir 糖炒栗子 *hot roasted chestnut – the ideal winter hand warmer*

túng·gwŏr 糖果 *lollies • candy*

túng·hóo·loo 糖葫芦 **(NC)** *toffeed crabapple stick*

tũng·làu 汤类 *soup*

tùng·tsòo 糖醋 *'sweet & sour' – piquant sauce composed of sugar & vinegar used to flavour meat or for dipping*

túng·tsòo lěe·yéw 糖醋鲤鱼 **(EC)** *sweet & sour fish*

túng·tsòo pái·goo 糖醋排骨 **(EC)** *sweet & sour pork ribs*

tyáir·bún kăo 铁板烤 *grilled on a hotplate*

tyén·bĭng 甜饼 *sweet biscuit • cookie*

tyăo·wày·pĭn 调味品 *flavour enhancer*

tyén 甜 *sweet*

tyén·jēe 田鸡 *'field chicken', ie, frog*

tyén·pĭn 甜品 *dessert*

tyén·tsài 甜菜 *beetroot*

W

wūn·tsài 皖菜 *Anhui cuisine*

wày·dào 味道 *flavour • taste*

wày·jīng 味精 *MSG*

wày·shìr·jēe 威士忌 *whisky*

wŏo·fùn 午饭 *lunch*

wóo·hwār gwŏr 无花果 *fig*

wōo·lóong·chá 乌龙茶 *oolong tea – delicious dark tea that is partially fermented before drying*

wŏr·tó 小窝头 **(NC)** *steamed yellow corn bun – rather dry & unappetising*

wŭn·dòu 豌豆 *pea*

wún·fùn 晚饭 *dinner*

Y

yā 鸭 duck

yā·bǐng 鸭饼 (SC) salted boned & pressed duck immersed in peanut oil then steamed

yàir·syāo 夜宵 practice of eating snacks in the late evening – popular items include eggs, beancurd & vegetables cooked in boiling stock & presented on a stick

yàir·syāo dyèn 夜宵店 snack shop

yéng·zir 椰子 coconut

yéng·rò jwā·fùn 羊肉抓饭 (WC) pilaf – cumin-flavoured rice cooked with carrot & lamb; an Uyghur speciality

yāo·gwŏr 腰果 cashew nut

yāo·zir 腰子 kidney

yén 盐 salt

yén·jèe 盐鸡 (SC) 'salt-baked chicken' – chicken stuffed with ginger, garlic & green onions & baked with rock salt

yèn·mài pyèn 燕麦片 oats

yéw 鱼 fish

yéw·gūn 鱼干 dried fish

yèw·mée bùng 玉米棒 corn cob

yéw·syūng 鱼香 'fragrant fish' – fish braised with either fish sauce or small dried fish

yéw·syūng chyáir·zir 鱼香茄子 (NC) shredded eggplant in a fish-flavoured sauce of vinegar, wine, garlic, ginger, pepper, spring onions & bean paste

yéw·to 芋头 (EC) yam

yéw·tūn 鱼摊 fish shop

yǐn·chá 饮茶 yum cha – a meal of snack-like portions taken from mid-morning to late afternoon

yīng·táo 樱桃 cherry

yín·lyào 饮料 cold drink

yó·chǎo myèn 油炒面 (NC) oily fried noodles

yó·jā 油炸 deep-fried

yèw·mēe 玉米 corn

yó·tsài 油菜 mustard greens – term covers a diverse range of greens which are often used in salads when young or pickled

yó·tyáo 油条 fried dough stick – a popular breakfast item

yó·yéw 鱿鱼 calamari • squid

yó·zir 柚子 grapefruit • pomelo

yúng·jō chǎo·fùn 扬州炒饭 (EC) Yangzhou fried rice – there are many variations of this dish but it may include shrimp & pieces of chicken or pork

yúng·jō shir·zir tó 扬州狮子头 (EC) 'lion's head meatballs' – oversized pork meatballs cooked with bok choy in a clay pot

yúng·jō zwày·syā 扬州醉虾 (EC) 'Yangzhou drunken prawns' – live prawns marinated in clear liquor & sometimes eaten while still alive

yúng·rò 羊肉 lamb

yúng·tsōong 洋葱 onion

ywàir·tsài 粤菜 Southern (Cantonese) cuisine – this style has the most varied range of ingredients & the most elaborate methods of preparation of any Chinese cuisine

ywèrn·lyào 原料 ingredient

Z

záo 枣 date

zǎo·fùn 早饭 breakfast

zìr·jòo·tsūn 自助餐 buffet

zìr·lái shwǎy 自来水 tap water

zír·tsài 紫菜 thin seaweed

zòong·zir 粽子 sticky rice wrapped in bamboo leaves

emergencies

紧急时刻

Fire!	走火啦！	zó·hwŏr la
Go away!	走开！	zŏ·kāi
Help!	救命！	jyò·mìng
Stop!	站住！	jùn·joo
Thief!	小偷！	syăo·tō
Watch out!	小心！	syăo·sīn

signs

急诊科	jée·jĕrn kēr	Emergency Department
医院	ēe·ywèn	Hospital
警察	jĭng·chá	Police
派出所	pài·chōo·swŏr	Police Station

It's an emergency.
有急事。 yŏ Jée·shìr

Call a doctor!
请叫医生
过来！ chĭng jyào ēe·shērng
gwòr·lái

Call an ambulance!
请叫一个
急救车！ chĭng jyào ēe·ger
jée·jyò chēr

I'm ill.
我生病了。 wŏr shērng·bìng ler

My friend/child is ill.
我的朋友/孩子
生病了。 wŏr·der pérng·yŏ/hái·zir
shērng·bìng ler

He/She is having a/an ...	他/她有……	tā yǒ ...
allergic reaction	过敏症	gwòr·mǐn·jèrng
asthma attack	哮喘发病	syào·chwǔn fā·bìng
baby	婴儿	yīng·ár
epileptic fit	癫痫病	dyēn·syén·bìng
	发作	fā·zwòr
heart attack	心脏病	sīn·zùng·bìng
	发作	fā·zwòr

I'm lost.
我迷路了。 wǒr mée lòr ler

Could you please help?
你能帮我吗？ něe nérng būng·wǒr ma

Can I use your phone?
我能借用 wǒr nérng jyàir·yòong
你的电话吗？ něe·der dyèn·hwà ma

Where are the toilets?
厕所在哪？ tsèr·swǒr zài nár

police

警察

In China, it's the Public Security Bureau or PSB (gōong·ūn·jǒo 公安局) that's responsible for introducing and enforcing regulations concerning foreigners. Turn to them for mediation in disputes with hotels, restaurants or taxi drivers.

Where's the police station?
哪里有派出所？ ná·lee yǒ pài·chōo·swǒr

Please telephone the PSB.
请叫公安局。 chǐng jyào gōong·ūn·jǒo

I want to report an offence.
我要报案。 wǒr yào bào·ùn

It was him/her.
是他/她做的。 shìr tā zwòr·der

I've been ...	我被······了。	wǒr bày ... ler
He/She has been ...	他/她被······了。	tā bày ... ler
assaulted	侵犯	chīn·fùn
raped	强奸	chyúng·jyèn
robbed	抢劫	chyǔng·jyáir
My ... was/were stolen.	我的······被偷了。	wǒr·der ... bày·tō ler
I've lost my ...	我的······给丢了。	wǒr·der ... gǎy·dyo ler
backpack	背包	bày·bāo
bags	行李	síng·lee
credit card	信用卡	sìn·yòong kǎ
handbag	手包	shǒ·bāo
jewellery	首饰	shǒ·shìr
money	钱	chyén
papers	文件	wérn·jyèn
passport	护照	hòo·jào
travellers cheques	旅行支票	lěw·síng jīr·pyào
wallet	钱包	chyén·bāo

What am I accused of?
我被指犯了
什么罪？
wǒr bày·jér fùn·ler
shér·mer zwày

I'm sorry.
我道歉。
wǒr dào·chyèn

I didn't realise I was doing anything wrong.
我没知道犯了
错误。
wǒr máy·jìr·dào fùn·ler
tswòr·woo

I didn't do it.
不是我做的。
bóo·shìr wǒr zwòr·der

Can I pay an on-the-spot fine?
我能交罚款吗？
wǒr nérng jyāo fá·kwǔn ma

I want to contact my embassy/consulate.
我要联系我的
大使馆/领事馆。
wǒr yào lyén·see wǒr·der
dà·shír·gwǔn/lǐng·shìr·gwǔn

Can I make a phone call?
我能打一个
电话吗？
wǒr nérng dǎ·ee·ger
dyèn·hwà ma

Can I have a lawyer who speaks English?

我想跟一个
英会说文的
律师联系。

wór·syüng gēn ēe·ger
hwày·shwōr yīng·wérn·der
lèw·shīr lyén·see

This drug is for personal use.

这个药品是
私用的。

jày·ger yào·pǐn shir
sīr·yòong·der

I have a prescription for this drug.

这个药我有处方。

jày·ger yào wór yǒ chòo·fūng

I (don't) understand.

我（不）明白。

wór (bòo) míng·bái

the police may say ...		
You're	你被指	něe bày·jér
charged with...	犯了……	fùn·ler ...
He/She is	他/她被	tā bày·jér
charged with ...	指犯了……	fùn·ler ...
assault	人身侵犯	rérn·shērn chīn·fùn
disturbing	破坏	pòr·hwài
the peace	秩序	jìr·sèw
possession	随带	swáy·dài
of illegal	禁物	jīn·wòo
substances		
not having	非法过境	fāy·fǎ
a visa	过期	gwòr·jìng
overstaying	签证	chyēn·jèrng
your visa	过期	gwòr·chēe
shoplifting	偷物	tō·wòo
theft	盗窃	dào·chyāir

SAFE TRAVEL

doctor

医生

Where's the nearest ...?	最近的……在哪？	zwày·jìn·der ... zài nǎr
(night) chemist	(昼夜)药房	(jō·yàir) yào·fǔng
dentist	牙科	yá·kēr
doctor	医生	ēe·shērng
emergency department	急诊科	jée·jěrn kēr
hospital	医院	ēe·ywèn
medical centre	医疗中心	ēe·lyáo jōong·sīn
optometrist	眼科	yén·kēr

I need a doctor (who speaks English).
我要看(会说
英文的)医生。
wǒr yào kùn (hwày·shwōr
yīng·wérn·der) ēe·shērng

Could I see a female doctor?
最好要看一位
女医生?
zwày·hǎo yào·kùn ēe·wày
něw·ēe·shērng

Could the doctor come here?
医生能到我
这儿来吗？
ēe·shērng nérng dào wǒr
jèr lái ma

Is there an after-hours emergency number?
有晚上急诊
电话吗？
yó wǔn·shùng jée·jěrn
dyèn·hwà ma

I've run out of my medication.
我用完了我的
处方药。

wŏr yòong·wŭn·ler wŏr·der
chòo·fūng·yào

This is my usual medicine.
我平时服这个药。

wŏr píng·shír fòo jày·ger yào

My child weighs (20 kilos).
孩子有（二十公斤）。

hái·zir yŏ (àr·shír gōong·jīn)

What's the correct dosage?
剂量是什么？

jèe·lyùng shir shér·mer

I don't want a blood transfusion.
我不药输血。

wŏr boo·yào shō·shyăir

Please use a new syringe.
请用一个新
针头。

chĭng yòong·ee·ger sīn
jĕrn·tó

I have my own syringe.
我自己带了针头。

wŏr zir·jĕe dài·ler jĕrn·tó

I've been vaccinated against …	我打过…… 的免疫针。	wór dă·gwòr … der myĕn·èe jĕrn
He/She has been vaccinated against …	他/她打过…… 的免疫针。	tā dă·gwòr … der myĕn·èe jĕrn
hepatitis A/B/C	甲/乙/丙 肝炎	jyă/ée/bĭng gūn·yén
rabies	狂犬病	kwúng·chwĕn·bìng
tetanus	破伤风	pòr·shùng·fērng
typhoid	伤寒	shùng·hŭn
I need new …	我要买新的……	wŏr yào·măi sīn·der …
contact lenses	隐形眼镜	yĭn·síng yĕn·jìng
glasses	眼镜	yĕn·jìng

the doctor may say ...

Do you ...?	你会……吗？	něe hwày ... ma
drink	喝酒	her·jyǒ
smoke	抽烟	chō·yēn
take drugs	吃毒品	chīr·dóo·pǐn

Are you ...?	你有……吗？	née yǒ ... ma
allergic to anything	过敏症	gwòr·mǐn·jèrng
on medication	处方药	chòo·fūng·yào

What's the problem?
有什么问题？ yǒ shér·mer wèrn·těe

Where does it hurt?
哪疼呢？ nár·térng ner

Do you have a temperature?
发烧吗？ fā·shāo ma

How long have you been like this?
这个情况持续了 jày·ger chǐng·kwùng chír·sèw·ler
多久？ dōr·jyǒ

Have you had this before?
以前有过这样的吗？ ěe·chyén yǒ·gwòr jày·yung·der ma

Are you sexually active?
你有性生活吗？ née yǒ sìng·shērng·hwór ma

Have you had unprotected sex?
你有过非安全 née yǒ·gwòr fāy·ūn·chwén
性交吗？ sìng·jyāo ma

How long are you travelling for?
你准备旅·行多久？ née jǒon·bày lěw síng dōr·jyǒ

You need to be admitted to hospital.
你需要住医院。 něe sēw·yào jòo ēe·ywèn

You should have it checked when you go home.
回国时要做检查。 hwáy·gwór shír yào·zwòr jyěn·chá

You should return home for treatment.
最好要回国养病。 zwày·hǎo yào hwáy·gwór yǔng·bìng

My prescription is …
我眼睛是……度。 wór yěn·jīng shìr … dòo

How much will it cost?
总共会要
多少钱? zóong·gòong hwày·yào
dōr·shǎo chyén

Can I have a receipt for my insurance?
我买的保险能
发票吗? wór mǎi·der báo·syěn nérng
fā·pyào ma

symptoms & conditions

病症与病态

I'm sick.
我病了。 wǒr bìng ler

My friend/child is sick.
我的朋友 / 孩子
病了。 wǒr·der pérng·yǒ/hái·zir
bìng ler

It hurts here.
这里痛。 jèr·lee tòong

I'm dehydrated.
我脱水了。 wǒr twōr·shwǎy ler

I feel ...	我感到……了。	wór gǔn·dào ... ler
anxious	忧虑	yō·lèw
better	好一些	hǎo ee·syāir
depressed	郁闷	yèw·mern
dizzy	头晕	tó·hōon
hot and cold	一会儿冷，	ēe·hwàr lěrng
	一会儿热	ēe·hwàr rèr
nauseous	反胃	fǔn·wày
shivery	全身发斗	chwén·shērn fā·dǒ
strange	奇怪	chée·gwày
weak	没有力气	máy·yǒ lèe·chee
worse	更不好	gērng bòo·hǎo

I've been ...	我……了。	wǒr ... ler
He/She has been ...	他/她……了。	tā ... ler
injured	受伤	shò·shūng
vomiting	常呕吐	chúng ǒ·tòo

I can't sleep.
我失眠了。　　　　　　　　wǒr shīr·myén ler

I think it's the medication I'm on.
好像跟我的　　　　　　　　hǎo·syùng gērn wǒr·der
处方药有关系。　　　　　　chòo·fūng·yào yǒ gwūn see

I'm on medication for ...
我有……的　　　　　　　　wór yǒ ... der
处方药。　　　　　　　　　chòo·fūng·yào

He/She is on medication for ...
他/她有……的处方药。　　tā yō ... der chòo·fūng·yào

I have (a/an) ...
我有……　　　　　　　　　wór yǒ ...

He/She has (a/an) ...
他/她有……　　　　　　　tā yǒ ...

I've recently had (a/an) ...
我最近有……　　　　　　　wǒr zwày·jìn yǒ ...

He/She has recently had (a/an) ...
他/她最近有……　　　　　　tā zwày·jìn yǒ ...

asthma	哮喘	syào·chǒown
cholera	霍亂	hwòr·lwùn
common cold	伤风	shùng·fēng
constipation	便秘	byēn·mèe
cough	咳嗽	kér·sò
diabetes	糖尿病	tǔng·nyào·bìng
diarrhoea	拉稀	lā·sēe
dysentry	赤痢	chìr·lèe
epilepsy	癫痫	dyèn·bèe
fever	发烧	fā·shāo
flu	感冒	gǔn·mào
giardiasis	鞭毛虫病	byèn·máo·chóng·bìng
malaria	疟疾	nwàir·jèe
nausea	反胃	fǔn·wày
pain	疼痛	térng·tòong
SARS	萨斯病	sà·sīr bìng
sore throat	喉咙疼	hǒ·lóong·térng

women's health

妇女卫生

(I think) I'm pregnant.
（我好像）　　　　(wór hǎo·syùng)
怀孕了。　　　　　hwáy·yèwn ler

I'm on the Pill.
我用避孕药。　　　wór yòong bèe·yèwn yào

I haven't had my period for (six) weeks.
我（六）个星期没　wǒr (lyò)·ger sīng·chēe máy
来过月经。　　　　lái·gwòr ywàir·jìng

I've noticed a lump here.
我发现长了一个　　wǒr fā·syèn jǔng·ler ee·ger
疙瘩。　　　　　　gēr·der

I need ...	我要买……	wǒr yào·mǎi ...
contraception	避孕品	bèe·yèwn pǐn
the morning-after pill	事后避孕药	shìr·hò bèe·yèwn yào
a pregnancy test	一个验孕测验	ee·ger yèn·yèwn tsèr·yen

Are you using contraception?
你用避孕
措施吗？   něe yòong bèe·yèwn
tswòr·shīr ma

Are you menstruating?
你的月经
还来吗？   něe·der ywàir·jìng
hái·lái ma

Are you pregnant?
你怀孕了吗？   něe hwày·yèwn ler ma

When did you last have your period?
上次流血是
什么时候？   shùng·tsir lyó·syǎir shìr
shér·mer shír·hò

You're pregnant.
你怀孕了。   něe hwày·yèwn ler

allergies

过敏症

I have a skin allergy. 我皮肤过敏。		wór pée·foo qwòr·mǐn
I'm allergic to ...	我对…… 过敏。	wǒr dwày ... gwòr·mǐn
He/She is allergic to ...	他/她对…… 过敏。	tā dwày ... gwòr·mǐn
antibiotics	抗菌素	kùng·jēwn·sòo
anti-inflammatories	抗炎药	kùng·yěn·yào
aspirin	埃斯匹林	āi·sir·pée·lín
bees	蜜蜂	mèe·fērng
codeine	可待因	kér·dài·yīn
penicillin	青霉素	chīng·máy·sòo
pollen	花粉	hwā·fěrn
sulphur-based drugs	硫基药物	lyó·jēe yào·wòr

I'm allergic to ...	我对……	wǒr dwày ...
	过敏。	gwòr·mín
He/She is	他/她对……	tā dwày ...
allergic to ...	过敏。	gwòr·mìn
butter	黄油	hwúng·yó
chilli	辣椒	là·jyāo
dairy produce	奶制品	nǎi·jìr·pín
eggs	鸡蛋	jēe·dùn
gelatine	明胶	míng·jyāo
gluten	面筋	myèn·jìn
honey	蜂蜜	fērng·mèe
MSG	味精	wày·jīng
nuts	果仁	gwǒr·rérn
peanuts	花生	hwā·shērng
seafood	海鲜	hái·syēn
shellfish	贝壳	bày·kér
antihistamines	抗组胺药	kùng·zóo·ūn yào
inhaler	吸入器	sēe·ròo chèe
injection	打针	dǎ·jērn

alternative treatments

非主流医疗

Herbal medicine (jōong·yào 中药) and acupuncture (jērn·jyǒ 针灸) are the most common medical systems in China.

I don't use (Western medicine).

我不吃(西药)。　　　　　wǒr bòo·chīr (sēe·yào)

I prefer ...	我更愿意……	wǒr gērng ywèn·ee ...
Can I see someone	哪里能看……	ná·lee nérng·kùn ...
who practices ...	大夫?	dài·foo
acupuncture	针灸	jērn·jyǒ
Chinese herbal medicine	中药	jōong·yào
Chinese medicine	中医	jōong·ēe
meridian massage	经络按摩	jīng·lwór ūn·mór

parts of the body

身体部位

My ... hurts.
我的……疼。　　　　　wŏr·der ... térng

I can't move my ...
我不能动我的……　　　wŏr bòo·nérng dòong wŏr·der ...

I have a cramp in my ...
我的……抽筋儿。　　　wŏr·der ... chō·jĭr

My ... is swollen.
我的……发肿了。　　　wŏr·der ... fā·jŏong ler

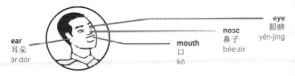

ear
耳朵
ăr·dŏr

mouth
口
kŏ

nose
鼻子
bée·zir

eye
眼睛
yĕn·jīng

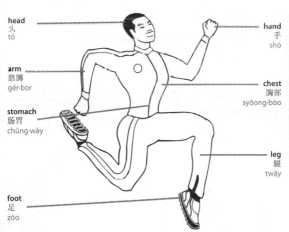

head
头
tó

arm
胳膊
gér·bor

stomach
肠胃
chŭng·wày

foot
足
zóo

hand
手
shŏ

chest
胸部
syōong·bòo

leg
腿
twăy

chemist

西药房

I need something for ...
我要……的药。 　　　　　wǒr yào ... der yào

Do I need a prescription for ...?
……需要处方吗? 　　　　　... sēw·yào chòo·fūng ma

I have a prescription.
我有处方。 　　　　　　　wór yǒ chòo·fūng

How many times a day?
每天吃几次? 　　　　　　máy·tyēn chīr jěe·tsìr

Will it make me drowsy?
吃后发困吗? 　　　　　　chīr·hò fā·kòon ma

antiseptic	消毒	syāo·dǒo
antibiotics	抗菌素	kùng·jēwn·sòo
bandage	绷带	bérng·dài
condom	避孕套	bèe·yèwn·tào
contraceptives	避孕品	bèe·yèwn·pǐn
cough medicine	感冒药	gǔn·mào yào
eye drops	眼泪水	yén·lày·shwǎy
gut blockers (for diahorrea)	止泻药	jǐr·syàir yào
herb (medicinal)	药材	yào·tsǎi
insect repellent	防虫剂	fúng·chǒong·jèe
iodine	碘水	dyén·shwǎy
lip balm	辰膏	chérn·gāo
moisturiser	护肤膏	hòo·foo gāo
painkillers	止痛药	jǐr·tòong yào
rehydration salts	补充水 冲剂	bǒo·chóong·shwǎy chōong·jèe
sleeping pills	安眠药	ūn·myén yào
sticking plaster	疮口铁	chwùng·kǒ tyāir
syringe	注射针	jòo·shèr jērn
thermometer	测温器	tsèr·wēn chèe
water purification tablets	清水药	chīng·shwǎy·yào

dentist

牙科

I have a ...	我有……	wó yǒ ...
broken tooth	崩牙	bērng·yá
cavity	牙洞	yá·dòong
toothache	牙疼	yá·térng

I've lost a filling.
我崩牙了。

wǒr bērng·yá ler

My dentures are broken.
我的假牙坏了。

wǒr·der jyǎ·yá hwày·ler

My gums hurt.
我齿龈好痛。

wór chǐr·yín hǎo·tòong

I don't want it extracted.
我不要把牙。

wǒr boo·yào bǎ·yá

Ouch!
哎呀, 疼!

āi·ya térng

I need a/an ...	我需要……	wǒr sēw·yào ...
anaesthetic	麻醉药	mǎ·zwày yào
filling	补牙	bǒo·yá

listen for ...

bóo·hwày térng 不会疼。	This won't hurt a bit.
byáir·dòong 别动。	Don't move.
hwáy·lai hái·máy wún 回来，还没完！	Come back, I haven't finished.
jūng·kāi kǒ 张开口。	Open wide.
shòo·kǒ 漱口！	Rinse!
yáo·ee·sya 咬一下。	Bite down on this.

The symbols ⑩, ⑧ and ⑨ (indicating noun, adjective and verb) have been added for clarity where an English term could be either.

A

abalone 鲍鱼 bāo·yéw

aboard 在······上 zài ... shùng

abortion 堕胎 dwòr·tái

about 关于 gwūn·yéw

above 以上 ěe·shùng

abroad 国外 gwór·wài

accident 事故 shìr·goo

accommodation 住宿 jòo·sōo

(bank) account 账单 jung·dun

across 对面 dwày·myen

actor 演员 yěn·ywén

acupuncture 针灸 jern·jyo

adaptor 双边插座
   shwūng·byen chā·zwòr

addiction 毒瘾 dóo·yin

address ⑩ 地址 dèe·jír

administration 行政部门
   síng·jèrng bòo·mern

admission price 票价 pyào·jyà

admit (let in) 允许 yěwn·sěw

adult ⑩ 大人 dà·rérn

advertisement 广告 gwúng·gào

advice 建议 jyèn·èe

aeroplane 飞机 fāy·jēe

Africa 非洲 fāy·jō

after 以后 ěe·hò

(this) afternoon (今天)下午
   (jīn·tyen) syà·wōo

aftershave 男用香水
   nún·yòong syūng·shwǎy

again 在一次 zài ee·tsìr

age ⑩ 年龄 nyén·líng

(three days) ago (三天)前
   (sun tyen) chyén

agree 同意 tóong·èe

agriculture 农业 nóong·yàir

ahead 前面 chyén·myen

AIDS 艾滋病 ài·zīr·bìng

air ⑩ 空气 kōong·chee

air-conditioned 有空调的 yó
   kōong·tyáo der

air-conditioning 空调 kōong·tyáo

airline 航空公司
   húng·kōong gōong·sīr

airmail 航运 húng·yèwn

airplane 飞机 fāy·jēe

airport 飞机场 fāy·jēe chǔng

airport tax 机场税 jēe·chǔng shwày

aisle (on plane) 走廊 zǒ·lúng

alarm clock 闹钟 nào·jōong

alcohol 酒精 jyǒ·jīng

all 所有的 swor·yo der

allergic 过敏 gwòr·mǐn

alleyway 胡同 hóo·toong

almond 杏仁 sìng·rérn

almost 差一点 chā ēe·dyǎr

alone 独一个人 dóo ēe·ger rérn

already 已经 ěe·jīng

also 也 yǎir

altitude 海拔 hǎi·bá

always 每次 máy·tsìr

ambassador 大使 dà·shír

ambulance 急救车 jée·jyò chēr

American football 美式橄榄球 máy·shìr gún·lŭn·chyó
anaemia 贫血 pín·syăir
ancestors 祖先 zŏo·syēn
ancestral home 老家 láo·jyā
ancient 古代 gŏo·dài
and 和 hér
angry 生气 shērng·chèe
animal 动物 dòong·woo
ankle 脚踝 jyăo·hwái
another 再一个 zài ēe·ger
answer 答复 dá·foo
ant 蚂蚁 má·ĕe
antibiotics 抗菌素 kùng·jēwn·sòo
antique ⓝ 古董 góo·dŏong
antique market 古董市场 góo·dŏong shìr·chŭng
antiseptic ⓝ 消毒剂 syāo·dóo jèe
any 任何 rèrn·hér
apartment (downmarket) 楼房 ló·fŭng
apartment (upmarket) 公寓 gōong·yèw
appendix (body part) 阑尾 lún·wăy
apple 苹果 píng·gwŏr
appointment (to meet someone) 有约 yó·ywāir
apricot 杏桃 sìng·táo
April 四月 sìr·ywàir
archaeology 考古学 káo·gŏo·shwáir
architect 建筑师 jyèn·joo·shīr
architecture 建筑学 jyèn·joo·shwáir
argue 吵架 chăo·jyà
arm 胳膊 gēr·bor
arrest 扣留 kò·lyó
arrivals 进港口 jìn·gúng·kŏ
arrive 到达 dào·dá
art ⓝ 艺术 èe·shoo
art gallery 艺术馆 èe·shoo·gwŭn
artist 艺术家 èe·shoo·jyā
ashtray 烟灰缸 yēn·hwāy·gūng
Asia 亚洲 yá·jō
ask (a question) 问 wèrn
ask (for something) 求 chyó
aspirin 阿斯匹灵 ā·sir·pée·líng
asthma 哮喘 syào·chwŭn
at 在 zài
athletics 田径 tyén·jīng
atmosphere (weather) 气候 chèe·ho
August 八月 bā·ywàir
aunt 阿姨 ā·ée
Australia 澳大利亚 ào·dà·lèe·yă
Australian Rules Football 澳式橄榄球 ào·shìr gún·lŭn·chyó
automated teller machine (ATM) 自动取款机 zìr·dòong chéw·kwŭn jēe
autumn ⓝ 秋天 chyō·tyēn
avenue 大街道 dà·jyāir·dào
awful 可恶 kĕr·wōo

B

B&W (film) 黑白（片） hāy·bái (pyēn)
baby ⓝ 小娃娃 syăo wā·wa
baby food 婴儿食品 yīng·ár shír·pĭn
baby powder 滑石粉 hwá·shír fĕrn
babysitter 临时保姆 lín·shír báo·mŏo
back (body) 背 bày
back (position) 后面 hò·myen
backpack 背包 bày·bāo
bacon 培根 páy·gērn
bad 坏 hwày
bag 包 bāo
baggage 行李 síng·lĕe
baggage allowance 免费行李 myĕn·fày síng·lĕe
baggage claim 行李领取处 síng·lĕe lĭng·chĕw chòo
balance (account) ⓝ 剩余额 shèrng·yew ér
balcony 阳台 yúng·tái
ball 球 chyó

ballet 芭蕾舞 bā·láy wǒo
bamboo shoots 笋 sǒon
banana 香蕉 syūng·jyāo
band (music) 乐队 ywàir dwày
bandage ⓝ 绷带 bérng·dài
Band-Aid 疮口铁 chwùng·kǒ tyáir
bank (money) 银行 yín·hǔng
bank account 银行账户
  yín·hǔng jùng·hoo
banknote 纸币 jír·bòo
baptism 洗礼 sée·lěe
bar 酒吧 jyǒ·ba
barbecued 烧烤 shāo·kǎo
barber 理发屋 lěe·fà wōo
baseball 棒球 bùng·chyó
basin 水盆 shwáy·pěn
basket 篮子 lún·zir
basketball 篮球 lún·chyó
bath ⓝ 浴缸 yèw·gūng
bathing suit 游泳衣 yó·yǒong·ēe
bathroom 浴室 yèw·shir
battery 电池 dyèn·chír
be (I want to be …) 当 dūng
beach ⓝ 沙滩 shā·tūn
beach volleyball 沙滩排球
  shā·tūn pái·chyó
bean 豆子 dò·zir
bean noodles 豆粉 dò·fěrn
beansprout 豆芽 dò·yá
beautiful 美丽 mǎy·lèe
beauty salon 美容店 mǎy·róong dyèn
because 因为 yīn·wáy
bed 床 chwúng
bed linen 床单 chwúng·dūn
bedding 被褥 bày·róo
bedroom 卧室 wòr·shir
bee 蜜蜂 mèe·fērng
beef 牛肉 nyó·rò
beer 啤酒 pée·jyǒ
before 以前 ěe·chyén
beggar 乞丐 chěe·gài

behind 背面 bày·myen
Beijing 北京 bǎy·jīng
Belgium 比利时 běe·lèe·shír
below 下面 syà·myen
beside 旁边 púng·byēn
best 最好的 zwày·hǎo der
bet ⓝ 赌博 dǒo·bór
better 更好 gērng·hǎo
between 中间 jōong·jyēn
bible 圣经 shèrng·jīng
bicycle 自行车 zir·síng·chēr
big 大 dà
bigger 更大 gērng·dà
biggest 最大 zwày·dà
bike ⓝ 自行车 zìr·síng·chēr
bike chain 车链 chēr lyén
bike lock 车锁 chīr·swǒr
bike path 自行车道 zir·síng·chēr dào
bike shop 修车店 syō·chēr dyèn
bill (restaurant etc) ⓝ 单子 dūn·zir
binoculars 望远镜 wùng·ywěn·jìng
bird 鸟 nyǎo
birth certificate 出生证
  chōo·shèrng·jèrng
birthday 生日 shērng·rìr
biscuit 饼干 bǐng·gūn
bite (dog) ⓝ 咬 yǎo
bite (insect) ⓝ 叮 dīng
bitter 苦 kǒo
bitter melon 苦瓜 kóo·gwā
black 黑色 hāy·sèr
bladder 膀胱 púng·qwūng
blanket 毛毯 máo·tūn
blind (unable to see) 眼瞎 yén·syā
blister ⓝ 起泡 chěe·pào
blocked (toilet) 堵塞 dǒo·sāi
blood 血液 yàir
blood group 血型 syàir·síng
blood pressure 血压 syàir·yā
blood test 验血 yèn·syàir
blue 蓝色 lún·sèr

board (a plane, ship etc) 登 dērng

boarding pass 登机卡 dērng·jēe kǎ

boat 船 chwún

body 身体 shērn·těe

boil ⊙ 煮 jǒo

bok choy 小白菜 syǎo bái·tsài

bone 骨头 góo·to

book ⊙ 书 shōo

book (make a booking) ⊙ 定 dìng

book shop 书店 shōo·dyèn

booked out 定满 dìng·mǔn

boots 靴子 shwāir·zir

border ⊙ 边界 byēn·jyàir

bored 闷 mèrn

boring 无聊 wóo·lyáo

borrow 借 jyàir

botanic garden 植物园 jír·woo ywén

both 两个都 lyǔng·ger·dō

bottle 瓶子 píng·zir

bottle opener 开瓶器 kāi·píng chèe

bottom (body part) 屁股 pèe·goo

bottom (position) 底 děe

bowl ⊙ 碗 wǔn

box ⊙ 箱子 syūng·zir

boxer shorts 小裤衩 syǎo kòo·chá

boxing 拳击 chwén·jēe

boy 男孩子 nún hái·zir

boyfriend 男朋友 nún·pérng·yo

(the) Boys (Beijing slang) 哥们儿 gēr·mer

bra 胸罩 syōong·jào

brakes 车闸 chēr·já

brandy 白兰地 bái·lún·dèe

brave 勇敢 yóong·gǔn

bread 面包 myèn·bāo

break ⊙ 折断 jěr·dwùn

break down ⊙ 崩溃 bērng·kwày

breakfast 早饭 zǎo·fùn

breast (body part) 乳房 róo·fúng

breathe 呼吸 hōo·sēe

bribe ⊙ 行贿 síng·hwày

bridge 桥 chyáo

briefcase 公文包 gōong·wén·bāo

brilliant (clever) 聪明 tsōong·ming

bring 带 dài

broccoli 西兰花 sēe·lún·hwā

brochure 说明书 shwōr·míng shōo

broken 坏了 hwài ler

broken down (car) 抛锚 pāo·máo

bronchitis 肺炎 fày·yén

bronze medal 铜牌 tóong·pái

brother 兄弟 syōong·dee

brother (elder) 哥哥 gēr·ger

brother (younger) 弟弟 dèe·dee

brothers 兄弟 syōong·dee

brown 咖啡色 kā·fāy sèr

bruise ⊙ 青肿 chīng·jǒong

brush ⊙ 毛笔 máo·běe

bucket 水桶 shwáy·tǒong

Buddha 大佛 dà·fór

Buddhism 佛教 fór·jyào

Buddhist 佛教徒 fór·jyào tóo

budget ⊙ 开支 kāi·jīr

buffet 自助餐 zir·jòo·tsūn

bug ⊙ 虫子 chóong·zir

build 建 jyèn

builder 泥匠 nèe·jyùng

building 楼 ló

bumbag 腰包 yào·bāo

burn ⊙ 烧伤 shāo·shùng

burnt 烧焦 shāo·jyāo

bus (city) 大巴 dà·bā

bus (intercity) 长途车 chúng·tóo chēr

bus station 长途车站 chúng·tǒo chēr·jùn

bus stop 车站 chēr·jùn

business ⊙ 生意 shērng·èe

business class 头等舱 tó·děrng tsūng

businessman 商人 shūng·rérn

businesswoman 商人 shūng·rérn

business trip 出差 chōo·chāi

busy (state of mind) 有事 yǒ·shìr
busy (at a certain time) 急急忙忙
  jée·jee múng·mung
but 但是 dàn·shir
butcher 刳了手 gwǎy·zǐr shǔ
butcher's shop 肉店 ròu·dyèn
butter ⓝ 黄油 hwúng·yó
butterfly 蝴蝶 hóo·dyáir
button ⓝ 纽扣 nyó·kò
buy ⓥ 买 mǎi

C

cabbage 白菜 bái·tsài
café 咖啡屋 kā·fāy wōo
cake 蛋糕 dùn·gāo
cake shop 糕点屋 gāo·dyèn wòo
calculator 计算器 jèe·swùn chèe
calendar 日历 rìr·lèe
call ⓥ 叫 jyào
camera 照相机 jào·syùng jee
camera shop 照相店 jào·syùng dyèn
camp ⓥ 野营 yěr·ying
can (be able) 能 néng
can (have permission) 可以 kér·ěe
can (tin) 罐头 gwùn·to
can opener 开罐器 kāi·gwùn chèe
Canada 加拿大 jyā·ná·dà
cancel 取消 chěw·syāo
cancer (illness) 癌症 ái·jèrng
candle 蜡烛 là·joo
candy 糖果 túng·gwǒr
cantaloupe 哈密瓜 hā·mì gwǎ
Cantonese (language) ⓝ 广东话
  gwǔng·dōong hwà
capitalism 资本主义 zīr·běn jǒo·èe
capsicum 青椒 chīng·jyāo
car 轿车 jyào·chēr
car hire 车租赁 chēr zōo·lín
car park 停车场 tíng·chēr chǔng
car registration 车号 chēr·hào

cardiac arrest 心脏病 sīn·zùng bìng
cards (playing) 扑克牌 pōo·kè pái
care (for someone) ⓥ 关心 gwūn·sīn
Careful! 小心 syǎo·sīn
carp (fish) 鲤鱼 lěe·yéw
carpenter 木匠 mòo·jyùng
carrot 胡萝卜 hóo·lwór·bor
carry 背 bày
cash ⓝ 现金 syèn·jīn
cash (a cheque) ⓥ 兑现 dwày·syèn
cash register 收银台 shò·yín tái
cashier 出纳 chōo·nà
casino 赌博场 dǔo·bór chǔng
cassette 录音带 lòo·yīn dài
casual work 零时工作
  líng·shír gōong·zwòr
cat 猫 māo
cathedral 大教堂 dà·jyào·túng
Catholic 天主教 tyēn·jǒo·jyào
cave 山洞 shūn·dòng
CD CD sēe·dèe
celebration 庆祝会 chìng·jòo hwày
cemetery ⓝ 坟地 fērn·dèe
cent 分 fērn
centimetre 厘米 lée·mēe
centre 中心 jōong·sīn
ceramics 陶瓷 táo·tsír
certificate 证明 jèrng·míng
chain ⓝ 莲子 lyén·zir
chair 椅子 ěe·zir
champagne 香槟 syūng·bīng
championships 竞赛 jìng·sài
chance 机会 jēe·hway
change ⓝ 换 hwùn
change (coins) 零钱 líng·chyén
change (money) ⓥ 换钱 hwùn·chyén
changing room 更衣室 gēng·ēe·shìr
charming 有魅力 yǒ mày·lèe
chat ⓥ 聊天 lyáo·tyēn
chat up 调情 tyáo·chíng
cheap 实惠 shír·hwày

cheat ⓝ 骗子 pyèn·zir

check ⓥ 确认 chwàir·rèrn

check (banking) 支票 jīr·pyào

check (bill) 账单 jùng·dūn

check-in (desk) 登记台 dērng·jèe tái

checkpoint 监察点 jyēn·chá dyěn

cheese 奶酪 nǎi·lào

chef 厨师 chóo·shīr

chemist (pharmacist) 药师 yào·shīr

chemist (shop) 药房 yào·fúng

cheque (bill) 账单 jùng·dūn

cherry 樱桃 yīng·táo

chess (Chinese) 象棋 syùng·chée

chess (Western) 国际象棋
gwór·jèe syùng·chée

chess board 棋盘 chée·pōon

chest (body) 胸 syūng

chestnut 栗子 lèe·zir

chewing gum 口香糖 kǒ·syūng·túng

chi 气 chèe

chicken 鸡 jēe

chicken pox 水痘 shwǎy·dò

child 宝贝 bǎo·bày

child seat 婴儿座 yīng·ǎr·zwòr

childminding 幼儿园 yò·ǎr·ywén

children 孩子们 hái·zir·mern

chilli 辣椒 là·jyāo

chilli sauce 辣椒酱 là·jyāo jyùng

China 中国 jōong·gwór

Chinese (language) 中文
jōong·wérn

Chinese flowering cabbage 菜心
tsài·sīn

Chinese medicine 中药 jōong·yào

Chinese medicine doctor 中医
jōong·ēe

chocolate 巧克力 chyáo·kěr·lèe

choose 选择 swěn·zér

chopping board 菜板 tsài·bǔn

chopsticks 筷子 kwài·zir

Christian 基督教徒 jēe·dōo jyào·tóo

Christmas 圣诞节 shèrng·dùn·jyáir

Christmas Day 圣诞日 shèrng·dùn·rìr

Christmas Eve 平安夜 píng·ūn yàir

chrysanthemum 菊花 jéw·hwā

chrysanthemum tea 菊花茶
jéw·hwā·chá

church 教堂 jyào·túng

cigarette 香烟 syūng·yēn

cigarette lighter 打火机 dá·hwǒr·jēe

cinema 电影院 dyèn·yǐng·ywèn

cinnamon bark 桂皮 gwày·pēe

circus 杂技 zǎ·jèe

citizenship 公民 gōong·mín

city 城市 chérng·shìr

city centre 市中心 shìr·jōong·sīn

civil rights 公民权 gōong·mín chwén

clams 蚌子 bùng·zir

class (category) 类 lày

class system 阶级制度 jyāir·jée jìr·dòo

classical 古典 góo·dyěn

clean ⓐ 干净 gūn·jìng

clean ⓥ 打扫 dá·sǎo

cleaning 清洁 chīng·jyáir

client 客户 kèr·hoo

cliff 悬崖 shwén·yá

climb (mountain) 攀山 pūn·shūn

cloakroom 寄存处 jèe·tsóon·chòo

clock 钟表 jōong·byǎo

close (shut) 关闭 gwūn·bèe

close (nearby) 附近 fòo·jìn

closed 关门 gwūn·mérn

clothesline 晾衣线 lyùng·ēe·syèn

clothing 衣服 ēe·foo

clothing store 服装店
fóo·jwūng·dyèn

cloud 云彩 yéwn·tsǎi

cloudy 有云 yǒ·yéwn

clutch (car) 换档踏板
hwùn·dǔng tā·bǔn

coach (bus) 大巴 dà·bā

coach (sports) 教练 jyào·lyèn

coast 海边 hǎi·byēn

coat 大衣 dà·ēe

cockroach 蟑螂 jūng·láng

cocktail 鸡尾酒 jēe·wǎy jyǒ

cocoa 巧克力分 chyǎo·kèr·lèe fēm

coffee 咖啡 kā·fāy

coins 硬币 yìng·bèe

(have a) cold 伤风 shùng·fērng

cold 冷 lěrng

colleague 同事 tóong·shìr

collect call 对方付款
dwày fūng fòo·kwǔn

college (university) 大学 dà·shwáir

colour 颜色 yěn sèr

comb 梳子 shōo·zir

come 来 lái

comedy 喜剧片 sēe·jòo pyēn

comfortable 舒服 shōo·foo

commission 代理费 dài·lěe fày

common people 老百姓 lǎo·bǎi·sìng

communications (profession) 交通
jyāo·tōong

communion 教会 jyāo·hwày

communism 共产主义
gòong chǔn jǒo èe

communist (party official) 干部
gùn·boo

communist (party member) 党员
dǔng·ywén

companion 同伙 tóong·hwǒr

company (business) 公司 gōong·sīr

compass 指南针 jǐr·nún jěrn

complain 抱怨 bào·ywen

complaint 投诉 tó·sòo

complimentary (tickets) 赠（票）
zèrng (pyào)

computer 电脑 dyèn·nǎo

computer game 电子游戏
dyèn·zǐr yó·sèe

comrade 同志 tóong·jìr

concert 音乐会 yīn·ywàir hwày

concussion 昏迷 hōon·mée

conditioner (hair) 润发剂 ròon·fā jèe

condom 避孕套 bèe·yèwn·tào

conference (big) 会议 hwày·èe

conference (small) 会合 hwày·hér

confession 坦白 tūn·bái

confirm (a booking) 确定 chwàir·dìng

congratulations 恭喜 gōong·sěe

conjunctivitis 结膜炎 jyáir·mor yén

connection 连接 lyén·jyāir

conservative 保守 bǎo·shǒ

constipation 便秘 byēn·mèe

consulate 领事馆 lǐng·shìr·gwǔn

contact lens solution 隐形眼镜水
yǐn·síng yěn·jìng shwǎy

contact lenses 隐形眼镜
yǐn·síng yěn jìng

contraceptives 避孕品 bèe·yèwn·pǐn

contract 合同 hér·toong

convenience store 小卖部
syǎo·mài·bòo

cook 厨子 chóo·zir

cook 炒菜 chǎo·tsài

cooking 做菜 zwòr·tsài

cool (temperature) 凉快 lyúng·kwài

corkscrew 螺丝开瓶器
lwǒr·sīr kāi·píng chèe

corn 玉米 yèw·měe

corner 角 jyǎo

corrupt 贪污 tún·wōo

cost (price) 价格 jyà·gér

cotton 棉花 myén·hwā

cough 咳嗽 kér·sò

cough medicine 感冒药 gǔn·mào yào

count 计算 jèe·swùn

counter (at hotel) 柜台 gwày·tái

country (nation) 国家 gwór·jyā

countryside 乡下 syūng·syà

coupon 票 pyào

court (legal) 法庭 fă·tíng

court (tennis) (网球)场 (wǔng·chyó)·chǎng

cover charge 入场费 ròo·chǔng fày

cow 牛 nyó

crafts 手艺 shǒu·èe

crash 撞车 jwùng·chēr

crazy 疯了 fērng·ler

cream (dairy) 奶酪 năi·lào

credit 信用 sìn·yòong

credit card 信用卡 sìn·yòong kǎ

crop (field) 农田 nóong·tyén

cross (religious) 十字架 shír·zìr·jyà

crowded 拥挤 yōong·jěe

cucumber 黄瓜 hwúng·gwā

cup 杯子 bāy·zir

cupboard 大柜 dà·gwày

cupping (traditional therapy) 刮痧 gwā·shā

currency exchange 货币兑换 hwòr·bèe dwày·hwùn

current (electricity) (电)流 (dyèn) lyó

current affairs 时事 shír·shìr

curry 咖喱 gā·lēe

custom 风俗 fērng·sóo

customs (immigration) 海关 hăi·gwūn

cut (wound) ⓝ 疮口 chwùng·kǒ

cut ⓥ 切 chyàie

cutlery 刀叉 dāo·chā

CV 简历 jyěn·lèe

cycle 骑自行车 chée zìr·síng·chēr

cycling 自行车赛 zìr·síng·chēr sài

cyclist 自行车骑手 zìr·síng·chēr chée·shǒ

cystitis 膀胱炎 púng·gwūng yén

D

dad 爸爸 bà·ba

daily 日常 rìr·chǔng

dance 跳舞 tyào·wǒo

dancing 舞蹈 wǒo·dǎo

dangerous 危险 wāy·syen

dark 黑暗 hāy·ùn

dark (of colour) 青色 chīng·sèr

date (appointment) 约会 ywāir·hwày

date (day) 日期 rìr·chēe

date (fruit) 枣 záo

date (a person) 谈朋友 tún pérng·yo

date of birth 出生日 chōo·shērng·rìr

daughter 女孩子 něw hái·zir

dawn 日出 rìr·chōo

day 白天 bái·tyēn

day after tomorrow 后天 hò·tyēn

day before yesterday 前天 chyén·tyēn

dead 死了 sǐr·ler

deaf 耳聋 ǎr·lóong

deal (cards) 发牌 fā (pái)

December 十二月 shír·àr ywàir

decide 决定 jwáir·dìng

deep 深 shērn

deforestation 乱砍乱伐 lwùn·kǔn lwùn·fá

degrees (temperature) 度 dòo

delay 往后退 wǔng·hò·twāy

deliver 递送 dèe·sòong

democracy 民主主义 mín·jǒo jǒo·èe

demonstration (protest) 游行 yó·síng

Denmark 丹麦 dūn·mài

dentist 牙科 yá·kēr

depart (leave) 离开 lée·kāi

department store 百货商店 băi·hwòr shūng·dyèn

departure 出发 chōo·fā

departure gate 登机口 dērng·jēe kǒ

deposit (bank) 存钱 tsóon·chyén

deposit (surety) 押金 yā·jīn

descendant 后裔 hò·èe

desert 沙漠 shā·mòr

design 设计 shèr·jee

dessert 甜点 tyén·dyěn

destination 目的地 mòo·dee·dèe
details 细节 sèe·jyáir
diabetes 糖尿病 tũng·nyào·bìng
dial tone 播音 bōr·yīn
diaper 尿裤 nyào·kòo
diaphragm (anatomical) 横隔膜
　　hérng gér·mór
diaphragm (contraceptive) 避孕药
　　bèe·yèwn yào
diarrhoea 拉稀 lā·sēe
diary 日记 rìr·jèe
dice 骰子 tó·zir
dictionary 词典 tsír·dyěn
die 去世 chèw·shìr
diet 减肥 jyěn·fáy
different 不同 bòo·tóong
difficult 困难 kòon·nũn
dim sum 點心 dyěn·sīn
dining car 餐车 tsūn·chēr
dinner 晚饭 wǔn·fùn
dipping sauce 黄酱 hwúng·jyùng
direct 直接 jír·jyāir
direct-dial 直播 Jír·bōr
direction 方向 fūng·syùng
director (business) 董事 dǒong·shìr
director (film) 导演 dǎo·yen
dirty 脏 zūng
disabled 残疾 tsún·jèe
disco 迪斯科 dēe·sīr·kēr
discount 折扣 jér·kòo
discrimination 歧视 chée·shìr
disease 疾病 jée·bìng
dish (food item) 盘 pún
disk (CD-ROM) 碟子 dyáir·zir
disk (floppy) 软盘 rwǔn·pún
diving (underwater) 潜水游
　　chyén·shwǎy·yó
diving equipment 潜水游设备
　　chyén·shwǎy·yó shèr·bày
divorced 离婚 lée·hōon
dizzy 头昏 tó·hōon
do 做 zwòr

doctor 医生 ēe·shērng
documentary 纪实片 jèe·shír pyēn
dog 狗 gǒ
dole 救济 jyò·jèe
doll 洋娃娃 yúng·wā·wa
(American) dollar (美) 叨 (máy) dāo
doona 被子 bày·zir
door 门 mérn
dope (drugs) 大麻 dà·má
double 双 chwūng
double bed 双人床
　　shwūng·rérn chwúng
double room 双人间
　　shwūng·rérn jyēn
down 下面 syà·myen
downhill 下坡 syà·pōr
dozen 打 dá
drama 戏剧 sèe·jèw
dream ⓝ 梦 mèrng
dress ⓐ 连衣裙 lyén·ēe·chèwn
dried 干 gūn
dried fruit 果干 gwór·gūn
drink (alcoholic) 酒料 jyǒ·lyào
drink (nonalcoholic) 饮料 yín·lyào
drink 喝 hēr
drive 开车 kāi·chēr
drivers licence 驾驶照 jyà shír jào
drug (illicit) 毒品 dóo·pǐn
drug (medication) 药品 yào·pǐn
drug addiction 毒品上瘾
　　dóo·pǐn shùng·yín
drug dealer 毒贩 dóo·fùn
drug trafficking 贩毒 fùn·dóo
drug user 吃毒瘾 chír·dóo yín
drugs (illicit) 毒品 dóo·pǐn
drugs (medication) 药品 yào·pǐn
drum (instrument) 鼓 gǒo
drunk 醉 zwày
(blow) dry (吹) 干 (chwāy) gūn
dry ⓐ 干 gūn
dry (eg, clothes) ⓥ 晾干 lyùng·gūn
duck 鸭子 yā·zir

dummy (pacifier) 奶嘴 nái·zwǎy
dumpling (boiled) 饺子 jyǎo·zir
dumpling (fried) 锅贴 gwōr·tyāir
dumpling (steamed) 包子 bāo·zir
durian 榴莲 lyó·lyén
DVD DVD dēe·wǎy·dèe

E

each 每个 mǎy·ger
ear 耳朵 ǎr·dōr
early 早 zǎo
earn (money) 挣 (钱) jèrng(·chyén)
earplugs 耳塞子 ǎr·sāi·zir
earrings 耳环 ǎr·hwún
Earth 地球 dèe·chyó
earthquake 地震 dèe·jèrn
east 东方 dōong·fūng
Easter 复活节 fòo·hwór·jyáir
easy 容易 róong·èe
eat 吃饭 chīr·fùn
economy class 经济舱 jīng·jee tsūng
ecstasy (drug) 迷幻剂 mée·hwùn·jèe
eczema 湿疹 shīr·jěn
editor 编辑 byēn·jee
education 教育 jyào·yew
egg (chicken) 鸡蛋 jēe·dùn
election 选举 shwén·jěw
electrical store 电子用品店
　　dyèn·zir yòong·pǐn dyèn
electricity 电 dyèn
elevator 电梯 dyèn·tēe
email 电子邮件 dyèn·zir yó·jyèn
embarrassed (slightly) 不好意思
　　bòo·hǎo èe·sīr
embarrassed (very) 尴尬 gūn·gà
embassy 大使馆 dà·shír·gwǔn
emergency 出事 chōo·shìr
emotional 有情份 yǒ chíng·fèrn
Emperor 皇帝 hwúng·dèe
employee 职员 jír·ywén
employer 老板 láo·bǔn

Empress 皇后 hwúng·hò
empty 空 kōong
end 结束 jyáir·shòo
endangered species 临危动物
　　lín·wāy dòong·woo
engaged (betrothed) 订婚 dìng·hōon
engaged (occupied) 有事 yó·shìr
engagement (appointment) 定婚会
　　dìng·hōon hwày
engine 发动机 fā·dòong·jēe
engineer 工程师 gōong·cherng shīr
engineering 工程学
　　gōong·cherng swāir
England 英国 yīng·gwór
English 英文 yīng·wérn
English teacher 英文老师
　　yīng·wérn lǎo·shīr
enjoy (oneself) 玩 wún
enough 足够 zōo·gò
enter 入场 ròo·chǔng
entertainment guide 娱乐指南
　　yéw·lèr jír·nún
entry 入口 ròo·kǒ
envelope 信封 sìn·fērng
environment 环境 hwún·jìng
epilepsy 癫痫 dyēn·bèe
equal opportunity 平等待遇
　　píng·děrng dài·yew
equality 平等 píng·děrng
equipment 设备 shèr·bay
escalator 扶梯 fóo·tēe
estate agency 房地产公司
　　fúng·dèe·chǔn gōong·sīr
euro 欧元 ō·ywén
Europe 欧洲 ō·jō
euthanasia 安乐死 un·lèr sīr
evening 晚上 wún·shùng
every 每次 mǎy·tsìr
everyone 每个人 mǎy·ger rérn
everything 一切 ee·chyàir
exactly 确切 chwàir·chyàir
example 举例 jěw·lèe

excellent 好极了 hǎo·jée·ler
excess (baggage) 过重(行李) gwòr·jòong (síng·lee)
exchange ⓝ 交换 jyāo·hwùn
exchange ⓥ 换 hwùn
exchange rate 兑换率 dwày·hwùn lèw
excluded 排除 pái·chóo
exhaust (car) 废气 fày·chèe
exhibition 展览 jún·lǔn
exit 出口 chōo·kǒ
expensive 贵 gwày
experience 经验 jīng·yen
exploitation 剥削 bōr·shwáir
express 快速 kwài·sòo
express (mail) 快递(信) kwài·dèe (sìn)
express mail (by) (寄)特快 jèe tè·kwài
extension (visa) (签证)延期 (chyēn·jèrng) yén·chēe
eye(s) 眼睛 yén·jing
eye drops 眼泪水 yén·lày·shwǎy

F

fabric 布料 hòo·lyào
face 脸 lyén
face cloth 毛巾 máo·jīn
factory 工厂 gōong·chǔng
factory worker 工人 gōong·rérn
fall (autumn) 秋天 chyōo·tyen
fall (down) 掉下 dyào·sya
family 家庭 jyā·tíng
family name 姓 sìng
famous 出名 chōo·míng
fan (hand held) 扇子 shùn·zir
fan (machine) 电风扇 dyèn·fērng·shùn
fan (sport etc) 球迷 chyó mée
far 远 ywěn
fare 票价 pyào·jyà
farm 农地 nóong·dèe

farmer (peasant) 农民 nóong·mǐn
fashion 时髦 shír·máo
fast 快 kwài
fat 胖 pùng
father 父亲 fòo·chin
father-in-law 岳父 ywàir·fòo
faucet 水龙头 shwǎy·lóong·tǒ
fault (someone's) 责任 zér·rèrn
faulty 有毛病 yǒ máo·hìng
fax machine 传真机 chwún·jērn·jēe
February 二月 àr·ywàir
feed (baby, animals) 喂 wày
feel (touch) 触摸 chōo·mór
feeling (physical) 情感 jwáir·gǔn
feelings 感情 gǔn·chíng
female 女性 něw·sìng
fen (measure) 分 fērn
fence 篱笆 lée·ba
fencing (sport) 剑术 jyèn·shòo
feng shui 风水 ferng·shwáy
ferry 渡船 dòo·chwún
festival 节日 jyáir·rìr
fever 发烧 fā·shǎo
few 些 syāir
fiancé 未婚夫 wày·hōon·fōo
fiancée 未婚妻 wày·hōon·chēe
fiction (novel) 虚构(小说) sēw·gòu (syǎu·shwōr)
fight ⓥ 打架 dǎ·jyà
fill 填满 tyén·mǔn
fillet 鱼片 yéw·pyèn
film (cinema) 电影 dyèn·yǐng
film (for camera) 胶卷 jyao·jwěn
film speed 感光度 gún·gwūng·dòo
filtered 过滤 gwòr·lèw
find 找到 jǎo·dào
fine ⓐ 满好 mún·hǎo
fine (penalty) 罚款 fā·kwún
finger 指头 jír·to
finish ⓝ 结束 jyáir·shòo
finish ⓥ 结头 jyáir·tó
Finland 芬兰 fērn·lún

fire 火 hwŏr
firewood 木柴 mòo·chái
first 第一 dèe·ēe
商业舱 shūng·yàir tsūng first class
first-aid kit 急救装备
   jée·jyò jwùng·bay
first name 名子 míng·zir
fish ⓝ 鱼 yéw
fish shop 鱼摊 yéw·tūn
fishing 钓鱼 dyào·yéw
flag 国旗 gwór·chée
flannel 擦布 tsā·bòo
flashlight (torch) 手电筒
   shŏ·dyèn·tŏong
flat (apartment) 楼房 ló·fúng
flat 贬 byĕn
flea 跳蚤 tyào·zăo
flight 航班 húng·būn
flood 洪水 hóong·shwăy
floor (ground) 地板 dèe·bún
floor (storey) 层 tsérng
florist 花店 hwā·dyèn
flour (wheat) 面粉 myèn·fĕrn
flower 花 hwā
flu 感冒 gŭn·mào
fly 飞 fāy
foggy 有雾 yŏ·wòo
folk music 民谣 mín·yáo
follow 跟随 gēn·swáy
food 吃的 chīr·der
food supplies 预备食品
   yèw·bày shír·pīn
foot 脚 jyăo
football (soccer) 足球 zóo·chyó
foot massage 脚按摩 jyăo ùn·mór
foreign (goods) 洋 yúng
foreigner 外国人 wài·gwór rérn
forest 森林 sērn·lín
forever 永远 yóong·ywĕn
forget 忘掉 wùng·dyào
forgive 原谅 ywèn·lyung
fork 叉子 chā·zir

fortune cookies 签饼 chyēn·bíng
fortune teller 阴阳先生
   yín·yŭng syēn·shērng
foul 犯规 fùn·gwāy
foyer 大堂 dà·túng
fragile 脆弱 tswày·ròr
France 法兰西 fă·gwór
free (available) 有空 yŏ·kòong
free (gratis) 免费 myĕn·fày
free (not bound) 自由 zìr·yŏ
freeze 冻结 dòong·jyáir
fresh 新鲜 sīn·syen
Friday 礼拜五 lĕe·bài wŏo
fridge 冰箱 bìng·syūng
fried (deep-fried) 炸 jà
fried rice 炒饭 chăo·fùn
friend 朋友 pérng·yo
Friendship Store 友谊商店
   yŏ·èe shūng·dyèn
from 从 tsóong
frost 双 shwūng
frozen 冰冻 bīng·dòong
fruit 水果 shwáy·gwŏr
fry (stir-fry) 炒 jà
full 满 mún
full-time 全时的 chwén·shír·der
fun 好玩 hăo·wár
(have) fun 出去玩 chōo·chèw wár
funeral 葬礼 zùng·lĕe
funny 可笑 kĕr·syào
furniture 家具 jyā·jew
future 将来 jyūng·lái

G

(the) Gals (Beijing slang) 姐们儿
   jyĕir·mer
game (football) 比赛 bĕe·sài
game (sport) 比赛 bĕe·sài
garage 车库 chēr·kòo
garbage 垃圾 lā·jēe
garbage can 垃圾箱 lā·jēe syūng

garden 花园 hwā·ywén
gardening 养花 yúng·hwā
garlic 大蒜 dà·swùn
gas (for cooking) 煤气 máy·chèe
gas (petrol) 汽油 chèe·yú
gastroenteritis 肠胃炎 chúng·wày·yén
gate (airport) 登机口 dērng·jee·kô
gate (general) 门 mérn
gauze 纱布 shā·bòo
gay (bar) 同志 (吧) tóng·jir (ba)
Germany 德国 dér·gwór
get (fetch) 接来 jyāir·lái
get off (a train, etc) 下 (车) syà (cher)
gift 礼物 lěe·wòo
gig 节目 jyáir·mòo
gin 金酒 jīn·jyó
ginger 姜 jyūng
ginseng 人参 rérn·shērn
girl 女孩子 něw·hái zir
girlfriend 女朋友 něw·pérng·yo
give 送 sòong
given name 名了 míng·zir
glandular fever 腺热 syèn rèr
glass (drinking) 玻璃杯 bōr·lée bāy
glass (material) 玻璃 bōr·lée
glasses (spectacles) 眼镜 yěn·jìng
glove(s) 手套 shǒ tào
glue 胶水 jyāo·shwǎy
go 去 chèw
go out 出去 chōo·chèw
go out with 谈朋友 tún pérng·yo
go shopping 逛街 gwùng jyáir
goal 目的 mòo·dee
(score a) goal 进门 jìn·mérn
goalkeeper 守门员 shǒ·mérn·ywén
goat 山羊 shūn·yúng
god 神 shérn
goggles (swimming) 游泳镜 yó·yǒong jìng
gold 黄金 hwúng·jīn
gold medal 金牌 jīn·pái

golf ball 高尔夫球 gāo·ér·foo chyó
golf course 高尔夫场 gāo·ér·foo chǔng
good 好 hǎo
goodbye 再见 zài·jyèn
goose 鹅 ér
government 政府 jèrng·fǔo
gram 克 kèr
grandchild 孙子 sōon·zir
grandfather (maternal) 外公 wài·gōong
grandfather (paternal) 爷爷 yáir·yair
grandmother (maternal) 外婆 wài·pó
grandmother (paternal) 奶奶 nǎi·nai
grapefruit 柚子 yó·zir
grapes 葡萄 póo·tao
grass 草 tsǎo
grasslands 草原 tsǎo·ywén
grateful 感谢 gǔn·syàir
grave 坟墓 férn·mòo
gray 灰色 hwāy·sèr
great (fantastic) 棒 bùng
Great Wall 长城 chúng·chérng
green 绿色 lèw·sèr
green beans 扁豆 byěn·dò
green tea 绿茶 lèw·chá
greengrocer 菜摊 tsài·tūn
grey 灰色 hwāy·ser
grocery 食品 shír·pīn
groundnut (peanut) 花生 hwā·shērng
grow 长大 jǒo·dà
guaranteed 有保证 yó bǎo·jèrng
guess 猜猜 tsāi·tsai
guesthouse 宾馆 bīn·gwǔn
guide (audio) 录音导游 lòo·yīn dǎo·yó
guide (person) 导游 dǎo·yó
guide dog 导盲犬 dǎo·múng chwěn
guidebook 指南书 jǐr·nǔn shōo
guided tour 团体旅行 twún·těe lěw·síng

guilty 有罪 yǒ·zwày
guitar 吉他 jée·tā
gum (chewing) 口香糖 kǒ·syūng·tǔng
gum (teeth) 齿龈 chǐr·yín
gun 手枪 shǒ·chyūng
gym (place) 健美中心
　jyèn·měy jōong·sīn
gymnastics 体操 těe·tsáo
gynaecologist 妇科医生
　fòo·kēr ēe·sherng

H

hair 头发 tó·fā
hairbrush 头刷子 tó shwā·zir
haircut 理发 lěe·fā
hairdresser 理发屋 lěe·fā wōo
halal 清真 chīng·jērn
half 半个 bùn·ger
hallucination 幻想 hwùn·syǔng
ham 火腿 hwǒr twǎy
hammer 锤子 chwǎy·zir
hammock 吊床 dyào·chwúng
hand 手 shǒ
handbag 手包 shó·bāo
handball 手球 shǒ·chyó
handicrafts 手艺 shǒ·èe
handkerchief 手绢 shǒ·jwèn
handlebars 车把 chēr·bǎ
handmade 手做的 shǒ·zwòr der
handsome 英俊 yīng·jèwn
happy 快乐 kwài·lèr
harassment 骚扰 sāo·rǎo
harbour 港口 gúng·kǒ
hard (difficult) 困难 kòon·nǔn
hard (not soft) 很硬 hérn yìng
hard seat 硬座 yìng·zwòr
hard sleeper 硬卧 yìng·wòr
hard-boiled egg (tea egg) 茶叶蛋
　chá·yàir dùn
hardware store 五金店 wǒo·jīn dyèn
hash 麻精 má·jīng

hat 帽子 mào·zir
have 有 yǒ
hay fever 花粉热 hwā·fěrn rèr
he 他 tā
head 头 tó
head massage 头按摩 tó ùn·mór
headache 头疼 tó·térng
headlights 车灯 chēr·dēng
health 身体 shērn·těe
hear 听到 tīng·dào
hearing aid 助听器 jòo·tīng chèe
heart 心脏 sīn·zùng
heart attack 心脏病突发
　sīn·zùng·bìng tòo·fā
heart condition 心脏病 sīn·zùng·bìng
heat 热气 rèr·chèe
heated 有暖气 yó nwǔn·chèe
heater 暖气管 nwǔn·chèe gwǔn
heating 暖气 nwǔn·chèe
heavy 重 jòong
Hello. (general greeting) 你好。
　née·hǎo
Hello. (polite, Beijing) 您好。
　nín·hǎo
Hello. (answering telephone) 喂。
　wày
helmet 头盔 tó·kwāy
help 帮助 bùng·joo
Help! 救人 jyò·rérn
hepatitis 肝炎 gūn·yén
her 她的 tā·der
herb (culinary) 香料 syūng·lyào
herb (medicinal) 药材 yào·tsǎi
herbalist 中药医生
　jōong·yào ēe·shērng
here 这里 jèr·lěe
heroin 海洛因 hǎi·lwòr·yīn
herring (canned salted fish)
　咸罐头 syén·yěw gwùn·to
high 高 gāo
high school 中学 jōong·shwáir
highchair 高凳 gāo·dèrng

highway 高速公路 gāo·soo gōong·lòo

hike ⓥ 步行 bòo·síng

hiking 狂野 gwùng·yǎir

hiking boots 步行靴子 bòo·síng swāir·zir

hiking route 步行道 bòo·síng dào

hill 山丘 shūn·chyó

Hindu 印度 yìn·doo

hire 租赁 zōo·lìn

his 他的 tā·der

historical (site) 名胜古迹 míng·shèng gǒo·jèe

history 历史 lèe·shír

hitchhike 搭车 tā·chēr

HIV 艾滋病毒 ài·zīr bìng·dóo

hockey 曲棍球 chēw·gòon chyó

holiday 度假 dòo·jyà

holidays 假期 jyà·chēe

home 家 jyā

homeless 无家可归 wóo·jyā kěr·gwāy

homemaker 管家 gwǔn·jyā

homosexual 同性恋 tóong·sìng lyèn

honey 蜂蜜 mèe·fēng

honeymoon 蜜月 mèe·ywàir

Hong Kong 香港 syūng·gǔng

horoscope 星象 sīng·syùng

horse 马 mǎ

horse riding 骑马 chée·mǎ

hospital 医院 êe·ywèn

hospitality 服务业 fóo·wòo yàir

hot 热 rèr

hot water 热水 rèr·shwǎy

hotel 酒店 jyǒ·dyèn

hour 小时 syǎo·shír

house 平房 píng·fúng

housework 家务 jyā·wòo

how 怎么 zěr·mer

how much 多少 dōr·shǎo

hug ⓝ 包住 bāo·jòo

huge 巨大 jèw·dà

human resources 人事 rérn·shìr

human rights 人权 rérn·chwén

humanities 文科 wén·kēr

hundred 百 bǎi

hungry (to be) 饿 èr

hunting 打猎 dǎ·lyàir

(to be in a) hurry 忙得 múng·der

hurt 疼 térng

husband 丈夫 jùng·foo

I

I 我 wǒr

ice 冰 bīng

ice axe 冰槌 bīng·chwáy

ice cream 冰激淋 bīng·jee·lín

ice hockey 冰球 bīng·chyó

ice skating 溜冰 lyó·bīng

identification 证件 jèrng·jyen

identification card (ID) 身份证 shèrn·fèrn jèrng

idiot 白痴 bái·chír

if 如果 róo·gwǒr

ill 有病 yǒ·bìng

immigration 移民 êe·mín

important 重要 jòong·yào

impossible 不可能 bòo kěr·nérng

in 在……里面 zài … lěe·myèn

in front of 在……前面 zài … chyén·myèn

included 包括 bāo·kwòr

income tax 个人税 gèr·rérn shwày

India 印度 yìn·doo

indicator 指标 jír·byāo

indigestion 肚子疼 dòo·zir tērng

indoor 室内 shìr·này

industry 行业 húng·yàir

infection 感染 gún·rǔn

inflammation 发炎 fā·yén

influenza 感冒 gǔn·mào

information 信息 sìn·sēe

ingredient 原料 ywén·lyào

inject 注射 jòo·shèr

injection 打针 dǎ·jērn
injured 受伤 shò·shūng
injury 伤害 shūng·hài
inner tube 内胎 này·tái
innocent 无辜 wóo·gòo
inside 里面 lēe·myèn
instructor 培训员 páy·sèwn ywén
insurance 保险 báo·syěn
interesting 有趣 yó·chèw
intermission 休息 syō·see
international 国际 gwór·jèe
Internet 因特网 yīn·tèr·wǔng
Internet café 网吧 wǔng·bā
interpreter 翻译 fún·èe
interview 采访 tsái·fǔng
invite 请客 chíng·kèr
Ireland 爱尔兰 ài·ár·lún
iron (for clothes) 熨斗 yèwn·dǒ
island 岛 dǎo
Israel 以色列 ēe·sìr·lyàir
it 它 tā
IT 信息技术 sìn·sēe jèe·shoo
Italy 意大利 èe·dà·lèe
itemised 分项的 fērn·syùng der
itinerary 日程表 rìr·chérng byǎo
IUD 宫内节育器
　　gōong·này jyǎir·yèw chèe

jacket 外壳 wài·kēr
jail 监狱 jyēn·yèw
jam 果酱 gwǒr·jyùng
January 一月 ēe·ywàir
Japan 日本 rìr·běrn
jar 玻璃罐头 bōr·lèe gwùn·tó
jasmine tea 花茶 hwā·chá
jaw 下巴 syà·bā
jealous 嫉妒 jèe·doo
jeans 牛仔裤 nyó·zǎi kòo
jeep 吉普车 jée·pōo chēr

jellyfish 海蜇 hǎi·jér
jet lag 时差反应 shír·chā fún·yìng
jewellery 首饰 shǒ·shìr
Jewish 犹太 yó·tài
jīn (measure) 斤 jīn
job 工作 gōong·zwòr
jogging 慢跑 mùn·pǎo
joke ⑪ 开玩笑 kāi wún·syào
journalist 记者 jèe·jǐr
journey 旅程 lěw·chérng
judge 法官 fǎ·gwūn
juice 果汁 gwǒr·jīr
July 七月 chēe·ywàir
jump 跳 pǎo
jumper (sweater) 毛衣 máo·ēe
June 六月 lyò·ywàir

K

kelp 海带 hǎi·dài
ketchup 番茄酱 fūn·chyáir jyùng
key 钥匙 yào·shir
keyboard 键盘 jyèn·pún
kick ⑫ 踢 tēe
kidney 肾 shèrn
kilogram 公斤 gōong·jīn
kilometre 公里 gōong·lěe
kind (nice) 善良 shàn·lyùng
kindergarten 幼儿园 yó·ǎr·ywèn
king 国王 gwór·wúng
kiosk 小卖部 syǎo mài·bòo
kiss ⑪ 亲吻 chīn·wérn
kiss ⑫ 亲 chīn
kitchen 厨房 chóo·fǔng
kiwifruit 猕猴桃 née·hó táo
knee 膝盖 chēe·gài
knife 刀 dāo
know 知道 jīr·dào
Korea (North) 朝鲜 cháo·syēn
Korea (South) 韩国 hún·gwór
Korean 朝鲜话 cháo·syēn hwà
kosher 清净 chīng·jìng
kuài (currency) 块 kwài

L

Labour Day 劳动节 láo·dòong·jyǎir
labourer 外劳 wài·láo
labyrinth 迷宫 mée·gōong
lace 花边 hwā·byēn
lake 湖 hóo
lamb 羊肉 yúng·rò
land 土地 tōo·dèe
landlady 房东 fáng·dōong
language 语言 yěw·yén
laptop 手提电脑 shǒ·tee dyén·nǎo
large 很大 hérn·dà
last (final) 最后的 zwày·hò·der
last (previous) 前一个 chyén·ēe·gèr
last (week) 上个 shùng·qer
late 迟到 chír·dào
later 以后 ēe·hò
laugh ⓥ 笑 syào
launderette 洗衣店 sěe·ēe·dyèn
laundry (clothes) 洗 sěe
law (study, professsion) 法律 fǎ·lèw
lawyer 律师 lèw·shīr
laxative 轻泻药 chīng·syàir yào
lazy 懒惰 lǔn·dòr
leader 领导 líng·dǎo
leaf 叶子 yàir·zir
leafy vegetables 青菜 chīng·tsài
learn 学习 swáir·sée
leather 皮革 pée·qér
lecturer 教师 jyào·shīr
ledge 边 byēn
left (direction) 左边 zwór·byēn
left luggage 行李寄存
   síng·lěe jèe·tsóon
left luggage (office) 寄存处
   jèe·tsóon chòo
left-wing 左派 zwór·pàl
leg 腿 twǎy
legal 法律 fǎ·lèw
legislation 法规 fǎ·gwǎy
legume 豆类 dò·lày

leisure 消遣 syāo·chyěn
lemon 柠檬 níng·mérng
lemonade 柠檬汁 níng·mérng jīr
lens 透镜 tò jìng
lentil 小扁豆 syáo·byěn·dò
lesbian 女同性恋
   něw tóong·sìng lyèn
less 少 shǎo
letter (mail) 信 sìn
lettuce 生菜 shērng·tsài
liar 骗子 pyèn·zir
library 图书馆 tóo shōo gwǔn
lice 头虱 tó·shīr
licence 执照 jír·jào
license plate number 车号 chēr·hào
lie (not stand) 躺下 tǔng·syà
life 生命 shērng·mìng
life jacket 救生衣 jyò·shērng ēe
lift (elevator) 电梯 dyén·tēe
light 光 gwūng
light (not heavy) 轻 chīng
light (of colour) 浅色 chyěn·sèr
light bulb 灯泡 dērng·pào
light meter 测光表 tser·gwūng byǎo
lighter (cigarette) 打火机
   dǎ·hwǒr jēe
like 同……一样 tóong … ēe·yùng
lime (chemical) 石灰 shír·hwǎy
linen (material) 亚麻布 yá·mǎ bòo
linen (sheets etc) 床单 chwúng dūn
lip balm 辰膏 chérn·gāo
lips 嘴辰 zwǎy·chérn
lipstick 口红 kǒ·hóong
liquor store 啤酒铺 pée·jyǒ tūn
listen (to) 听 tīng
litre 公升 gōong·shērng
little 小 syǎo
(a) little 一点 ēe·dyěn
live (inhabit) 住 jòo
liver 肝 gūn
lizard (gecko) 壁虎 bèe·hóo
local 地方 dèe·fūng

lock ⓝ 锁 swŏr

lock ⓥ 锁上 swŏr·shùng

locked (door, etc) 锁上了 swŏr·shùng ler

lollies 糖果 túng·gwŏr

long 长 chúng

look 看 kùn

look after 照顾 jào·goo

look for 找 jăo

lookout 望景台 wùng·jĭng tái

loose 很松 hĕrn·sōong

loose change 零钱 líng·chyén

lose 丢 dyō

lost (one's way) 迷路 mĕe·lòo

lost property 遗失物 ée·shìr wòo

(a) lot 好多 hăo·dōr

loud 吵 chăo

love ⓝ 爱情 ài·chíng

love ⓥ 爱 ài

lover 爱人 ài·rérn

low 低 dēe

lubricant 润滑油 ròon·hwá yó

luck 运气 yùn·chee

lucky 有福气 yó fŏo·chèe

luggage 行李 síng·lĕe

luggage lockers 行李寄存 síng·lĕe jèe·tsóon

luggage tag 行李标签 síng·lĕe byāo·chyén

lump 疙瘩 gēr·der

lunch 午饭 wŏo·fùn

lung 肺 fày

luxury 奢侈 shēr·chĭr

lychee 荔枝 lèe·jīr

lychee-flavoured soft drink 荔枝 lèe·jīr jìr

M

machine 机器 jēe·chee

magazine 杂志 zá·jìr

Mahjong 麻将 má·jyùng

mail (letters) 来信 lái·sìn

mail (postal system) 邮电 yó·dyèn

mailbox 信箱 sìn·syūng

main 主要 jŏo·yào

main road 干道 gŭn·dào

make 制作 jìr·zwòr

make-up 打扮 dă·bùn

mammogram 肉眼 rò·yěn

man (male person) 男人 nún·rérn

man (mankind) 人 rérn

manager 经理 jīng·lĕe

mandarin 橘子 jéw·zir

Mandarin 普通话 pŏo·tōong hwà

mango 芒果 múng·gwŏr

manual worker 手工 shŏ·gōong

many 好多 hăo·dōr

maotai (Chinese vodka) 茅台酒 máo·tái jyŏ

map 地图 dèe·tóo

March 三月 sūn·ywàir

marijuana 大麻 dà·má

marital status 婚姻身份 hōon·yīn shèrn·fèrn

market 市场 shìr·chŭng

marriage 婚姻 hōon·yīn

married 已婚 ěe hōon

marry 结婚 jyáir·hōon

martial arts 武术 wŏo·shòo

mass (Catholic) 礼拜 lĕe·bài

massage 按摩 ùn·mór

masseur/masseuse 按摩师傅 ùn·mór shìr·foo

mat 地毯 dèe·tún

match (sports) 比赛 bĕe·sài

matches (for lighting) 火柴 hwŏr·chái

mattress 垫子 dyèn·zir

May 五月 wŏo·ywàir

maybe 可能 kĕr·nérng

mayor 市长 shìr·jŭng

me 我 wŏr

meal 一顿饭 èe·dòon fùn

measles 麻疹 má·jĕrn

meat 肉 ròu

mechanic 车修理师 chēr syō·lěe shīr

medal tally 奖牌数 jyǔng·pái shòo

media 媒体 máy·tēe

medicine (study, profession) 医学 ēe·shwǎir

medicine (medication) 医药 ēe·yào

meditation 静坐 jìng·zwòr

meet 会见 hwày·jyèn

melon 瓜 gwā

member 成员 chérng·ywén

menstruation 月经 ywàir·jīng

menu 菜单 tsài·dūn

message 信条 sìn·tyáo

metal 金属 jīn·shoo

metre 米 měe

meter (taxi) 表 byāo

metro (train) 地铁 dèe·tyáir

metro station 地铁站 dèe·tyáir jùn

microwave (oven) 微波炉 wāy·bōr lōo

midday/noon 中午 jūng·wǒo

midnight 午夜 wǒo·yàir

migraine 偏头疼 pyēn tó·těrng

military 国防 gwór·fáng

military service 兵役 bīng·èe

milk 牛奶 nyó·nǎi

millet 小米 syáo·měe

millimetre 毫米 háo·měe

million 百万 bǎi·wùn

mince 肉馅 ròu·syèn

mineral water 矿泉水 kwùng·chwén shwǎy

minute 分钟 fēn·jōong

mirror 镜子 jìng·zir

miscarriage 流产 lyó·chǔn

miss (feel absence of) 想念 syǔng·nyèn

mistake 过失 gwòr·shīr

mix 调拌 tyáo·bùn

mobile phone 手机 shǒ·jēe

modem 猫 māo

modern 现代 syèn·dài

moisturiser 护肤膏 hòo·foo gāo

monastery (Buddhist) 佛寺 fór·sìr

Monday 星期一 sīng·chēe ēe

money 钱 chyén

Mongolia 蒙古 mérng·gǒo

monk 和尚 hér·shung

month 月 ywàir

monument 纪念碑 jèe·nyèn bēy

moon 月亮 ywàir·lyung

more 多 dōr

morning (after breakfast) 早上 zǎo·shùng

morning (before lunch) 上午 shùng·wǒo

morning sickness 晨吐症 chérn·ŏ·jèrng

mosque 清真寺 chīng·jērn sìr

mosquito 蚊子 wérn·zir

mosquito coil 蚊香 wérn·syūng

mosquito net 蚊帐 jūng·perng

mother 母亲 mǒo·chīn

mother-in-law 岳母 ywàir·mǒo

motorbike 摩托车 mó·twōr chēr

motorboat 赛船 sài·chwún

motorcycle 摩托车 mó·twōr chēr

motorway (tollway) 收费公路 shō·fày gōong·lòu

mountain 山 shūn

mountain bike 山地车 shūn·dèe chēr

mountain climbing 爬山 pá·shūn

mountain path 山路 shūn·lòu

mountain range 山脉 shūn·mài

mouse 耗子 hào·zir

mouth 口 kǒ

movie 电影 dyèn·yǐng

Mr 先生 syēn·shērng

Mrs 女士 něw·shìr

Ms/Miss 小姐 syáo·jyǎir

MSG 味精 wày·jīng

mud 泥巴 née·bā

mum 妈妈 mā·ma

mumps 麻疹 má·jěrn

mung beans (red) 红豆 hóong·dò

murder ⓝ 杀人犯 shā·rérn fùn

murder ⓥ 杀 shā

muscle 瘦肉 shò·rò

museum 博物馆 bó·wòo gwǔn

mushroom 蘑菇 mó·gōo

music 音乐 yīn·ywàir

music shop 音像店 yīn·syung dyèn

musician 音乐家 yīn·ywàir jyā

Muslim 穆斯林 mòo·sīr·lín

mussel 青蚌 chīng·bùng

mustard 芥末 jyàir·mor

mustard greens 油菜 yó·tsài

mute 哑巴 yǎ·ba

my 我的 wǒr·der

N

nail clippers 剪指刀 jyén·jǐr dāo

name 名字 míng·zìr

napkin 餐巾 tsūn·jīn

nappy 尿裤 nyào·kòo

nappy rash 尿裤疹 nyào·kòo·jěrn

National Day 国庆节 gwór·chìng·jyáir

national park 自然保护区
    zìr·rún bǎo·hòo chēw

nationality 国籍 gwór·jée

nature 大自然 dà zìr·rún

nausea 反胃 fǔn·wày

near 近 jìn

nearby 附近 fòo·jìn

nearest 最近 zwày·jìn

necessary 必要的 bèe·yào der

necklace 项链 syùng·lyèn

nectarine 油桃 yó·táo

need ⓥ 需要 sēw·yào

needle (sewing) 针线 jērn·syèn

needle (syringe) 注射针 jòo·shèr jērn

negative 消极 syāo·jée

neither 两个都不 lyǔng·ger dō bòo

net 网 wǔng

Netherlands 荷兰 hér·lún

never 从来不 tsóong·lái bòo

new 新 sīn

New Year's Day 元旦 ywén·dùn

New Year's Eve 元旦除夕
    ywěn·dùn chóo·sēe

New Zealand 新西兰 sīn·sēe·lún

news 新闻 sīn·wérn

news stand 报纸摊 bào·jǐr tūn

newspaper 报纸 bào·jǐr

next (month) 下个 syà·ger

next to 旁边 púng·byēn

nice 善良 shùn·lyùng

nickname 昵称 nèe·chērng

night 晚上 wǔn·shùng

night out 晚上活动
    wǔn·shùng hwór·dòong

nightclub 夜总会 yàir·zōong·hwàiy

no 不对 bóo·dwày

no vacancy 没空 máy·kòong

noisy 吵 chǎo

none 一个也没有 ēe·gèr yǎir máy·yǒ

nonsmoking 不吸烟 bòo sēe·yēn

noodle house 面摊 myèn·tūn

noodles 面条 myèn·tyáo

noon 中午 jūng·wǒo

north 北边 bǎy·byēn

Norway 挪威 nór·wāy

nose 鼻子 bée·zir

not 不是 bóo·shìr

notebook 笔记本 běe·jèe běrn

nothing 一无所有 ēe·woo swór·yǒ

November 十一月 shír·ēe ywàir

now 现在 syèn·zài

nuclear energy 核发电 hér·fā·dyèn

nuclear testing 核试验 hér·shìr·yèn

nuclear waste 核废物 hér·fày·wòo

number 号码 hào·mǎ

numberplate 车牌 chēr·pái

nun 尼姑 née·gōo

nurse 护士 hòo·shìr

nut 果仁 gwǒr·rérn

O

oats 燕麦片 yèn·mài pyèn
occupation 工作 gōong·zwòr
occupied 有事 yǒ·shìr
ocean 大海 dà·hǎi
October 十月 shír·ywàir
off (spoiled) 过时 gwòr·shír
office 办公室 bùn·gōong shír
office worker 白领工 bái lǐng gōong
often 经常 jīng·chǔng
oil (food) 白油 shír yó
oil (petroleum) 汽油 chèe·yó
old 老 lǎo
old man (derogatory) 老头 lǎo·tó
old man (respectful) 大爷 dà·yair
old woman (derogatory) 老太太
  lǎo·tài·tai
old woman (respectful) 大妈 dà·mā
Olympic Games 奥运会
  ào·yèwn hwày
Olympic record 奥运纪录
  ào·yèwn jèe·lòo
omelette 炒鸡蛋 chǎo jēe·dùn
on 以上 ēe shùng
on time 准时 jǒn·shír
once 一次 ēe·tsìr
one 一个 ēe·gèr
one-way (ticket) 单程 dūn·chéng
onion 洋葱 yúng·tsōong
only 只有 jír·yǒ
oolong tea 乌龙茶 ōo·lóong chá
open ⓐ 开放 kāi·fùng
open ⓥ 打开 dà·kāi
opening hours 营业时间
  yíng·yàir shír·jyēn
opera (Chinese) 京剧 jīng·jèw
opera (Western) 歌剧 gēr·jèw
opera house 剧场 jèw·chǔng
operation (medical) 手术 shǒ·shòo
operator 操作工 tsāo·zwòr·gōong
opinion 看法 kùn·fǎ

opposite 对面 dwày·myèn
optometrist 眼科医生
  yěn·kēr ēe·sherng
or 或者 hwòr·jǐr
orange (fruit) 橙子 chéng·zir
orange (colour) 橙色 chéng·sèr
orange juice 橙汁 chéng·jīr
orchestra 交响乐队
  jyāo·syǔng ywàir·dwày
order (arrangement) 顺序 shòon·sew
order (food) 点菜 dyěn·tsài
ordinary 普通 pǒo·tōong
orgasm 高潮 gāo·cháo
original 开拓性 kāi twòr àing
other 其他 chée·tā
our 我们的 wǒr·mern
out of order 坏了 hwài·ler
outside 外面 wài·myen
ovarian cyst 卵巢胀包
  lwǔn·tsáo nóong·bāo
ovary 卵巢 lwǔn·tsáo
oven 烤箱 kǎo·syūng
overcoat 大衣 dà·ēe
overdose 过量 gwòr·lyùng
overnight 过夜 gwòr·yàir
overseas 海外 hǎi·wài
owe 欠 chyèn
owner 主人 jǒo·rérn
oxygen 氧气 yúng·chèe
oyster 蚝 háo
oyster sauce 蚝油 háo·yó
ozone layer 臭氧气层
  chò yúng·chèe tsérng

P

pacemaker 心律调节器
  sīn·lòo tyáo·jyáir chèe
pacifier (dummy) 奶嘴 nái·zwǎy
package 包裹 bāo·gwǒr
packet (general) 包 bāo
padlock 锁 swǒr

page 页 yàir

pagoda 八角塔 bā·jyǎo·tá

pain 疼 térng

painful 很疼 hěrn·térng

painkiller 止痛药 jǐr·tòong·yào

painter 画家 hwà·jyā

painting (a work) 画 hwà

painting (the art) 画画儿 hwà·hwàr

pair 对 dwày

Pakistan 巴基斯坦 bā·jēe·sīr·tún

palace 宫殿 gōong·dyèn

pan 小锅 syǎo·gwōr

panda 熊猫 syúng·māo

pants (trousers) 长裤 chúng·kòo

panty liners 卫生巾 wày·shērng·jīn

pantyhose 长袜 chúng·wà

pap smear 抹片检查
tsā·pyèn jyěn·chá

papaya 木瓜 mòo·gwā

paper 织 jīr

papers (official documents) 证件
jèrng·jyèn

paperwork 手续 shǒ·sèw

paraplegic 双肢障 shwūng·jīr·jùng

parcel 包裹 bāo·gwǒr

parents 父母 fòo·mǒo

park 公园 gōong·ywén

park (a car) 停 (车) tíng (chēr)

parliament 议会 èe·hwày

part (component) 部分 bòo·fern

part-time 零时工 líng·shír·gōong

party (night out) 逛酒吧
gwùng jyǒ·bā

party (politics) 党 dǔng

pass (mountain) 关口 gwūn·kǒ

pass (permit) 许可证 séw·kěr·jèrng

pass 通过 tòong·gwòr

passenger 乘客 chérng·kèr

passionfruit 鸡蛋果 jēe·dùn gwǒr

passport 护照 hòo·jào

passport number 护照号码
hòo·jào hào·mǎ

past 过去 gwòr·chèw

pasta 意大利面 èe·dà·lèe myèn

pastry (French bread) 法式面包
fǎ·shìr myèn·bāo

path 小路 syǎo·lòo

pavillion 亭子 tíng·zir

pawpaw 木瓜 mòo·gwā

pay ⊙ 付 fòo

payment 付款 fòo·kwǔn

pea shoots 豆苗 dò·myáo

peace 和平 hér·píng

peach 桃子 táo·zir

peak (mountain) 山顶 shūn·dǐng

peanut 花生 hwā·shērng

pear 梨 lée

peasant 农民 nóong·mín

pedal 脚凳 jyǎo·dèrng

pedestrian 行人 síng·rérn

pedicab 三轮车 sūn·lóon·chēr

Peking duck 北京烤鸭
běy·jīng kǎo·yā

Peking opera 京剧 jīng·jòo

pen (ballpoint) 钢笔 gūng·běe

pencil 铅笔 chyén·běe

penis 阳具 yúng·jòo

penknife 小刀 syǎo·dāo

pensioner 退休职工
twày·syō jír·gōong

people 人 rérn

pepper (vegetable) 青椒 chīng·jyāo

pepper (spice) 辣椒 là·jyāo

per (day) 每 (天) máy·tyēn

per cent 百分比 bǎi·fērn·běe

perfect 完美 wún·měy

performance 演出 yén·chōo

perfume 香水 syūng·shwǎy

period pain 月经痛 ywàir·jīng tòong

permission 许可 séw·kěr

permit 许可证 séw·kěr jèrng

persimmon 柿子 shìr·zir

person 人 rérn

petition 投诉 tó·sòo

petrol 汽油 chèe·yó
petrol station 汽油站 chèe·yó jùn
pharmacy 西药房 sēe·yào fúng
phone box 公用电话
　gōong·yòong dyèn·hwà
phone card 电话卡 dyèn·hwà kǎ
photo 照片 jào·pyèn
photographer 摄影家 shèr·yǐng jyā
photography 摄影 shèr·yǐng
phrasebook 语句书 yěw·jèw·shōo
pickles 咸菜 syén·tsài
picnic 野餐 yěr·tsūn
ple 馅饼 syèn·bǐng
piece 块 kwài
pig 猪 jōo
pigeon 鸽子 gēr·zir
pill 药片 yào·pyèn
Pill (the) 避孕药 bèe·yèwn yào
pillow 枕头 jěn·tó
pineapple 菠萝 bōr·lór
pink 粉色 fēn·sèr
pistachio 开心果 kāi·sīn·gwǒr
PLA (People's Liberation Army)
　解放军 jyǎir·fàng jēwn
PRC (People's Republic of China)
　中华人民共和国
　jōong·hwá rérn·mín gòong·hér gwór
PSB (Public Security Bureau)
　公安局 gōong·ūn jéw
place 地方 dèe·fūng
place of birth 出生地
　chōo·shērng dèe
plane 飞机 fāy·jēe
planet 星球 sīng·chyó
plant 植物 jír·wòo
plastic 塑料 sòo·lyào
plate 盘子 pún·zir
plateau 高原 gāo·ywén
platform 站台 jùn·tái
play (cards) 打 dǎ
play (guitar) 弹 tún
play (theatre) 剧 jèw

plug (bath) 塞子 sāi·zir
plug (electricity) 插头 chā·tó
plum 梅子 máy·zir
pocket 口袋 kǒ·dài
pocket knife 小刀 syǎo·dāo
poetry 诗歌 shīr·gēr
point ⓝ 点 dyěn
point ⓥ 指 jír
poisonous 有毒 yǒ·dóo
police 警察 jǐng·chá
police officer 警察 jǐng·chá
public security office 公安 gōong·ūn
police station 派出所 pài·chōo swǒr
policy 政策 jèrng·tsèr
politician 政治家 jèrng·jìr jyā
politics 政治 jèrng·jìr
pollen 花粉 hwā·fěn
pollution 污染 wōo·rǔn
pool (game) 台球 tái·chyó
pool (swimming) 游泳池
　yó·yǒong chír
poor 穷 chyóong
popular 流行 lyó·síng
pork 猪肉 jōo·ò
pork sausage 香肠 syāng chúng
port (sea) 港口 gǔng·kǒ
portrait sketcher 画像师
　hwà syùng shīr
positive 正 jèrng
possible 有可能 yó·kěr·nérng
post code 邮电号码 yó·dyèn hào·mǎ
post office 邮局 yó·jéw
postage 邮电 yó·dyèn
postcard 明信片 míng·sìn·pyèn
poster 画报 hwà·bào
pot (ceramics) 瓶 píng
pot (dope) 大麻 dà·má
potato 土豆 tǔo·dò
pottery 陶器 táo·chèe
pound (money, weight) 镑 bùng
poverty 贫穷 pín·chyóong
powder 粉 fěn

power 权利 chwén·lèe
prawn 虾子 syā·zir
prayer 祈祷 chée·dǎo
prayer book 祈祷书 chée·dǎo shōo
prefer 偏喜欢 pyēn sēe·hwūn
pregnancy test kit 妊娠试验 rèrn·shērn shìr·yèn
pregnant 怀孕 hwái·yèwn
prehistoric art 原始艺术 ywén·shǐ èe·shoo
premenstrual tension 经前紧张 jīng·chyén jǐn·jūng
prepare 准备 jún·bày
prescription 药方 yào·fūng
present (gift) 礼物 lée·wòo
present (time) 现在 syèn·zài
president 总统 zóong·tŏong
pressure 压力 yā·lèe
pressure point massage 经纬按摩 jīng·wáy ùn·mór
pretty 漂亮 pyào·lyung
price 价格 jyà·gér
priest 牧师 mòo·shir
prime minister 首相 shŏu·syùng
printer (computer) 打印机 dǎ·yìn·jēe
prison 监狱 jyēn·yèw
prisoner 罪犯 zwày·fùn
private 私人 sīr·rérn
produce ⓥ 生产 shēng·chǔn
profit 利润 lèe·ròon
program 节目 jyáir·mòo
projector 投影机 tó·yǐng·jēe
promise 发誓 fā·shìr
prostitute 妓女 jèe·něw
protect 保护 báo·hòo
protected (animal, etc) 受保护动物 shò báo·hòo dòong·woo
protest ⓝ 游行 léw·síng
protest ⓥ 抗议 kùng·èe
provisions 预备品 yèw·bày·pín
pub (bar) 酒吧 jyŏ·bā
public gardens 公园 gōong·ywén

public relations 公共关系 gōong·gòong gwūn·see
public telephone 公用电话 gōong·yòong dyèn·hwà
public toilet 公厕 gōong·tsèr
publishing 出版 chōo·bǔn
pull 拉 lā
pump ⓝ 打气筒 dǎ·chèe·tóong
pumpkin 南瓜 nún·gwā
pumpkin seeds 瓜子 gwā·zir
puncture 穿孔 chwūn·kǒong
pure 纯 chóon
purple 紫色 zǐr·sèr
purse 钱包 chyén·bāo
push 推 twāy
put 放 fùng

Q

qi 气 chèe
quadriplegic 四肢障 sìr·jīr·jùng
qualifications 学历 shwáir·lèe
quality 质量 jìr·lyùng
quarantine 免疫站 myén·èe·jùn
quarter 四分之一 sìr·fèrn jir êe
queen 女王 něw·wúng
question 问题 wèrn·tèe
queue 排队 pái·dwày
quick 快 kwài
quiet 安静 ūn·jìng
quit 辞职 tsír·jír

R

rabbit 兔子 tòo·zir
race (sport) 比赛 běe·sài
racetrack 赛场 sài·chǔng
racing bike 赛车 sài·chēr
racism 种族歧视 jŏong·zóo chée·shìr
racquet 拍子 pái·zir
radiator 暖气管 nwún·chèe·gwūn
radio 收音机 shò·yīn·jēe
radish 萝卜 lór·bor

railway station 火车站 hwŏr·chēr·jùn

rain ⓝ 下雨 syà·yĕw

raincoat 雨衣 yĕw·ēe

raisin 葡萄干 póo·tào·gūn

rape ⓝ 强奸 chyúng·jyēn

rare (uncommon) 罕见 hūn·jyèn

rare (about food) 半熟半生
bùn·shó bùn·shērng

rash 疹子 jĕrn·zir

raspberry 山楂 shūn·máy

rat 老鼠 láo·shòo

rave 电子舞会 dyùn·air wŭu·hwày

raw 生 shērng

razor 剃刀 tēe·dāo

razor blade 剃刀片 tēe·dāo·pyèn

read 读 dóo

reading 看书 kùn·shōo

ready 做好了 zwòr·hăo·ler

real estate agent 房产代理
fúng·chún dài·lĕe

realistic 现实 syèn·shír

rear (seat etc) 后 hò

reason 原因 ywén·ìn

receipt 发票 fā·pyào

recently 最近 zwày·jìn

recommend 推荐 twāy·jyèn

record ⓥ 录 lòo

recording 录音 lòo·yīn

recyclable 可回收 kĕr hwáy·shō

recycle 回收 hwáy·shō

red 红色 hóong·sèr

referee 裁判 tsái·pùn

reference (letter) 推荐（信）
twāy·jyèn·(sìn)

reflexology 反射疗法 fún·shèr lyáo·fă

refrigerator 冰箱 bīng·syūng

refugee 难民 nùn·mín

refund ⓝ 退钱 twày·chyén

refuse 拒绝 jèw·jwáir

regional 地方性 dèe·fūng sìng

registered mail/post 挂号 gwà·hào

rehydration salts 补液盐 bŏo·yàir·yén

reiki 灵气按摩 líng·chèe ùn·mór

relationship 关系 gwūn·see

relax 放松 fùng·sōong

relic 活恐龙 hwór kŏong·lóong

religion 宗教 zōong·jyào

religious 宗教性的
zōong·jyào sìng·der

remote 偏僻 pyēn·pèe

remote control 遥控 yáo·kòong

rent 租赁 zōo·lín

repair 修理 syō·lĕe

republic 共和国 gòong·hér·gwór

reservation (booking) 预定 yèw·dìng

rest 休息 syō·see

restaurant 饭馆 fùn·gwŭn

resumé (CV) 简历 jyén·lèe

retired 退休 twày·syō

return (come back) 回来 hwáy·lăi

return (ticket) 双程（票）
shwūng·chéng·(pyào)

review ⓝ 复查 fòo·chá

rhythm 节奏 jyáir·zò

ribs (beef) 排背 pái·gŏo

rice (raw) 大米 dà·mĕe

rice (cooked) 米饭 mĕe·fùn

rice cake 黏糕 nyén·gāo

rice vinegar (white) 白醋 bái·tsòo

rich (wealthy) 有钱 yŏ·chyén

ride (horse) ⓥ 骑 chée

right (correct) 对 dwày

right (direction) 右边 yò·byēn

right-wing 右派 yò·pài

ring (on finger) 戒指 jyài·jīr

ring (on phone) 打（电话）dă (dyèn·hwà)

rip-off 宰人 zāi·rérn

risk ⓝ 风险 fērng·syĕn

river 川 chwūn

road 道路 dào·loo

road map 交通地图 jyāo·tōong·dèe·tóo

rob 偷 tō

rock (stone) 石头 shír·to

rock (music) 摇滚 yáo·gŏon

rock climbing 攀岩 pūn·yén
rock group 摇滚乐队 yáo·gŏon ywàir·dwày
roll (bread) 小面包 syăo myèn·bāo
rollerblading 旱冰 hùn·bīng
romantic 浪漫 lùng·mùn
room 房间 fúng·jyēn
room number 房间号 fúng·jyēn hào
rope 绳子 shérng·zir
round 圆 ywén
roundabout 圆环岛 ywén·hwún·dǎo
route 路线 lòo·syen
rowing 划船 hwā·chwún
rubbish 垃圾 lā·jēe
rubella 德国麻疹 dér·gwór má·jěrn
rug 地毯 dèe·tǔn
rugby 英式橄榄球 yīng·shìr gún·lǔn chyó
ruins 废墟 fày·sēw
rule ⑩ 规定 gwǎy·dìng
run 跑 pǎo
running (sport) 跑步 pǎo·bòo
runny nose 流鼻涕 lyó bée·tèe

S

sad 郁闷 yèw·mern
saddle 马鞍 mǎ·ūn
safe 安全 ūn·chwén
safebox 保险箱 báo·syěn syúng
safe sex 安全性交 ūn·chwén sìng·jyáo
saint 圣人 shèrng·rérn
salad 沙拉 shā·lā
salami 香肠 syúng·chúng
salary 薪水 sīn·shwǎy
sale 大甩卖 dà shwāi·mài
sales tax 销售税 syāo·sho shwày
salmon 三文鱼 sūn·wérn yéw
salt 盐 yén
same 一样 ēe·yùng
sand 沙子 shā·zir
sandal 凉鞋 lyúng·syǎir

sanitary napkin 卫生巾 wày·shērng·jīn
sardine 咸鱼 syén·yéw
SARS 萨斯 sǎ·sīr
Saturday 星期六 sīng·chēe lyò
sauce 浆 jyùng
sauna 桑那 sūng·ná
sausage 香肠 syúng·chúng
say 说 shwōr
scarf 头巾 tó·jīn
scenic area 风景区 fērng·jǐng·chēw
school 学校 shwáir·syào
science 科学 kēr·shwáir
scientist 科学家 kēr·shwáir jyā
scissors 剪刀 jyén·dāo
score 进球 jìn·chyó
Scotland 苏克兰 sōo·kèr·lún
scrambled (stir-fried) 炒(鸡蛋) chăo
sculpture 塑像 sòo·syùng
sea 海 hǎi
sea cucumber 海参 hǎi·shērn
seafood 海鲜 hǎi·syēn
seasick 晕船 yèwn·chwún
seaside 海边 hǎi·byēn
season 季节 jèe·jyáir
seat (place) 座位 zwòr·wày
seatbelt 安全带 ūn·chwén·dài
second ⑩ 秒 myāo
second ⓐ 第二 dèe·àr
second-class 二等 àr·děrng
second-hand 二手 àr·shó
second-hand shop 二手店 àr·shó dyèn
secretary 秘书 mèe·shoo
see 看见 kùn·jyèn
self service 自助 zír·jòo
self-employed 个体户 gèr·těe hòo
selfish 自私 zìr·sīr
sell 卖 mài
send 寄送 jèe·sòong
sensible 有理的 yó·lěe·der
sensual 肉体的 rò·těe·der

separate 分开的 fērn·kāi·der
September 九月 jyŏ·ywàir
serious 严肃 yěn·sòo
service 服务 fóo·wòo
service charge 服务费 fóo·wòo fày
service station 加油站 jyā·yó jùn
serviette 纸巾 jír·jín
sesame paste 芝麻酱 jīr·ma jùng
several 好几个 háo jěe·ger
sew (mend) 补 bŏo
sew (not mend) 缝纫 fěrng·rèrn
sex 男女事 nún·něw shìr
sexism 重男轻女
　　jòong·nún chīng·něw
sexy 性感 sìng·gŭn
shade ⓝ 树荫 shòo·yín
shadow 影子 yĭng·zir
shallots 小葱 syáo tsoong
shampoo 香波 syūng·bōr
Shanghai 上海 shùng·hǎi
shape ⓝ 形状 síng·jwùng
share 公用 gōong·yòong
shave 刮脸 gwā·lyěn
shaving cream 剃须膏 tèe·sēw·gāo
she 她 tā
sheep 绵羊 myěn·yúng
sheet (bed) 床单 chwúng·dūn
shelf 架子 jyà·zir
shiatsu 指压按摩 jír·yā ùn·mór
shingles (illness) 带状泡疹
　　dài·jwùng pào·jěrn
ship 船 chwún
shirt 衬衫 chérn·shūn
shoe 鞋 syáir
shoe shop 鞋店 syáir·dyèn
shoes 鞋子 syáir·zir
shoot 打枪 dǎ·chyūng
shop ⓝ 店 dyèn
shop ⓥ 买东西 mái dōong·see
shopping 逛街 gwùng·jyāir
shopping centre 商场 shūng·chúng
short (height) 矮 ǎi

short (length) 短 dwǔn
shortage 紧缺 jǐn·chwáir
shorts 短裤 dwǔn·kòo
shoulder 肩膀 jyēn·bǔng
shout 喊 hǔn
show 表演 byáo·yěn
shower 浴室 yèw·shir
shrine 庙 myào
shut 关 gwūn
shy 害羞 hài·syō
sick 病 bìng
side 旁边 púng·byēn
sign 牌子 pái·zir
signature 签名 chyēn·míng
silk 丝绸 sīr·chó
silver 银子 yín·zir
silver medal 银牌 yín·pái
similar 同样 toong·yùng
simple 简单 jyěn·dūn
since (May) 从 (五月)
　　tsóong (wǒo ywàir)
sing 唱歌 chùng·gēr
Singapore 星加坡 sīng·jyā·pōr
singer 歌手 gēr·shó
single (person) 单人 dūn·rérn
single room 单人间 dūn·rérn jyēn
singlet 背心 bày·sīn
sister (elder) 姐姐 jyǎir·jyáir
sister (younger) 妹妹 mày·may
sisters 姐妹 jyǎir·mày
sit 坐下 zwòr·syà
size (general) 大小 dà·syáo
skateboarding 滑板 hwá·bǔn
ski ⓥ 滑雪 hwá·shwǎir
skiing 滑雪 hwá·shwǎir
skin 皮肤 pée·foo
skirt 裙子 chéwn·zir
skull 窟窿 kōo·loong
sky 天 tyēn
sleep 睡觉 shwày·jyào
sleeping bag 睡袋 shwày·dài
sleeping berth 卧铺 wōr·pòo

S

english-mandarin

229

sleeping car 卧铺车厢
wŏr·pòo chēr·syūng

sleeping pills 安眠药 ūn·myén yào

sleepy 发困 fā·kùn

slice (cake) 蛋糕 dùn·gāo

slide (film) 幻灯片 hwùn·dērng pyèn

slippers 拖鞋 twōr·syáir

slow 慢 mùn

slowly 慢慢的 mar·mùn·der

small 小 syăo

smaller 更小 gērng·syăo

smallest 最小 zwày·syăo

smell 味道 wày·dào

smile 微笑 wāy·syào

smoke 抽烟 chō·yēn

snack 小吃 syăo·chīr

snail 蜗牛 wōr·nyó

snake 蛇 shér

snorkelling 潜水游 chyén·shwăy·yó

snow 雪 shwāir

snow pea 荷兰豆 hér·lún dò

snowboarding 滑雪板
hwá·shwáir·bŭn

soap 肥皂 fáy·zào

soap opera 肥皂剧 fáy·zào jèw

soccer 足球 zóo·chyó

social welfare 社会福利
shèr·hwày fóo·lèe

socialism 社会主义 shèr·hwày jŏo·èe

socialist 社会主义战士
shèr·hwày jŏo·èe jùn·shir

sock(s) 袜子 wà·zir

soft drink 汽水 chèe·shwăy

soft seat 软座 rún·zwòr

soft sleeper 软卧 rún·wòr

soldier 军人 jēwn·rérn

some 一些 ēe·syāir

someone 某人 mŏ·rérn

something 一个什么的
èe·ger shér·mer der

sometimes 偶尔 ó·ăr

son 儿子 ăr·zir

song 歌曲 gēr·chĕw

soon 快 kwài

sore 疮口 chwùng·kŏ

soup 汤 tūng

sour plum drink 酸梅汤
swūn·máy·tūng

south 南 nún

souvenir 纪念品 jèe·nyèn pĭn

souvenir shop 纪念品店
jèe·nyèn·pĭn dyèn

soybean 黄豆 hwúng·dò

soy milk (fresh) 豆浆 dò·jyūng

soy milk (powdered) 豆奶粉
dò·năi fĕrn

soy sauce 酱油 jyūng·yó

space 空间 kōong·jyēn

Spain 西班牙 sēe·būn·yă

sparkling wine 香槟 syūng·bīn

speak 说话 shwōr·hwà

special 特别 tèr·byáir

specialist 专家 jwūn·jyā

speed 速度 sòo·dòo

speed limit 最高车速
zwài·gāo chēr·sòo

speedometer 速度表 sòo·dòo byăo

spider 蜘蛛 jīr·jòo

spinach 菠菜 bór·tsài

spirits (Chinese alcohol) 白酒 bái·jyŏ

spoiled 烂掉了 lùn·dyào·ler

spoon 勺 sháo

sport 体育 tĕe·yèw

sports store 体育用品店
tĕe·yèw yòong·pĭn dyèn

sportsperson 体育家 tĕe·yèw jyā

sprain 扭伤 nyŏ·shwūng

spring (coil) 弹簧 tún·hwúng

spring (season) 春天 chōon·tyēn

Spring Festival 春节 chōon·jyáir

square (town) 广场 gwúng·chŭng

stadium 体育场 tĕe·yèw chŭng

stairway 台阶 tái·jyáir

stale 过时 gwòr·shír

stamp 邮票 yó·pyào

stand-by ticket 站台票 jùn·tái pyào

star 星星 sīng·sing

(four-)star (四)星级 (sìr) sīng·jée

star anise 八角 bā·jyáo

start 开头 kāi·tó

start 开始 kāi·shír

station 车站 chēr·jùn

stationer's (shop) 文具店 wérn·jèw dyèn

statue 塑像 sòo·syùng

stay (at a hotel) 住 jòo

stay (in one place) 留住 lyó·zài

steak (beef) 排骨 pái·gǔo

steal 偷 tō

steamed bun 馒头 mún·tó

steep 陡 dō

step 台阶 tái·jyāir

stereo 音响 yīn·syǔng

still water 净水 jìng·shwǎy

stockings 长袜 chúng·wà

stolen 盗窃的 dào·chyàir·der

stomach 肚子 dòo·zir

stomachache (to have a) 肚子疼 dòo·zir térng

stone 石头 shír·to

stoned (drugged) 吃毒晕晕的 chír·dóo yèwn·yèwn·der

stop (bus, tram, etc) 停 tíng

stop (cease) 停止 tíng·jǐr

stop (prevent) 防止 fúng·jǐr

Stop! 救人 jyò·rérn

storm 风暴 fēng·bào

story 故事 gòo·shìr

stove 炉子 lóo·zir

straight 直接 jír·jyāir

strange 奇怪 chée·gwài

stranger 陌生人 mòr·shērng·rérn

strawberry 草莓 tsǎo·máy

stream 山泉 shūn·chwén

street 街头 jyāir·tó

street market 街市 jyāir·shìr

strike 罢工 bà·gōng

string 绳子 shérng·zir

stroke (medical) 中风 jòong·fērng

stroll 散步 sùn·bòo

stroller 婴儿推车 yīng·ár twǎy·chēr

strong 有劲 yǒ·jìn

stubborn 固执 gòo·jír

student 学生 shwǎir·shērng

studio 工作室 gōong·zwòr shìr

stupid 愚蠢 yéw·chǒon

style 风格 fēng·gúr

subtitles 字幕 zìr·mòo

suburb 郊区 jyāo·chēw

subway 地铁 dèe·tyǎir

suffer 吃苦 chír·kǒo

sugar 砂糖 shā·túng

sugar cane 甘蔗 gūn·jér

suitcase 旅行箱 lěw·sìng syūng

summer 夏天 syà·tyēn

sun 太阳 tài·yúng

sunblock 防晒油 fúng·shài yó

sunburn 晒伤 shài·shung

Sunday 星期天 sīng chēe tyēn

sunflower seeds 瓜子 gwā·zir

sunglasses 墨镜 mòr·jìng

sunny 很晒 hérn·jyǒ

sunrise 日出 rìr chōo

sunset 日落 rìr·lwòr

sunstroke 中暑 jòong·shǒo

supermarket 超市 chāo·shìr

superstition 迷信 mée·sìn

supporter (politics) 支持者 jīr·chír jěr

supporter (sport) 球迷 chyó·mée

surf (waves) 海浪 hǎi·lùng

surface mail (land) 陆运 lòo·yèwn

surface mail (sea) 海运 hǎi·yèwn

surfboard 冲浪板 chōong·lùng bǔn

surfing 冲浪 chōong·lùng

surname 姓 sìng

surprise 惊讶 jīng·yà

sweater 上衣 shùng·ēe

Sweden 瑞典 rày·dyèn
sweet 甜 tyén
sweet potato 地瓜 dèe·gwā
sweets 甜点 tyén·dyèn
swim 游泳 yó·yǒong
swimming (sport) 游泳 yó·yǒong
swimming pool 游泳池 yó·yǒong chír
swimsuit 游泳衣 yó·yǒong êe
Switzerland 瑞士 rày·shir
swollen 肿了起来 jòong·ler chêe·lái
synagogue 犹太教堂 yó·tài jyào·tǔng
synthetic 人为的 rérn·wéi·der
syringe 注射针 jòo·shìr jèrn

T

table 桌子 jwōr·zir
table tennis 乒乓球 pīng·pūng chyó
tablecloth 桌布 jwōr·bòo
tail 尾巴 wǎy·ba
tailor 裁缝 tsái·fèrng
Taiwan 台湾 tái·wūn
take 拿走 nár·zǒ
take a photo 照相 jào·syùng
talk 谈话 tún·hwà
tall 高 gāo
tampon 棉条 myén·tyáo
Taoism 道教 dào·jyào
tap 水龙头 shwǎy·lóong·tó
tap water 自来水 zìr·lái shwǎy
tape (recording) 磁带 tsír·dài
tasty 好香 hǎo·syūng
tax 税 shwày
taxi 出租车 chōo·zōo chēr
taxi stand 出租车站
　chōo·zōo chēr jùn
tea 茶 chá
teahouse 茶馆 chá·gwǔn
tea pot 茶壶 chá·hóo
teacher 老师 lǎo·shìr
team 运动队 yèwn·dòong dwày
technique 做法 zwòr·fǎ
teeth 牙齿 yá·chǐr

telegram 电报 dyèn·bào
telephone 电话 dyèn·hwà
telephone 打电话 dǎ dyèn·hwà
telescope 望远镜 wùng·yěwn jìng
television 电视 dyèn·shìr
tell 告诉 gào·soo
temperature (weather) 温度
　wērn·doo
temperature (fever) 发烧 fā·shāo
temple 寺庙 sìr·myào
tennis 网球 wǔng·chyó
tennis court 网球场
　wǔng·chyó chǔng
tent 帐篷 jùng·perng
terrible 可怕的 kěr·pà der
test 考试 kǎo·shìr
thank 道谢 dào·syàir
thankyou 谢谢 syàir·syàir
that (one) 那个 này·ger
theatre 剧场 jèw·chǔng
their 他们的 tā·mern der
there 那边 này·byēn
thermos 热水瓶 rèr·shwáy·píng
they 他们 tā·mern
thick 厚 hò
thief 小偷 syǎo·tō
thin 薄 báo
think 想 syǔng
third 第三 dèe·sūn
thirsty (to be) 渴 kěr
this (month) 这个(月) jày·ger (ywàir)
this (one) 这个 jày·ger
thread 棉线 myén·syèn
throat 脖子 bór·zir
thrush (health) 鹅口疮 ér·kǒ·chwūng
thunderstorm 雷雨 láy·yěw
Thursday 星期四 sīng·chēe sìr
Tibet 西藏 sēe·zùng
ticket 票 pyào
ticket collector 售票员
　shò·pyào ywén
ticket office 票房 pyào·fǔng

tide 潮流 cháo·lyó
tight 很紧 hérn·jǐn
time 时间 shír·jyen
time difference 时差 shír·chā
timetable 时刻表 shír·kèr byáo
tin (can) 罐头 gwùn·to
tin opener 开罐器 kāi·gwùn·chèe
tiny 微小 wāy·syáo
tip (gratuity) 消费 syáo·fày
tired 累 lày
tissues 纸巾 jír·jīn
tó (go to, come to) 到 dào
toast 烤面包 kǎo·myèn·bāo
tobacco 烟丝 yēn·sīr
tobacco kiosk 烟摊 yēn·tūn
today 今天 jīn·tyēn
toe 脚指头 jyǎo·jír·to
tofu 豆腐 dò·fǒo
together 一起 ee·chée
toilet 厕所 tsèr·swǒr
toilet paper 手纸 shó·jǐr
tomato 西红柿 sée·hóong·shìr
tomato sauce 番茄酱
　　fūn·chyáir jyùng
tomb 坟墓 férn·mòo
tomorrow 明天 míng·tyēn
tomorrow afternoon 明天下午
　　míng·tyēn syà·wǒo
tomorrow evening 明天晚上
　　míng·tyēn wǔn·shùng
tomorrow morning 明天早上
　　míng·tyēn zǎo·shùng
tonight 今天晚上 jīn·tyēn wǔn·shùng
too (expensive, etc) 太 tài
tooth 牙齿 yá·chír
toothache 牙齿疼 yá·chír térng
toothbrush 牙刷 yá·shwā
toothpaste 牙膏 yá·gāo
toothpick 牙签 yá·chyēn
torch (flashlight) 手电筒
　　shǒ·dyèn·tǒong

touch 触摸 chòo·mó
tour 向导游 syùng·dǎo yó
tourist 旅客 lěw·kèr
tourist hotel 旅店 lěw·dyèn
tourist office 旅行社 lěw·síng dyèn
towards 向 syùng
towel 毛巾 máo·jīn
tower (telecom) (电视)塔
　　(dyèn·shìr) tǎ
toxic waste 有毒废物 yǒ·dòo fày·wòo
toy shop 玩具店 wún·jèw dyèn
track (path) 山路 chūn·lòo
track (sport) 田径 tyén·jīng
trade 行业 húng·yàlr
tradesperson 工匠 gōong·jyùng
traffic 交通 jyāo·tōong
traffic light 红绿灯 hóong·lèw·dērng
trail 步行路 bùo·síng lòu
train 火车 hwǒr·cher
train station 火车站 hwǒr·chēr jùn
tram 电车 dyèn·chēr
transit lounge 转机室 jwǔn·jēe shír
translate 翻译 fūn·èe
transport 运输 yèwn·shoo
travel 旅游 lěw·yó
travel agency 旅行社 lěw·síng shèr
travel sickness 晕车 yèwn·chēr
travellers cheque(s) 旅行支票
　　lěw·síng jír·pyào
tree 树 shòo
trip (journey) 旅程 lěw·chérng
trolley 车子 chēr·zir
trousers 休闲裤 syō·syén kòo
truck 卡车 kǎ·chēr
trust 信用 sìn·yòong
try 尝试 chǔng·shìr
try (attempt) 试图 shìr·tóo
T-shirt T恤 tēe·sèw
tube (tyre) 内胎 này·tāi
Tuesday 星期二 sīng·chēe àr
tumour 肿瘤 jǒong·lyó
tuna 土拿鱼 tǒo·ná yěw

tune 曲调 chēw·dyào
turkey 火鸡 hwŏr·jēe
turn 转身 jwŭn·shērn
TV 电视 dyèn·shìr
tweezers 镊子 nyáir·zir
twice 两次 lyúng·tsìr
twin room 双人房 shwūng·rérn fúng
twins 双胞胎 shwūng·bāo tāi
two 两个 lyŭng·ger
type 类型 lày·síng
typical 通常 tōong·chúng
tyre 轮胎 lóon·tái

U

ultrasound 超声检查 chāo·shērng jyĕn·chá
umbrella 雨伞 yéw·sŭn
uncomfortable 不舒服 bòo shōo·foo
understand 懂 dŏong
underwear 内衣 này·ēe
unemployed 事业 shìr·yàir
unfair 不公平 bòo gōong·píng
uniform 工作服 gōong·zwòr foo
universe 宇宙 yéw·jò
university 大学 dà·shwáir
unleaded 无铅 wóo·chyén
unsafe 不安全 bòo ūn·chwén
until (Friday, etc) 一直到 èe·jír dào
unusual 反常 fŭn·chúng
up 上 shùng
uphill 上坡 shùng·pōr
urgent 要紧 yào·jĭn
urinary infection 尿道感染 nyào·dào gún·rŭn
USA 美国 mǎy·gwór
useful 有用的 yŏ·yòong der

V

vacancy 空房 kōong·fúng
vacant 有空 yŏ·kòong
vacation 度假 dòo·jyà

vaccination 免疫针 myén·ēe jērn
vagina 阴经 yín·jīng
validate 确认 chwàir·rèrn
valley 山谷 shūn·gŏo
valuable 贵重 gwày·jòong
value (price) 实价 shír·jyà
van 面地 myèn·dēe
veal (beef) 牛肉 nyó·rò
vegetable 蔬菜 shōo·tsài
vegetarian 吃素的 chīr·sòo der
vein 血脉 sywäir·mài
venereal disease 性病 sìng·bìng
venue 地点 dèe·dyén
vermicelli 粉丝 fĕrn·sīr
very 很 hĕrn
video recorder 录像机 lòo·syùng jēe
video tape 录像带 lòo·syùng dài
Vietnam 越南 ywàir·nún
view 视野 shìr·yäir
villa 别墅 byáir·shòo
village 村庄 tsūn·jwūng
vine (creeper) 攀藤 pún·térng
vinegar 醋 tsòo
vineyard 葡萄场 póo·tao chūng
virus 病毒 bìng·dóo
visa 签证 chyēn·jèrng
visit 拜访 bài·fúng
vitamins 维生素 wáy·shērng·sòo
vodka 伏特加 fóo·tèr·jyā
voice 声音 shērng·yīn
volleyball (sport) 排球 pái·chyó
volume 声音大小 shērng·yīn dà·syǎo
vote 投票 tó·pyào

W

wage 工资 sīn·shwǎy
wait (for) 等 dĕrng
waiter 服务员 fóo·wòo ywén
waiting room 等候室 dĕrng·hò shír
wake (someone) up 叫醒 jyào·sĭng
walk 走路 zŏ·lòo

wall (outer) 墙壁 chyúng·bèe
want 想要 syǔng·yào
war 战争 jùn·jērng
wardrobe 衣柜 ēe·gwày
warehouse 仓库 tsūng·kòo
warm 暖和 nwǔn·hwór
warn 警告 jīng·gào
wash 洗 sěe
wash cloth (flannel) 毛巾 máo·jīn
washing machine 洗衣机 sěe·ēe·jēe
watch 观望 gwūn·wùng
watch 手表 shó·byǎo
water 水 shway
water bottle (hot) 热水袋 rèr·shwǎy dài
waterfall 瀑布 póo·bòo
watermelon 西瓜 sēe·gwǎr
waterproof 防水 fúng·shwǎy
waterskiing 滑水 hwá·shwǎy
wave 海浪 hǎi·lùng
way 道 dào
we 我们 wǒr·mern
weak 弱 rùo
wealthy 富裕 fòo·yew
wear 穿 chwūn
weather 气候 chèe·ho
wedding 婚礼 hōon·lěe
wedding cake 喜糖 sěe·túng
wedding present 红包 hóung·bāo
Wednesday 星期三 sīng·chēe sūn
week 星期 sīng·chēe
(this) week (这个) 礼拜 (jày·ger) lěe·bài
weekend 周末 jō·mòr
weigh 称 chērng
weight 重量 jòong·lyùng
weights (lift) 健身 jyèn·shērn
welcome 欢迎 hwūn·íng
welfare 福利 fōo·lèe
well 很好 hérn·hǎo
west 西 sēe
wet 湿透 shír·tò

what 什么 shér·mer
wheel 车轮 chēr·lóon
wheelchair 轮车 lóon·chēr
when 什么时候 shér·mer shír·hò
where 哪里 ná·lěe
which 哪个 nǎy·ger
whisky 威士忌 wày·shir·jèe
white 白色 bái·sèr
who 谁 sháy
wholemeal bread 粗谷面包 tsòo·góo myèn·bāo
why 为什么 wày shér·mer
wide 宽 kwūn
wife 老婆 lǎo·pōr
wild rice root 茭日 jyāo·bāi
win 胜利 shèrng·lèe
wind 风 fērng
window 窗 chwūng
windscreen 防风屏 fúng·fērng píng
windsurfing 滑浪風帆 hwá·lùng fērng·fún
wine 葡萄酒 póo·tào jyǒ
wings 翅膀 chìr·bǔng
winner 胜利者 shèrng·lèe·jer
winter 冬天 dōong·tyēn
wire 金属丝 jīn·shǒo sīr
wish ⓥ 祝愿 jòo·ywèn
with 跟 gērn
within (an hour) (一个小时) 以内 (ēe·ger syǎo·shír) ěe·này
without 以外 ěe·wài
wok 锅 gwōr
woman 女人 něw·rérn
wonderful 奇妙 chēe·myào
won ton soup 混沌 hóon·dòon
won ton stall 混沌摊 hóon·dòon tūn
wood 木柴 mòo·chái
wool 羊毛 yúng·máo
word 单词 dūn·tsír
work 工作 gōong·zwòr
work 打工 dǎ·gōong
work experience 实习 shír·sěe

work permit 工作证 gōong·zwòr shír
work unit 单位 dūn·wày
workout 锻炼 dwùn·lyèn
workshop 工作室 gōong·zwòr·shír
world 世界 shìr·jyàir
World Cup 世界杯 shìr·jyàir bāy
world record 世界纪录
　　shìr·jyàir jèe·lòo
worm 蚯蚓 chyōo·yǐn
worried 着急 jáo·jée
worship 崇拜 chōong·bài
wrist 手腕 shó·wǔn
write 写 syǎir
writer 作家 zwòr·jyā
wrong 错 tswòr

Y

year 年 nyén
(this) year （今)年 (jīn) nyén

yellow 黄色 hwúng·sèr
yes 是 shìr
yesterday 昨天 zwór·tyēn
(not) yet 还（没有）hǎi (máy·yǒ)
yoga 瑜伽 yèw·jyā
yoghurt 酸奶 swùn·nǎi
you (inf) 你 něe
you (polite, Beijing) 您 nín
you (plural) 你们 něe·mern
young 年轻 nyén·chīng
your 你的 něe·der
youth hostel 旅栈 lěw·jùn

Z

zip/zipper 拉链 lā·lyèn
zodiac 星象 sīng·syùng
zoo 动物园 dòong·woo ywén
zucchini 西葫芦 sēe hóo·loo

mandarin–english

The Mandarin–English dictionary is arranged according to the number of strokes in the first character of the Chinese word. Thus, the dictionary commences with 一个 ēe·ger 'one' (the character 一 ēe has one stroke), and concludes with 罐头 gwùn·tó (罐 gwùn has 23 strokes). As there are many first characters with the same number of strokes, the characters within this number-of-strokes classification system are then ordered according to radical – the element of a character which conveys the meaning of a word.

The symbols ⓝ, ⓐ and ⓥ (indicating noun, adjective and verb) have been added for clarity where an English term could be either.

这是一个中英文单词对照表,可用于帮助这位老外明白你想说的话,请从表种查出相关的中文单词,再指示所对应的英文词条。中文词条安排的次序按首字笔画数目多少,同画数字按起笔 (即书写首笔画) 一 (衡, 横钩, 提) 丨 (竖, 竖钩) 撇丿、(捺点) ㇀ (折, 钩等) 排序。多谢您的热心帮助。

(Translation: This is a Chinese–English vocabulary correspondence table, which has been developed to help this foreigner understand what you wish to say. Please find the relevant word from the table, and point to the corresponding English word on the right. The Chinese words on the left are listed by number of strokes. Characters with the same number of strokes are ordered according to their first stroke in order of cross stroke, down stroke, left down, right down and hook. Many thanks for your kind help.)

一画 1 stroke

一个 ēe·ger one
一无所有 ēe·woo swór·yǒ nothing
一切 ēe·chyàir everything
一月 ēe·ywàir January
一直到 ēe·jír dào until (Friday, etc)
一起 ēe·chěe together
一顿饭 ēe·dòon fùn meal ⓝ

二画 2 strokes

二月 àr·ywàir February
二等 àr·děrng second class ⓝ
十一月 shír·ēe ywàir November
十二月 shír·àr ywàir December
十月 shír·ywàir October
七月 chēe·ywàir July

人 rérn mankind
人参 rérn·shēm ginseng
入口 ròo·kǒ entry
入场费 ròo·chǔng fày cover charge
八月 bā·ywàir August
儿子 ăr·zir son
九月 jyǒ·ywàir September
刀 dāo knife

三画 3 strokes

三月 sūn·ywàir March
十 gūn dry
干净 gūn·jìng clean ⓥ
干部 gùn·boo communist party
  official
上 shùng up

上衣 shùng·ēe **sweater**
工人 gōong·rérn **factory worker**
工作 gōong·zwòr **job**
工程师 gōong·chérng·shīr **engineer**
工程学 gōong·cherng swǎir
  engineering
下 (车) syà·chēr **get off (a train, etc)**
下个 syà·ger **next (month)**
(今天) 下午 (jīn·tyēn) syà·wǒo
  (this) afternoon
下雨 syà·yěw **rain** (n)
下面 syà·myen **down**
大 dà **big**
大小 dà·syǎo **size** (n)
大夫 dài·foo **doctor**
大巴 dà·bā **bus (city)**
大米 dà·měe **rice (raw)**
大衣 dà·ēe **coat** (n)
大佛 dà·fór **Buddha**
大使 dà·shír **ambassador**
大使馆 dà·shír·gwǔn **embassy**
大学 dà·shwáir **university**
大麻 dà·má **dope (drugs)** (n)
川 chwūn **river** (n)
小 syǎo **small**
小刀 syǎo·dāo **penknife**
小心 syǎo·sīn **Careful!**
小吃 syǎo·chīr **snack** (n)
小时 syǎo·shír **hour**
小卖部 syǎo mài·bòo
  convenience store • kiosk
小姐 syáo·jyǎir **Ms/Miss**
小娃娃 syǎo wǎ·wa **baby**
小路 syǎo·lòo **path**
口 kǒ **mouth**
口红 kǒ·hóong **lipstick**
山 shūn **mountain**
勺 shǎo **spoon** (n)
广东话 gwǔng·dōong hwà
  Cantonese (language) (n)
女人 nǚ·rérn **woman**
女士 něw·shìr **Mrs**
女同性恋 něw tóong·sìng lyèn
  lesbian (n)
女性 něw·sìng **female**
女朋友 něw·pérng·yo **girlfriend**
女孩子 něw·hái·zir **girl**

已婚 ēe·hōon **married**
卫生巾 wày·shěrng·jīn **panty liners •
  sanitary napkin**
叉子 chā·zir **fork**
广场 gwúng·chǔng **square (town)**
飞 fāy·fy (v)
飞机 fāy·jēe **aeroplane**
飞机场 fāy·jēe chǔng **airport**
乡下 syūng·syà **countryside**

四画 4 strokes

开车 kāi·chēr **drive** (v)
开放 kāi·fùng **open** (a)
开罐器 kāi·gwùn·chèe **can/tin opener**
无聊 wóo·lyǎo **boring**
元旦 ywěn·dùn **New Year's Day**
元旦除夕 ywěn·dùn chóo·sēe
  New Year's Eve
艺术 èe·shoo **art**
艺术馆 èe·shoo·gwǔn **art gallery**
艺术家 èe·shoo·jyā **artist**
不可能 bòo kěr·nérng **impossible**
不对 bóo·dwày **no**
不同 bòo·tóong **different**
不吸烟 bòo sēe·yēn **nonsmoking**
不舒服 bòo shōo·foo **uncomfortable**
长 chúng **long**
长城 chúng·chérng **Great Wall**
长途车 chúng·tǒo chēr
  bus (intercity)
长途车站 chúng·tóo chēr·jùn
  bus station
长袜 chúng·wà **pantyhose**
长裤 chúng·kòo **pants (trousers)**
木柴 mòo·chái **wood**
支票 jīr·pyào **cheque**
太阳 tài·yúng **sun**
比赛 bēe·sài **match (sports)** (n)
五月 wǒo·ywàir **May**
车子 chēr·zir **trolley**
车号 chēr·hào **car registration**
车灯 chēr·dērng **headlights**
车闸 chēr·já **brakes**
车站 chēr·jùn **bus station/stop**
车租赁 chēr zōo·lín **car hire**

牙齿疼 yá·chǐr térng **toothache**
牙科 yá·kēr **dentist**
牙刷 yá·shwā **toothbrush**
牙膏 yá·gāo **toothpaste**
切 chyàir **cut** ⓥ
止痛药 jǐr·tòong·yào **painkiller**
少 shǎo **less**
中午 jūng·wǒo **midday**
中文 jōong·gwór rérn **Chinese (language)**
中心 jōong·sīn **centre** ⓝ
中国 jōong·gwór **China**
中华人民共和国 joong·hwá rérn·mín goong·hér gwór **PRC**
中医 jōong·ēe **Chinese medicine doctor**
中药 jōong·yào **Chinese medicine**
日本 rìr·běrn **Japan**
日出 rìr·chōo **dawn** ⓝ
日常 rìr·chǔng **daily**
日期 rìr·chēe **date (day)**
月 ywàir **month**
日出 rìr·chōo **sunrise**
日落 rìr·lwòr **sunset**
水 shwǎy **water** ⓝ
水龙头 shwǎy·lóong·tóu **tap • faucet**
水果 shwǎy·gwǒr **fruit** ⓝ
内衣 này·ēe **underwear**
牛仔裤 nyó·zāi kòo **jeans**
牛奶 nyó·nǎi **milk**
牛肉 nyó·rò **beef**
午饭 wǒo·fùn **lunch** ⓝ
午夜 wǒo yàir **midnight**
气 chèe **chi • qi**
手 shǒ **hand**
手工艺 shǒ gōng·èe **handicrafts**
手工的 shǒ·gōng der **handmade**
手电筒 shǒ·dyèn·tǒong **torch • flashlight**
手包 shó·bāo **handbag**
手提包 shó·tǐ·bāo **briefcase**
手机 shǒ·jēe **mobile phone**
手套 shǒ·tào **glove(s)**
手纸 shó·jǐr **toilet paper**
手续 shǒ·sèw **paperwork**
手表 shó·byǎo **watch** ⓝ

毛巾 máo·jīn **towel**
毛衣 máo·ēe **jumper • sweater**
毛毯 máo·tǔn **blanket**
斤 jīn jīn **(measure)**
什么时候 shér·mer shír·hò **when**
反胃 fǔn·wày **nausea**
父亲 fòo·chín **father**
从 tsóong **from**
父母 fòo·mǒo **parents**
火车 hwǒr·chēr **train**
火车站 hwǒr·chēr·jùn **railway station**
火柴 hwǒr·chái **matches (for lighting)**
今天 jīn·tyēn **today**
今天晚 | jīn·tyēn wǔn·shùng **tonight**
分 fēn fēn **(measure)**
分钟 fēn·jōong **minute** ⓝ
公斤 gōong·jīn **kilogram**
公司 gōong·sīr **company (business)**
公用 gōong·yòong **share** ⓥ
公用电话 gōong·yòong dyèn·hwà **public telephone**
公园 gōong·ywén **park** ⓝ
公安 gōong·ūn **police officer (in country)**
公安局 gōong·ūn jéw **PSB**
公里 goong·lee **kilometre**
公厕 gōong·tsèr **public toilet**
公寓 gōong·yèw **apartment (upmarket)**
风俗 fēng·sóo **custom**
风水 fēng·shwǎy **feng shui**
方向 fūng·syùng **direction**
六月 lyò·ywàir **June**
文具店 wérn·jèw dyèn **stationer's (shop)**
计算器 jèe·swùn chèe **calculator**
计算机 jèe·swùn·jēe **computer**
心脏 sīn·zùng **heart**
心脏病 sīn·zùng·bìng **heart condition**
为什么 wày shér·mer **why**
双头插座 shwūng·byèn chā·zwòr **adaptor**
双人床 shwūng·rérn chwúng **double bed**
双人间 shwūng·rérn jyēn **double room**
双人房 shwūng·rérn fúng **twin room**

四画

mandarin-english

239

双程(票) shwūng·chérng (pyào) **return (ticket)**

书 shōo **book** ⓝ

幻灯片 hwùn·dērng pyèn **slide (film)**

五画 5 strokes

未婚夫 wày·hōon·fòo **fiancé**

未婚妻 wày·hōon·chēe **fiancée**

去 chèw **go**

玉米 yèw·mēe **corn**

打开 dǎ·kāi **open** ⓥ

打火机 dǎ·hwǒr·jēe **cigarette lighter**

打电话 dǎ dyèn·hwà **telephone** ⓥ

打印机 dǎ·yìn·jēe **printer (computer)**

打扫 dá·sǎo **clean** ⓐ

打扮 dǎ·bùn **make-up** ⓝ

打针 dǎ·jērn **injection**

古代 gǒo·dài **ancient**

古典 góo·dyěn **classical**

古董 góo·dǒong **antique** ⓝ

古董市场 góo·dǒong shìr·chǔng **antique market**

艾滋病 ài·zīr·bìng **AIDS**

节日 jyáir·rìr **festival**

左边 zwǒr·byēn **left (direction)**

右边 yò·byēn **right (direction)**

石油 shír·yó **oil (food)**

头 tó **head** ⓝ

头巾 tó·jīn **scarf**

头疼 tó·tērng **headache**

头等舱 tó·děrng tsūng **business class**

商业舱 shūng·yàir tsūng **first class**

东方 dōong·fūng **east**

北边 bǎy·byēn **north**

北京烤鸭 bǎy·jīng káo·yā **Peking duck**

以上 ěe·shùng **on**

以外 ěe·wài **without**

以后 ěe·hò **after · later**

目的地 mòo·dee dèe **destination**

兄弟 syōong·dee **brother**

叫 jyào **call** ⓥ

叫醒 jyào·sǐng **wake (someone) up**

(美) 叨 (máy) dāo **dollar (American)**

号码 hào·mǎ **number** ⓝ

电子用品店 dyèn·zir yòong·pǐn dyèn **electrical store**

电子邮件 dyèn·zir yó·jyèn **email** ⓝ

电子舞会 dyèn·zir wǒo·hwày **rave** ⓝ

电风扇 dyèn·fērng·shùn **fan (machine)**

电池 dyèn·chír **battery** ⓝ

电报 dyèn·bào **telegram**

电视 dyèn·shìr **television**

电话 dyèn·hwà **telephone** ⓝ

电话卡 dyèn·hwà kǎ **phone card**

电梯 dyèn·tēe **lift · elevator**

电影 dyèn·yǐng **movie**

电影院 dyèn·yǐng·ywèn **cinema**

四月 sìr·ywàir **April**

生日 shērng·rìr **birthday**

生意 shērng·èe **business** ⓝ

皮革 pēe·gér **leather** ⓝ

付款 fòo·kwǔn **payment**

代理费 dài·lěe fày **commission**

他 tā **he**

他的 tā·der **his**

乐队 ywàir·dwài **band (music)**

冬天 dōong·tyēn **winter**

外壳 wài·kér **jacket**

外国人 wài·gwór rérn **foreigner**

外面 wài·myen **outside**

包 bāo **bag · packet**

包子 bāo·zir **dumpling (steamed)**

包括 bāo·kwòr **included**

包裹 bāo·gwǒr **package · parcel** ⓝ

写 syǎir **write**

市中心 shìr·jōong·sīn **city centre**

市场 shìr·chǔng **market** ⓝ

白天 bái·tyēn **day**

白色 bái·sèr **white**

半个 bùn·ger **half**

礼物 lée·wòo **present** ⓝ

记者 jèe·jǐr **journalist**

民主主义 mín·jǒo jǒo·èe **democracy**

出口 chōo·kǒ **exit**

出去 chōo·chèw **go out**

出发 chōo·fā **departure**

出生日 chōo·shērng·rìr **date of birth**

出生证 chōo·shērng·jèrng **birth certificate**

出纳 chōo·nà **cashier**
出事 chōo·shìr **emergency** ⓝ
出差 chōo·chāi **business trip**
出租车 chōo·zōo chēr **taxi**
出租车站 chōo·zōo chēr jùn **taxi stand**
奶奶 nǎi·nai **grandmother (paternal)**
奶酪 nǎi·lào **cream (dairy)**
加油站 jyā·yó jùn **service station**
加拿大 jyā·ná·dà **Canada**
发动机 fā·dòong·jee **engine**
发烧 fā·shǎo **fever**
发票 fā·pyào **receipt**
边界 byēn·jyàii **border** ⓝ
圣诞节 shèrng·dùn·jyáir **Christmas**
对方付款 dwày·fūng fòo·kwǔn **collect call**
台阶 tái·jyāir **stairway**
台湾 tái·wūn **Taiwan**
母亲 mǒo·chīn **mother** ⓝ
幼儿园 yò·ǎr·ywén **childminding** ⓝ
丝绸 sīr·chó **silk** ⓝ

六画 6 strokes

买 mǎi **buy** ⓥ
买东西 mǎi dōong·see **shop** ⓥ
亚麻布 yá·mā bòo **linen (material)**
交换 jyāo·hwùn **exchange** ⓝ
价格 jyà·gér **cost · price**
休闲裤 syo·syén kòo **trousers**
休息 syo·see **intermission** ⓝ
会议 hwày·èe **conference (big)**
会合 hwày·hér **conference (small)**
传真机 chwún·jērn·jee **fax machine**
伤害 shūng·hài **injury**
先生 syēn·shērng **Mr**
光 gwūng **light** ⓝ
光盘 (CD) sēe·dèe **CD**
共产主义 gòong·chǔn jǒo·èe **communism**
关 gwūn **shut**
关口 gwūn·kǒ **pass (mountain)**
关门 gwārn·mérn **closed**
关闭 gwārn·bèe **close** ⓐ
再一个 zài ēe·ger **another**
再见 zài·jyèn **goodbye**

军人 jēwn·rérn **soldier**
农民 nóong·mīn **farmer (peasant)**
冰 bīng **ice** ⓝ
冰冻 bīng·dòong **frozen**
冰箱 bīng·syūng **refrigerator**
动物 dòong·woo **animal** ⓝ
动物园 dòong·woo ywén **zoo**
危险 wāy·syén **dangerous**
吃饭 chīr·fùn **eat**
吃的 chīr·der **food**
吃素的 chīr·sòo der **vegetarian** ⓐ
同……一样 tóong …… ee·yùng **like** ⓥ
同伙 tóong·hwǒr **companion**
同志 (吧) tóong·jìr (ba) **gay (bar)**
同事 tóong·shìr **colleague**
同性恋 tóong·sìng lyèn **homosexual** ⓝ
名字 míng·zìr **given name · name**
后 hò **rear (seat etc)**
后天 hò·tyēn **day after tomorrow**
团体旅行 twún·těe lěw·síng **guided tour**
因特网 yīn·tèr·wǔng **Internet**
回来 hwáy·lái **return (come back)**
在……上 zài … shùng **aboard**
在……里面 zài … lěe·myèn **in**
地方 dèe·fūng **local**
地址 dèe·jír **address** ⓝ
地图 dèe·tóo **map** ⓝ
地铁 dèe·tyǎir **subway**
地铁站 dèe·tyǎir jùn **subway station**
抽筋 dèe·jērn **earthquake**
(网球) 场 (wǔng·chyó) chǔng **court (tennis)**
多 dōr **more**
她的 tā·der **her**
好 hǎo **good**
好香 hǎo·syūng **tasty**
字幕 zìr·mòo **subtitles**
存钱 tsóon·chyén **deposit (bank)**
孙子 sōon·zìr **grandchild**
安全 ūn·chwén **safe** ⓐ
安全性交 ūn·chwén sìng·jyāo **safe sex**
安全带 ūn·chwén·dài **seatbelt**
安静 ūn·jìng **quiet**
导游 dǎo·yó **guide (person)** ⓝ
年 nyén **year**

年龄 nyén·líng **age** ⓝ
忙得 múng·der **in a hurry**
收费公路 shō·fày gōong·lòo
 motorway (tollway)
收音机 shò·yīn·jēe **radio** ⓝ
收银台 shò·yín tái **cash register**
早 zǎo **early**
早上 zǎo·shùng **morning** ⓝ
早饭 zǎo·fùn **breakfast** ⓝ
有毛病 yǒ máo·bìng **faulty**
有约 yó·ywàir **appointment**
有事 yó·shìr **engaged (occupied)**
有空 yǒ·kòong **free (available)** •
 vacant
有空调的 yó kōong·tyáo der
 air-conditioned
有保证 yó bǎo·jèrng **guaranteed**
有病 yǒ·bìng **ill**
有暖气 yó nwǔn·chèe **heated**
机场税 jēe·chǔng shwày **airport tax**
杂技 zǎ·jèe **circus**
灰色 hwāy·sèr **grey**
爷爷 yáir·yair **grandfather (paternal)**
百货商店 bǎi·hwòr shūng·dyèn
 department store
米 měe **metre**
米饭 měe·fùn **rice (cooked)**
红色 hóong·sèr **red**
纪念品 jèe·nyèn pǐn **souvenir**
纪念品店 jèe·nyèn·pǐn dyèn
 souvenir shop
网吧 wǔng·bā **Internet café**
网球 wǔng·chyó **tennis**
网球场 wǔng·chyó chǔng **tennis
 court**
羊毛 yúng·máo **wool**
羊肉 yúng·rò **lamb**
耳朵 ěr·dōr **ear**
老 lǎo **old**
老公 lǎo·gōong **husband**
老师 lǎo·shīr **teacher**
老百姓 láo·bǎi·sìng **common people**
老婆 lǎo·pōr **wife**
肉 rò **meat**
肉店 rò·dyèn **butcher's shop**
自动取款机 zìr·dòong chéw·kwǔn jēe
 automated teller machine (ATM)

自行车 zìr·síng·chēr **bicycle** ⓝ
自行车骑手 zìr·síng·chēr chée·shǒ
 cyclist
自助 zìr·jòo **self service**
血型 syǎir·síng **blood group**
血液 syǎir yàir **blood**
行李 síng·lěe **luggage**
行李寄存 síng·lěe jèe·tsóon
 luggage lockers
行李领取处 síng·lěe líng·chēw chòo
 baggage claim
衣服 ēe·foo **clothing**
西 sēe **west**
西药房 sēe·yào fúng **pharmacy**
西班牙 sēe·būn·yǎ **Spain**
西藏 sēe·zùng **Tibet**
许可证 séw·kěr·jèrng **pass (permit)**
过时 gwòr·shír **off (spoiled)**
过夜 gwòr·yàir **overnight**
过重(行李) gwòr·jòong síng·lee
 excess (baggage)
那个 này·ger **that (one)**
那边 này·byēn **there**
防晒油 fúng·shài yó **sunblock**

七画 7 strokes

两个 lyǔng·ger **two**
两个都 lyǔng·ger·dō **both**
住宿 jòo·sòo **accommodation** ⓝ
体育用品店 těe·yèw yòong·pǐn dyèn
 sports store • **sports shop**
体育场 těe·yèw chǔng **stadium**
体育家 těe·yèw jyā **sportsperson**
佛寺 fór·sìr **monastery (Buddhist)**
佛教 fór·jyào **Buddhism**
佛教徒 fór·jyào tóo **Buddhist**
你 nēe **you (inf)**
克 kèr **gram**
免疫针 myèn·ēe jērn **vaccination**
免费 myěn·fày **free (gratis)**
免费行李 myěn·fày síng·lěe
 baggage allowance
兑现 dwày·syèn **cash (a cheque)**
兑换率 dwày·hwùn lèw **exchange
 rate**
冷 lěrng **cold**

务孩子 něw hái·zir daughter
医学 ēe·shwáir medicine (study, profession)
医药 ēe·yào medicine (medication)
医院 ēe·ywèn hospital
吵 chǎo loud
听 tīng listen (to)
坏了 hwài·ler out of order
坟地 férn·dèe cemetery
妓女 jèe·něw prostitute
尿裤 nyào·kòo nappy • diaper
层 tsérng floor (storey)
岛 dǎo island
床 chwúng bed
床单 chwúng·dūn bed linen
弟弟 dèe·dee brother (younger)
快 kwài fast • soon
快乐 kwài·lèr happy
快递(信) kwài·dèe sìn express (mail)
怀孕 hwái·yèwn pregnant
我 wǒr I • me
我们的 wǒr·mern our
我的 wǒr·der my
戒指 jyàir·jǐr ring (on finger)
扶梯 fóo·tēe escalator
投诉 tó·sòo complaint
折扣 jér·kò discount ⓝ
抗菌素 kùng·jěwn·sòo antibiotics
护士 hòo·shìr nurse ⓝ
护照 hòo·jào passport
护照号码 hòo·jào hào·mǎ passport number
扭伤 nyǒ·shūng sprain ⓝ
报纸 bào·jǐr newspaper
抛锚 pāo·máo broken down (car)
时刻表 shír·kèr byǎo timetable ⓝ
时差反应 shír·chā fún·yìng jet lag
更大 gèrng·dà bigger
更小 gèrng·syǎo smaller
更好 gèrng·hǎo better
更衣室 gèrng·ēe·shìr changing room
来信 lái·sìn mail (letters)
步行 bòo·síng hike ⓥ
每(天) mǎy·tyēn per (day)
每个 mǎy·ger each
每个人 mǎy·ger rérn everyone
每次 mǎy·tsìr every

沙滩 shā·tūn beach
沙漠 shā·mòr desert
汽油 chèe·yó petrol • oil (petroleum)
汽油站 chèe·yó jùn petrol station
没空 máy·kòong no vacancy
狂野 gwùng·yǎir hiking
男人 nún·rérn man (male person)
男女事 nún·něw shìr sex
男朋友 nún·pérng·yo boyfriend
男孩子 nún·hái·zir boy
社会主义战士 sher·hwày joo·ēe jun·shìr socialist
私人 sīr·rérn private
纸巾 jǐr·jīn tissues
纸币·钞 jǐr·bòo banknote
罕见 hūn·jyèn rare (uncommon)
肚子 dòo·zir stomach
肚子疼 dòo·zir térng indigestion • stomachache
肠胃炎 chúng·wày·yén gastroenteritis
花园 hwā·ywén garden ⓝ
花粉热 hwā·fěrn rèr hay fever
苏克兰 sōo·kèr·lún Scotland
证件 jèrng·jyèn identification • papers (official documents)
词典 tsír·dyěn dictionary
豆浆 dò·jyúng soy milk (fresh)
豆腐 dò·fóo tofu
走廊 zǒ·lúng aisle (on plane)
走路 zǒ·lòo walk ⓥ
足够 zóo·gò enough
足球 zóo·chyó football (soccer)
身份证 shèrn·fèrn jèrng identification card (ID)
近 jìn near
这个 jày·ger this (one)
这里 jèr·lěe here
进港口 jìn·gúng·kǒ arrivals
远 ywěrn far
连衣裙 lyén·ēe·chéwn dress ⓝ
连接 lyén·jyàir connection
迟到 chír·dào late
邮寄 yó·dyèn mail (postal system)
邮电号码 yó·dyèn hào·mǎ post code
邮局 yó·jéw post office
邮票 yó·pyào stamp ⓝ

针灸 jērn·jyǒ **acupuncture**
针线 jērn·syèn **needle (sewing)**
阿姨 ā·ée **aunt**
阿斯匹灵 ā·sir·pée·líng **aspirin**
附近 fòo·jìn **nearby**
陆运 lòo·yèwn **surface mail (land)**
饭馆 fùn·gwǔn **restaurant**
饮料 yín·lyào **drink** ⓝ
鸡 jēe **chicken**
鸡蛋 jēe·dùn **egg (chicken)**

八画 8 strokes

现代 syèn·dài **modern**
现在 syèn·zài **now**
现金 syèn·jīn **cash** ⓝ
表演 byáo·yěn **show** (ⓝ, ⓥ)
青色 chīng·sèr **dark (of colour)**
武术 wǒo·shòo **martial arts**
其他 chée·tā **other**
取消 chěw·syāo **cancel**
抽烟 chō·yēn **smoke** ⓥ
拉稀 lā·sēe **diarrhoea**
拉链 lā·lyèn **zip · zipper**
事故 shìr·gòo **accident**
卧室 wòr·shìr **bedroom**
卧铺车厢 wòr·pòo chēr·syūng
    sleeping car
直接 jír·jyāir **direct**
直播 jír·bōr **direct-dial**
苦 kǒo **bitter**
英文 yīng·wérn **English**
英文老师 yīng·wérn lǎo·shīr
    English teacher
英国 yīng·gwór **England**
英俊 yīng·jèwn **handsome**
雨伞 yěw·sǔn **umbrella**
雨衣 yěw·ēe **raincoat**
杯子 bāy·zir **cup** ⓝ
枕头 jēn·tó **pillow**
画 hwà **painting (a work)**
画画儿 hwà·hwàr **painting (the art)**
画家 hwà·jyā **painter**
厕所 tsèr·swǒr **toilet**
矿泉水 kwùng·chwén shwǎy
    mineral water

转机室 jwǔn·jēe shír **transit lounge**
软卧 rún·wòr **soft sleeper**
软座 rún·zwòr **soft seat**
软盘 rwǔn·pún **disk (floppy)**
轮车 lóon·chēr **wheelchair**
轮胎 lóon·tai **tyre** ⓝ
欧元 ō·ywén **euro**
欧洲 ō·jō **Europe**
到 dào **to (go to, come to)**
垃圾 lā·jēe **garbage**
垃圾箱 lā·jēe syūng **garbage can**
周末 jō·mòr **weekend**
味道 wày·dào **smell** ⓝ
咖啡 kā·fāy **coffee**
咖啡色 kā·fāy sèr **brown**
咖啡屋 kā·fāy wōo **café**
国际象棋 gwór·jèe syùng·chée
    chess (International)
国家 gwór·jyā **country (nation)**
明天 míng·tyēn **tomorrow**
明天下午 míng·tyēn syà·wǒo
    tomorrow afternoon
明天早上 míng·tyēn zǎo·shùng
    tomorrow morning
明天晚上 míng·tyēn wǔn·shùng
    tomorrow evening
明信片 míng·sìn·pyèn **postcard**
朋友 pérng·yo **friend**
服务 fóo·wòo **service** ⓝ
服务员 fóo·wòo ywén **waiter**
服务费 fóo·wòo fày **service charge**
服装店 fóo·jwūng·dyèn
    clothing store
肥皂 fáy·zào **soap**
图书馆 tóo·shōo gwǔn **library**
账单 jūng·dūn **(bank) account**
账单 jùng·dūn **check (bill)**
钓鱼 dyào·yéw **fishing**
刮脸 gwā·lyén **shave**
刮痧 gwā·shā **cupping (therapy)**
季节 jèe·jyáir **season**
岳父 ywàir·fòo **father-in-law**
岳母 ywàir·mǒo **mother-in-law**
昏迷 hōon·mēe **concussion**
货币兑换 hwòr·bèe dwày·hwùn
    currency exchange
往后退 wǔng·hò·twǎy **delay** ⓝ

炒 jà **fry (stir-fry)**
炒菜 chǎo·tsài **cook** (v)
贪污 tún·wōo **corrupt**
鱼 yéw **fish** (n)
鱼摊 yéw·tūn **fish shop**
狗 gǒ **dog**
京剧 jīng·jòo **classical theatre**
京剧 jīng·jèw **opera (Chinese)**
夜总会 yàir·zǒong·hwày **nightclub**
店 dyèn **shop** (n)
废墟 fày·sēw **ruins**
闹钟 nào·jōong **alarm clock**
定 dìng **book (make a booking)**
定满 dìng·mǔn **booked out**
宝贝 bǎo·bày **child**
空 kōong **empty**
空房 kōong·fǔng **vacancy**
法兰西 fǎ·gwór **France**
法律 fǎ·lèw **law (study, professsion)**
注射针 jòo·shèr jērn **needle (syringe)**
浅色 chyěrn·sèr **light (of colour)**
单人 dūn·rérn **single (person)**
单人间 dūn·rérn jyēn **single room**
单子 dūn·zir **bill (restaurant etc)**
单程 dūn·chéng **one-way (ticket)**
学生 shwáir·sherng **student**
房东 fǔng·dōong **landlady**
房地产公司 fǔng·dèe·chǔn gōong·sīr **estate agency**
房间 fǔng·jyēn **room**
房间号 fúng·jyēn hào **room number**
肩膀 jyēn·bǔng **shoulder**
衬衫 chèrn·shūn **shirt**
视野 shìr·yǎir **view** (n)
建筑师 jyèn·joo·shīr **architect**
建筑学 jyèn·joo·shwáir **architecture**
录像机 lòo·syùng jēe **video recorder**
录像带 lòo·syùng dài **video tape**
妹妹 mày·may **sister (younger)**
姐姐 jyǎir·jyair **sister (elder)**
姓 sìng **family name**
驾驶照 jyà·shír·jào **drivers licence**
织 jīr **paper**
经纬点按摩 jīng·wáy ùn·mór **pressure point massage**
经济舱 jīng·jee tsūng **economy class**

九画 **9 strokes**

春天 chōon·tyēn **spring (season)**
毒品 dóo·pǐn **drug (illicit)**
玻璃杯 bōr·lée bāy **glass (drinking)**
玻璃 bōr·lée **glass (material)**
帮助 bùng·joo **help** (n)
帮 bùng **help** (v)
城市 chéng·shìr **city**
项链 syùng·lyèn **necklace**
挂号 gwa·hào **registered mail/post** (n)
指头 jǐr·to **finger**
指南书 jǐr·nǔn shōo **guidebook**
按摩 ùn·mór **massage** (n)
按摩师傅 ùn·mór shīr·foo **masseur + masseuse**
垫子 dyèn·zir **mattress** (n)
指 jǐr **point** (v)
政治 jèrng·jìr **politics**
胡同 hóo·toong **alleyway**
药片 yào·pyèn **pill**
药方 yào·fūng **prescription**
药师 yào·shīr **chemist (pharmacist)**
药房 yào·fǔng **chemist (shop)**
药品 yào·pǐn **drug (medication)**
茶馆 chá·gwǔn **teahouse**
南 nún **south**
要紧 yào·jǐn **urgent**
树荫 shòo·yín **shade** (n)
迷路 mēe·lòo **lost (one's way)**
厘米 lée·mēe **centimetre**
残疾 tsún·jēe **disabled**
面包 myèn·bāo **bread**
面摊 myèn·tūn **noodle house**
面条 myèn·tyáo **noodles**
轻泻药 chīng·syàir yào **laxative**
轻 chīng **light (not heavy)**
背 bày **back (body)**
背包 bày·bāo **backpack**
背面 bày·myen **behind**
尝试 chúng·shìr **try** (v)
恤 tēe·sèw **T-shirt**
星加坡 sīng·jyā·pōr **Singapore**
星期 sīng·chēe **week**
星期一 sīng·chēe ēe **Monday**
星期二 sīng·chēe àr **Tuesday**

星期三 sīng·chēe sūn **Wednesday**
星期四 sīng·chēe sìr **Thursday**
星期五 sīng·chēe wŏo **Friday**
星期六 sīng·chēe lyò **Saturday**
星期天 sīng·chēe·tyēn **Sunday**
哪里 ná·lěe **where**
哪个 nǎy·ger **which**
是 shìr **yes**
昨天 zwór·tyēn **yesterday**
贵 gwày **expensive**
罚款 fā·kwūn **fine (penalty)**
贵重 gwày·jòong **valuable**
钥匙 yào·shir **key** ⓝ
钢笔 gūng·bēe **pen (ballpoint)**
重 jòong **heavy**
重要 jòong·yào **important**
香烟 syūng·yēn **cigarette**
香港 syūng·gǔng **Hong Kong**
秋天 chyō·tyēn **autumn • fall**
科学 kēr·shwáir **science**
科学家 kēr·shwáir jyā **scientist**
复活节 fòo·hwór·jyáir **Easter**
饺子 jyáo·zir **dumpling (boiled)**
便秘 byēn·mèe **constipation**
保险 báo·syěn **insurance**
修理 syō·lěe **repair** ⓥ
信 sìn **letter (mail)**
信用 sìn·yòong **credit**
信用卡 sìn·yòong kǎ **credit card**
信条 sìn·tyáo **message**
信息技术 sìn·sēe jèe·shoo **IT**
信箱 sìn·syūng **mailbox**
很硬 hérn yìng **hard (not soft)**
很疼 hěrn·térng **painful**
食品 shír·pǐn **grocery**
受伤 shò·shūng **injured**
独自一个人 dóo ēe·ger rérn **alone**
急救车 jée·jyò chēr **ambulance**
急救忙忙 jée·jee múng·mung
　busy (at a certain time)
急救装备 jée·jyò jwùng·bay
　first-aid kit
临时保姆 lín·shír báo·mōo
　babysitter

亭子 tíng·zir **pavillion**
疮口 chwùng·kǒ **cut (wound)**
度假 dòo·jyà **vacation**
音乐会 yīn·ywàir hwày **concert**
音乐 yīn·ywàir **music**
音像店 yīn·syung dyèn **music shop**
皇帝 hwúng·dèe **Emperor**
皇后 hwúng·hò **Empress**
美丽 mǎy·lèe **beautiful**
姜 jyūng **ginger**
美国 mǎy·gwór **USA**
首饰 shǒ·shìr **jewellery**
前一个 chyén ēe·gèr
　last (previous) ⓐ
前天 chyén·tyēn
　day before yesterday
宫殿 gōong·dyèn **palace** ⓝ
客户 kèr·hoo **client**
洪水 hóong·shwǎy **flood**
洋 yáng **foreign (goods)**
洗 sēe **wash (something)**
洗衣店 sēe·ēe dyèn **launderette**
洗衣服 sēe ēe·foo **laundry (clothes)**
洗衣机 sēe·ēe jēe **washing machine**
测光表 tsèr·gwūng byǎo
　light meter ⓝ
派出所 pài·chōo swŏr
　police station
剃刀 tēe·dāo **razor**
剃刀片 tēe·dāo pyèn **razor blade**
语言 yěw·yén **language**
语句书 yěw·jèw·shōo **phrasebook**
祖先 zǒo·syēn **ancestors**
说明书 shwōr·míng shōo **brochure**
退休职工 twāy·syō jír·gōong
　pensioner
退钱 twày·chyén **refund** ⓝ
孩子们 hái·zir·mern **children**

十画 10 strokes

换 hwùn **change • exchange**
换钱 hwùn·chyén **change (money)**
热 rèr hot ⓐ
热气 rèr·chèe **heat** ⓝ
热水瓶 rèr·shwáy·píng **thermos**

热水袋 rèr·shwǎy dài **hot water bottle**
哥哥 gēr·ger **brother (elder)**
恭喜 gōong·sēe **congratulations**
荷兰 hér·lún **Netherlands**
桥 chyáo **bridge**
粉色 fěrn·sèr **pink**
夏天 syà·tyēn **summer**
党员 dǔng·ywén **communist (party member)**
轿车 jyào·chēr **car**
晒伤 shài·shūng **sunburn**
晕车 yèwn·chēr **travel sickness**
晚上 wǔn·shùng **evening • night**
晚上活动 wǔn·shùng hwór·dòong **night out**
晚饭 wǔn·fùn **dinner**
胳膊 gē·bor **arm** (n)
胶卷 jyáo·jwěn **film (for camera)**
胸 syoong **chest (body)**
脆弱 tswày·ròr **fragile**
脏 zūng **dirty**
钱 chyén **money**
钱包 chyén·bāo **purse**
铅笔 chyén·běe **pencil**
乘客 chérng·kèr **passenger**
租赁 zōo·lín **rent** (v)
透镜 tò·jìng **lens**
预定 yèw·dìng **reservation (booking)**
饿 èr **hungry (to be)**
笔记本 běe·jèe běrn **notebook**
健美中心 jyèn·měy jōong·sīn **gym (place)**
烟斗 yēn·sǐr **tobacco**
烤面包 kǎo myèn·bāo **toast** (n)
烧伤 shāo·shùng **burn** (n)
烧焦 shāo·jyāo **burnt**
爱 ài **love** (v)
爱尔兰 ài·ǎr·lún **Ireland**
爱情 ài·chíng **love** (n)
连酒吧 gwùng jyǒ·bā **party (night out)**
浆油 jyūng·yó **soy sauce**
离开 lée·kāi **depart (leave)**
离婚 lée·hōon **divorced**
高 gāo **high** (a)
高尔夫场 gāo·ér·foo chǔng **golf course**

高速公路 gāo·soo gōong·lòo **highway**
准时 jǒon·shír **on time**
座位 zwòr·wày **seat (place)** (n)
病 bìng **sick**
疼 térng **pain**
旁边 púng·byēn **beside**
站台 jùn·tái **platform**
站台票 jùn·tái pyào **stand-by ticket**
资本主义 zīr·běn jǒo·èe **capitalism**
旅行支票 lěw·síng jīr·pyào **travellers cheque**
旅行社 lěw·síng dyèn **tourist office**
旅行社 lěw·sìng shèr **travel agency**
旅行箱 lěw·síng·syùng **suitcase**
旅店 lěw·dyèn **tourist hotel**
旅栈 lěw·jùn **youth hostel**
旅程 lěw·chérng **journey**
航运 húng·yèwn **airmail**
航空公司 húng kōong goong·sīr **airline**
航班 húng·būn **flight**
家 jyā **home**
家具 jyā·jew **furniture**
家庭 jyā·tíng **family**
宾馆 bīn·gwǔn **guesthouse**
酒吧 jyǒ bā **bar** (n)
酒店 jyǒ·dyèn **hotel**
酒料 jyǒ·lyào **drink (alcoholic)**
酒精 jyǒ·jīng **alcohol**
消毒剂 syāo·dóo·jèe **antiseptic**
消费 syāo·fày **tip (gratuity)** (n)
海 hǎi **sea**
海外 hǎi·wài **overseas** (n)
海关 hǎi·gwūn **custom (immigration)**
海运 hǎi·yèwn **surface mail (sea)**
浴室 yèw·shìr **bathroom • shower** (n)
浴缸 yèw·gūng **bath**
润滑油 ròon·hwá yó **lubricant**
(电)流 (dyèn) lyó **current (electricity)**
递送 dèe·sòong **deliver**
浪漫 lùng·mùn **romantic**
瓶子 píng·zìr **bottle** (n)
逛街 gwùng·jyāir **go shopping** (v)
谁 sháy **who**
袜子 wà·zìr **sock(s)**
剧 jèw **play (theatre)**
剧场 jèw·chǔng **theatre**

展览 jún·lǔn exhibition
陶瓷 táo·tsír ceramics
娱乐指南 yéw·lèr jír·nún entertainment guide
预备食品 yèw·bày shír·pǐn food supplies

十一画 11 strokes

理发 lěe·fā haircut
理发屋 lěe·fā wōo hairdresser
推荐 twày·jyèn recommend
博物馆 bó·wòo gwǔn museum
塔车 tā·chēr hitchhike
票 pyào ticket
票价 pyào·jyà admission price • fare
票房 pyào·fúng ticket office
黄色 hwúng·sèr yellow
黄金 hwúng·jīn gold ⓝ
剪刀 jyěn·dāo scissors
剪指刀 jyén·jǐr dāo nail clippers
菊花 jéw·hwā chrysanthemum
菜单 tsài·dūn menu
营业时间 yíng·yàir shír·jyēn opening hours
萨斯 sǎ·sīr SARS
雪 shwǎir snow ⓝ
救人 jyò·rérn Stop!
厨子 chóo·zir cook ⓝ
厨房 chóo·fúng kitchen
奢侈 shēr·chǐr luxury
插头 chā·tó plug (electricity)
帽子 mào·zir hat
喝 hēr drink
啤酒 pée·jyǒ beer
啤酒摊 pée·jyǒ tūn liquor store
眼睛 yén·jīng eye(s)
眼镜 yén·jìng glasses (spectacles)
累 lày tired
脖子 bór·zir throat
脚 jyǎo foot
脚踝 jyǎo·hwái ankle
脸 lyén face
野餐 yěr·tsūn picnic ⓝ
银子 yín·zir silver ⓖ
银行 yín·hǔng bank (money)
银行账户 yín·hǔng jùng·hoo bank account

甜 tyén sweet
剩余额 shèng·yew ér balance (account)
停 (车) tíng·chēr park (a car) ⓥ
您 nín you (pol)
假期 jyà·chēe holidays
领事馆 lǐng·shìr·gwǔn consulate
象棋 syùng·chée chess (Chinese)
猪肉 jōo·rò pork
猫 māo modem
毫米 háo·měe millimetre
痒 yúng itch ⓝ
麻将 má·jyùng Mahjong
商人 shūng·rérn businessman • businesswoman
商场 shūng·chúng shopping centre
盗窃的 dào·chyàir·der stolen
船 chwún boat
奥运会 ào·yèwn hwày Olympic Games
盘 pún dish (food item)
盘子 pún·zir plate
寄存处 jèe·tsóon·chòo cloakroom • left luggage office
寄特代 jèe tè·kwài express mail (by)
清洁 chīng·jyáir cleaning
清真 chīng·jērn halal
清真寺 chīng·jērn sìr mosque
隐形眼镜 yǐn·síng yěn·jìng contact lenses
绷带 bérng·dài bandage ⓝ
绿色 lèw·sèr green
骑马 chée·mǎ horse riding
骑自行车 chēe zìr·sīng·chēr cycle

十二画 12 strokes

裁缝 tsái·fèrng tailor ⓝ
超市 chāo·shìr supermarket
越南 ywàir·nún Vietnam
朝鲜 cháo·syēn Korea (North)
葡萄酒 póo·tào jyǒ wine
韩国 hún·gwór Korea (South)
棉条 myén·tyáo tampon
森林 sērn·lín forest
硬币 yìng·bèe coins
硬卧 yìng·wōr hard sleeper

硬座 yìng·zwòr **hard seat**
确认 chwàir·rèrn **validate**
确定 chwàir·dìng **confirm (a booking)**
紫色 zǐr·sèr **purple**
最大 zwày·dà **biggest**
最小 zwày·syǎo **smallest**
最后的 zwày·hò·der **last (final)**
最好的 zwày·hǎo der **best**
最近 zwày·jìn **nearest**
最高车速 zwài·gāo chēr·sòo
speed limit
晾干 lyùng·gūn **dry (clothes)**
遗失物 ée·shīr wòo **lost property**
黑白(片) hāy·bái (pyēn) **B&W (film)**
黑色 hāy·sèr **black**
黑暗 hāy·ùn **dark**
锁 swǒr **padlock**
锁上 swǒr·shùng **lock** ⓥ
锁上了 swǒr·shùng ler **locked (door)**
锅 gwōr **wok**
锅贴 gwōr·tyāir **dumpling (fried)**
等 děrng wait (for)
等候室 děrng·hò shír **waiting room**
街道 jyāir·tó **street**
街市 jyāir·shìr **street market**
舒服 shōo·foo **comfortable**
短 dwǔn **short (length)**
短裤 dwǔn·kòo **shorts**
窗 chwūng **window**
湖 hóo **lake**
温度 wērn·doo **temperature
(weather)**
渴 kěr **thirsty (to be)**
滑雪 hwá·shwàir **skiing**
渡船 dòo·chwún **ferry**
游泳 yó·yǒong **swim** ⓥ
游泳池 yó·yǒong chír **swimming pool**
游泳衣 yó·yǒong ēe **swimsuit**
普通话 pǒo·tōong hwà **Mandarin**
道教 dào·jyào **Taoism**
道路 dào·loo **road**
裙子 chéwn·zir **skirt**
谢谢 syàir·syàir **thankyou**
登 dērng **board (a plane, ship etc)** ⓥ
登记台 dērng·jèe tái **check-in (desk)**
登机卡 dērng·jèe kǎ **boarding pass**

摄影 shèr·yǐng **photography**
摄影家 shèr·yǐng jyā **photographer**
摇滚 yáo·gǒon **rock (music)**
蒙古 mérng·gǒo **Mongolia**
蓝色 lún·sèr **blue**
零钱 líng·chyén **change (coins)**
楼 ló **building**
楼房 ló·fúng **apartment
(downmarket)**
感光度 gǔn·gwung·doo **film speed**
感冒 gǔn·mào **influenza**
感冒药 gǔn·mào yào **cough medicine**
感染 gún·rǔn **infection**
感谢 gǔn·syàir **grateful**
碗 wǔn **bowl** ⓝ
暖气管 nwǔn·chèe gwǔn **heater**
暖和 nwǔn·hwór **warm**
照相 jào·syùng **take a photo**
照片 jào·pyen **photo**
照相机 jào·syùng jēe **camera**
睡觉 shwày·jyào **sleep** ⓥ
睡袋 shwày·dài **sleeping bag**
腿 twǔy **leg**
跳舞 tyào·wǒo **dance**
矮 ǎi **short (height)**
筷子 kwài·zir **chopsticks**
签证 chyēn·jèrng **visa**
微波炉 wēi·bōr lǒo **microwave
(oven)** ⓝ
解放军 jyāir·fùng jěwn **People's
Liberation Army (PLA)**
煤气 máy·chèe **gas (for cooking)**
遥控 yáo·kòong **remote control**
新 sīn **new**
新西兰 sīn·sēe·lún **New Zealand**
新闻 sīn·wérn **news**
新鲜 sīn·syen **fresh**
塑像 sòo·syùng **sculpture**
塞子 sāi·zir **plug (bath)**
满 mún **full**

碟子 dyáir·zir **disk (CD-ROM)**
磁带 tsír·dài **tape (recording)** ⓝ
榜 bùng **great (fantastic)**

慢慢的 màr·mùn·der **slowly**
墨镜 mòr·jìng **sunglasses**
舞蹈 wóo·dǎo **dancing**
辣椒 là·jyāo **chilli**
辣椒酱 là·jyāo jyùng **chilli sauce**
鼻子 bēe·zir **nose**
演出 yén·chōo **performance**
演员 yěn·ywén **actor**
蜜月 mèe·ywàir **honeymoon**
熊猫 syúng·māo **panda**

十五画 **15 strokes**

蔬菜 shōo·tsài **vegetable**
醉 zwày **drunk**
鞋 syáir **shoe**
鞋店 syáir·dyèn **shoe shop**
膝盖 chēe·gài **knee**
镊子 nyáir·zir **tweezers**
镑 bùng **pound (money, weight)**
箱子 syūng·zir **box** ⓝ
德国 dér·gwór **Germany**

摩托车 mó·twōr chēr **motorcycle** ⓝ
颜色 yén·sèr **colour**
澳大利亚 ào·dà·lèe·yǎ **Australia**

十六至二十三画
16 to 23 strokes

橙色 chérng·sèr **orange (colour)**
糖尿病 tǔng·nyào·bìng **diabetes**
赠（票）zèrng (pyào)
  complimentary (tickets)
穆斯林 mòo·sir·lín **Muslim**
避孕套 bèe·yèwn·tào **condom**
餐巾 tsūn·jīn **napkin**
餐车 tsūn·chēr **dining car**
點心 dyěn·sīn **dim sum**
翻译 fūn·èe **interpreter • translator**
警察 jǐng·chá **police • police officer
  (in city)**
罐头 gwùn·to **can • tin**

don't just stand there, say something!

What kind of traveller are you?

A. You're eating chicken for dinner *again* because it's the only word you know.

B. When no one understands what you say, you step closer and shout louder.

C. When the barman doesn't understand your order, you point frantically at the beer.

D. You're surrounded by locals, swapping jokes, email addresses and experiences – other travellers want to borrow your phrasebook.

If you answered A, B, or C, you NEED Lonely Planet's phrasebooks.

- **Talk to everyone everywhere**
  Over 120 languages, more than any other publisher

- **The right words at the right time**
  Quick-reference colour sections, two-way dictionary, easy pronunciation, every possible subject

- **Lonely Planet Fast Talk** – essential language for short trips and weekends away

- **Lonely Planet Phrasebooks** – for every phrase you need in every language you want

'Best for curious and independent travellers' – *Wall Street Journal*

Lonely Planet Offices

Australia
90 Maribyrnong St, Footscray,
Victoria 3011
☎ 03 8379 8000
fax 03 8379 8111
✉ talk2us@lonelyplanet.com.au

USA
150 Linden St, Oakland,
CA 94607
☎ 510 893 8555
fax 510 893 8572
✉ info@lonelyplanet.com

UK
72-82 Rosebery Ave,
London EC1R 4RW
☎ 020 7841 9000
fax 020 7841 9001
✉ go@lonelyplanet.co.uk

www.lonelyplanet.com